CW00971020

Dog Smart

Evidence-based Training with
The Science Dog

Linda P. Case

Dog Smart
Evidence-based Training with The Science Dog

Linda P. Case

AutumnGold Publishing
A Division of AutumnGold Consulting
Mahomet, IL 61853
www.autumngoldconsulting.com

Copyright © 2018 Linda P. Case
Cover illustration: Mike Case

All rights reserved. No part of this book may be reproduced or transmitted in any form or by any means, electronic, digital or mechanical, including photocopying, recording, or by any information storage or retrieval system without permission in writing from the author,

ISBN-13: 978-1979380317
ISBN-10: 1979380317

Other Books by Linda P. Case

Beware the Straw Man: The Science Dog Explores Dog
Training Fact & Fiction

Dog Food Logic: Making Smart Decisions for your Dog
in an Age of Too Many Choices

Only Have Eyes for You: Exploring Canine Research
with The Science Dog

Canine and Feline Nutrition: A Resource for Companion
Animal Professionals

The Dog: Its Behavior, Nutrition and Health

The Cat: Its Behavior, Nutrition and Health

For Vinny & Chip

Contents

Acknowledgments

This book would not have been possible without the help of longtime dog training friends and colleagues who have not only helped with this project in particular but have been outstanding mentors, scientists, trainers, teachers and friends. My deepest appreciation for your willingness to chat with me about the many topics that this book involved, for providing your expertise, training experiences, and research study results. Most of all, thank you for your continued dedication to dogs and science and to "pushing the peanut forward" as we continue to learn more about our canine best friends. The dogs of the world are the better for your care and your passion. In alphabetical order, my sincere appreciation to Roger Abrantes, Marjie Alonso, Eileen Anderson, Lisa Burgoon, Jill Cline, Gail Czarnecki, Steve Dale, Leighann Daristotle, Maria de Godoy, George Fahey, Julie Hecht, Nancy Kerns, Lindsay Lilly, Pam Lowrey, Patricia McConnell, Jackie Mertens, Sandy Myers, Mary Owens, Dan Rode, Amanda Rodriguez, Mary Stuart, Nancy Tucker, Mary Ellen Tuveson, Cheryl Weber, Sarah Whitehead, Lauren Zverina, and Carla Zych. And very special thanks always to my husband Mike, who served as editor, voice of reason and humor, and lifelong best friend for this project and so many before. This book has been both a labor of love and a passion – I hope that dog lovers everywhere enjoy reading it as much as I enjoyed writing it.

Introduction

I was lucky enough to grow up in an animal-loving family. As a young child, I had an auspicious start to pet ownership with Beany the Bird, a parakeet who I trained to fly from his cage to land on top of my head. As a pre-teen, Shelley the Sheltie joined our family, followed shortly thereafter by my horse, Hickory. (Clearly, alliteration and I share a long history). I trained Shelley in 4-H and competed with her in 4-H dog shows and AKC obedience trials. By my teen years, my mom was training and showing her own dogs, first a Belgian Tervuren named Tina and eventually a succession of Border Collies. We shared many years of traveling around the east coast and Midwest together to dog shows, training seminars and conferences. I have wonderful memories of those shared adventures and of our love of dogs. I would not change a thing.

Well, okay. I might change one thing.

I started training dogs in the early 1970's. In those years, established dog training methods involved choke collars, corrections, and very generous use of the word "<u>NO</u>!." Another popular aversive was that throat-clearing, grandpa-in-the-bathroom, "*EE-HHHH*" sound. (Really? Who was responsible for inventing *that*?) These methods were standard and accepted training practice, originally developed by military trainers during WWII.

Here are two examples from those early training years. When I first began training Shelley in 4-H, the club leader strictly informed her budding group of young trainers that we must "*never look our dogs in the eye.*" Rather we were instructed to stare out into space, at a spot located somewhere above the dog's head. I guess the premise was that my sweet and gentle Shetland Sheepdog would suddenly revert back to her wolf-like ancestor and launch for my throat should I make the error of making eye contact and thus challenge her status. A few years later, I attended a weekend seminar with my mom in which the presenter, a nationally recognized obedience competitor, instructed his students to yank on a long lead attached to their dog's choke collar, immediately after yelling "COME!" The collar correction was intended to ensure that their dogs came running as quickly as possible. This was a time during which dogs were assumed to be in a constant battle for dominance with their owners, negative reinforcement and punishment reigned in dog training, and the use of food was viewed as bribery or even worse "cheating." Luckily, just a few years later, around the mid-80's, things began to change for the better for dogs - and for trainers.

After finishing my undergraduate degree, getting married, and adding two Golden Retrievers to our family, Mike and I spent four pre-graduate school years moving around the East Coast as Mike completed his ROTC commitment to the Navy. (They had very generously paid for his engineering education at Cornell, so he owed them a bit of time in return). During our time in Massachusetts, I was lucky enough to become friends with a group of dog trainers who were as passionate as I was about dogs and training. We would meet regularly to train and walk our dogs together in area parks. One day, one of these friends excitedly showed up with a new training book in hand. This book was *"Don't Shoot the Dog"* by Karen Pryor. We all read it. Devoured it, really.

As dog trainers, we never looked back.

The era of reward-based training methods had begun. Karen's book was based on the science of behaviorism, encouraged positive reinforcement and strongly discouraged punishment. She promoted using food treats as a primary reinforcer and introduced the concept of using a marker word as a conditioned reinforcer. Karen's seminal book and those that followed caused a paradigm shift in thinking and led to the development of an entirely new philosophy of dog training. Out went confrontational and correction-based methods that assumed dogs must be dominated to be trained and in came a gentler, kinder approach to training that also happened to be firmly grounded in learning theory and the behavioral sciences.

The changes of the 1980's were followed by another remarkable development – this time in the academic world. After decades of being completely ignored in almost all fields of scientific study, the *domestic dog* was suddenly becoming a hot topic for scientists in a host of disciplines. It began with programs in canine and feline nutrition (upon which my own graduate studies centered), and was rapidly followed by studies of the evolutionary history and domestication of dogs, by new examinations of canine behavior that challenged previously accepted dog-as-wolf archetypes, and most recently, with studies of the dog's unique talents in social cognition and emotional complexities. Although not focusing on dogs per se, the 1990's also witnessed the serious philosophical consideration of animal consciousness, animal welfare and animal rights at universities around the world.

Collectively, these many areas of study expanded our understanding of and appreciation for the inner mental lives of non-human animals and directly challenged many long held beliefs about how we should view and treat other animals, including dogs. While in graduate school and later, when teaching at the university, I read and studied the work of these scientists and philosophers. I brought their studies to my students for review, for group discussions, and as examples to practice their critical thinking skills. More personally, the evidence for complex animal minds and the arguments for changes in the ways that society has traditionally viewed animals had the effect of further modifying how I lived with, trained, and cared for my own dogs.

In 1989, Mike and I built a dog training facility on the land adjacent to our home and opened AutumnGold Dog Training Center. I had just started teaching in the Companion Animal Science program in the University of Illinois. I taught undergraduates during the day and obedience classes at our school in the evenings. In its early years, when we were still competing in obedience trials, AutumnGold offered both competitive obedience classes and basic manners classes. Today we employ a group of talented trainers and instructors and teach classes that are primarily designed for pet dog owners. These include puppy and adult manners classes, a set of dog sports (for fun) classes, and a series that we call "LifeSkills" for teaching behaviors that promote harmony between owners and their dogs and help dogs to be well-behaved and comfortable in many situations.

This book, "*Dog Smart: Evidence-based Training with The Science Dog*" is a product of my years owning and developing classes for AutumnGold, teaching, researching, and writing about dogs during my work at the University of Illinois, and training, living with and loving a long succession of beloved dogs. It focuses on solid, scientifically-acquired knowledge about dogs and attempts to dispel many of the prevailing myths that continue to persist, even among professed dog lovers. It is also a testimony to just how far we have come in our understanding of and empathy for the amazing dogs who are in our care and with whom we are privileged to share our lives with.

"*Dog Smart*" has two primary objectives. The first is to provide accurate summaries of some of the most important evidence regarding present day understanding of the dog's history and domestication, behavior, social cognition, and learning process. Some of this information is not new. For example, we have had an understanding of the principles of associative learning (behaviorism) for more than a century. However, scientists continue to study the benefits and limitations of these principles when used to train dogs (you may be surprised at some of their results). Other bodies of knowledge are quite recent and include studies of the dog's ability to understand human communication signals, examinations of perspective-taking ability, and the importance of observation and emotion as factors in learning.

The second objective of "*Dog Smart*" is to apply this information to practical dog training methods and to provide means for communicating this information and teaching these methods in ways that are both interesting and useful to *all* dog owners. If you are a trainer, these people include your students, professional colleagues, show buddies and private clients. For all of us, it also includes the many other dog owners who we know – who in most cases make up a majority of dog owners in our lives. These are distant (and not-so-distant) family members, work acquaintances, people you meet at the pet supply store, most of your neighbors, and of course, neighbor Joe (who happens to know a lot about dogs). We all have a Joe (or two) in our lives. He is that neighbor or relative or client who has had dogs "all of his life" and, "happens to know a lot about them." Joe is everywhere. Most of the Joes who we know sincerely like and often deeply love dogs. Joe also enjoys sharing his vast knowledge about dogs with others. Sometimes he is spot-on correct; other times, well, not so much. The icon below is your warning that Joe is on his way and it is time to chat with him, converting what you have learned about the science into language that is accessible and useable to the Joes of your world – look for this *"Talking to Joe"* icon at the end of each chapter.

TALKING TO JOE

"Dog Smart" is arranged into three sections. *"Who is Dog"* tackles the question that no one ever seems to answer completely – how are dogs related to wolves and how (if at all) should this relationship influence how we train our dogs? While I do not profess to have a complete answer to this question, there is sufficient evidence to inform us, at the very least, about training practices. Similarly, dog owners live with a wide variety of dog breeds and breed-mixes and may not have a thorough understanding of why their terrier likes to dig or their Aussie likes to chase. Chapter 2 reviews the history of breeds, how this has influenced behavior, and how owners may perceive and react to these differences. Developmental behavior is the topic of the third chapter. I focus primarily on the somewhat overused concept of puppy socializa-

tion and how it can help (and possibly hinder) raising a well-adjusted puppy. The final two chapters of this section examine the world from the dog's point of view – first how their special senses differ from our own, followed by an examination of basic forms that canine communication that should be important to all dog owners.

In the first chapters of Section 2, "*How Dogs Learn*", my focus shifts to the principles of behaviorism. These precepts have formed the scaffolding upon which dog training (both correction-based and reward-based) has rested for many years. The emotional component of the dog's mind and the role of social behavior and cognition is examined in detail in the latter chapters of this section. Our continually expanding understanding of the dog's skills in social cognition can be incorporated into dog training practices and used to modify accepted methods based upon associative learning. Although there appears to be some tension existing between those who fall firmly in the behaviorism camps and those who focus on the dog's cognitive skills, I make an attempt to bring these two camps together in a shared desire to effectively train, understand and respect dogs as the highly responsive and cognitive beings that they are.

The final section of "*Dog Smart*" combines what we know about canine behavior, learning, and social cognition to provide practical dog training practices, specifically presenting the approaches that we use at AutumnGold. General training procedures and my personal opinions and experiences about their uses are the topics of Chapters 10 and 11. These are followed with chapters addressing puppy training, general manners training, and finally, solutions for a set of common behavior problems. (Serious behavior problems such as aggression and separation anxiety are beyond the scope of this book). AutumnGold's methods are consistent with the science that is presented throughout the book. However, they are not the *only* way in which to apply this knowledge. They are methods that we have developed at AutumnGold over the last 30 years, modifying and sometimes making even major changes as new information has become available. In these chapters, I share many of the student guidelines and handouts that we use in our classes (see shaded boxes). If you are an instructor, rescue or shelter professional, work with private clients, or simply wish to give one to your neighbor Joe, you are welcome to reproduce and share them.

Dogs are smart – this is known. They are also highly emotional, socially aware beings. We must match this by being *Dog Smart* ourselves regarding how we view them, care for them, and train them. It you are already a practitioner of evidence-based and reward-based methods, I hope that this book further supports your understanding of the science and provides new and helpful techniques for your training tool box. If you are not yet convinced of the cogency of scientifically acquired knowledge, I hope that this book helps to persuade you of its importance. My ultimate hope is that *"Dog Smart"* will provide all readers with the communication tools to impart solid training advice (and to dispel myths) to students, training friends and to our pal "neighbor Joe", who may be a challenge at times, but truly loves his dog, just as we all love our own.

Linda Case
February, 2018

Part 1 – Who Is Dog?

Chapter 1
Dogs vs. Wolves –
Let's Settle this Once and For All

Just recently, during my school's Beginner Class orientation, a new student asked this:

"My neighbor Joe, (who knows a lot about dogs), told me that because wolves are the ancestors of dogs, we should train dogs according to how wolves behave in packs. He told me that I need to be "alpha" and that my dog must recognize my dominant status during training. Will we be making sure that my dog Muffin (a Mini-Doodle) knows that I am dominant?"

And I think, *"Here we go again."*

The problem with this rationale (the dog's primary wild ancestor is the wolf; therefore we should base our training practices on what is known about wolf behavior) is that, like many folklores, it contains elements of truth plus a slew of falsehoods and mythologies.

How do you answer in one minute or less to a skeptical student, friend or neighbor (Joe)?

The best way is to arm yourself with facts and then condense those facts into a short and easily understandable response. In this chapter, we review current knowledge regarding the dog's ancestry, domestication and basic social behavior. Then, as in all of the chapters that follow, I will provide you with a few *"Talking to Joe"* responses that you can use in your classes, when teaching seminars, talking to other dog owners, and when attempting to convince neighbor Joe (who may need a lot of convincing).

It's all Greek (er, Latin) to me: Let's start with the dog's taxonomy, which is the hierarchical system that we use to classify animals. Although this information may seem somewhat academic, it is important for trainers to know the dog's taxonomy because it allows us to see just how closely related the dog is to the wolf and other canid species. The broadest classification groups are domain and kingdom, followed by the increasingly narrow groups of phylum, class, order, family, genus and species. The genus and species Latin names are how we typically identify commonly known animals, including the dog.

Taxonomic Group	Dog's Classification	Wolf's Classification
Phyla	Animalia	Animalia
Class	Mammalia	Mammalia
Order	Carnivora	Carnivora
Family	Canidae	Canidae
Genus	*Canis*	*Canis*
Species	*familiaris*	*lupus*

The domestic dog is classified within the phylum Animalia, the class, Mammalia and the order Carnivora. Carnivora includes 17 families and about 250 different species. Carnivores are so named because of a set of enlarged teeth (the carnassials) which comprise the enlarged upper fourth premolar and the lower first molar on each side of the mouth. Take a moment to open your dog's mouth and take a look at those teeth. If you live with anything larger than a Chihuahua, you will notice that these are some mighty big chompers.

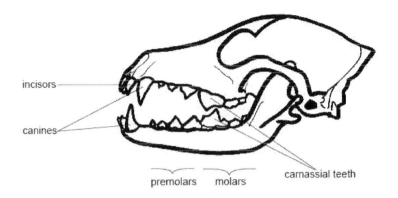

incisors

canines

premolars   molars   carnassial teeth

If you brush your dog's teeth regularly, you are already familiar with the carnassials because they present the flattest and largest tooth surface that you run your brush across and are also a popular spot for plaque and calculus to deposit. All of the species that are classified with dogs in this order have these impressive teeth, which are adapted for shearing and tearing prey. Carnivores also have small, sharp incisors at the front of the mouth for holding and dissecting prey. These are the teeth that Muffin uses to de-fluff her new stuffed squeaky toy. The four elongated canine teeth evolved for both predation and defense. Interestingly, despite these dental modifications, not all of the present day species that are found in Carnivora are strict carnivores. Some, such as bears and raccoons, are omnivorous and at least one species, the Panda, is primarily vegetarian.

Families are groups within the orders, with dogs found in the family Canidae and in the genus *Canis*. Other canids within the Canidae family are wolves (two species), coyotes (one species) and foxes (five species). The wolf and the dog hang together taxonomically all the way down through genus and only separate when classified as separate species; wolves are *Canis lupus* and dogs are *Canis familiaris*. (Note: There is still a bit of disagreement about this among scientists. Some argue that dogs should be classified as a sub-species of wolf – *Canis lupus familiaris*.

There is no consensus about this and you will see dogs classified in both ways*).*

So, this is where you can start with your answer to Joe: Dogs and present-day wolves are different species within the same genus. The Latin name for the domestic dog is *Canis familiaris* and the present-day Gray wolf is *Canis lupus.*

Cousin, *not* Ancestor: To which, Joe replies: *"Yeah, but the wolf is the dog's ancestor, right?"* This is one of those pesky partial truths. The domestic dog and today's gray wolf share a common ancestor, a type of wolf that lived at least 45,000 years ago and has since gone extinct. Much in the same way that the Chimpanzee (*Pan troglodytes*) is the closest living relative to present day humans (*Homo sapiens*), we do not (and should not) refer to the Chimpanzee as our ancestor. This is incorrect. Just as we share a *common* ancestor with present-day great apes, so too do dogs share a common ancestor with today's wolves.

Oldest Best Friend: However closely dogs may be related to wolves from an evolutionary perspective, they are different in many important ways. The first distinction is that dogs, unlike wolves, are a domesticated species. They are in fact, the very first animal that humans domesticated. We were hanging out with dogs several thousand years before we began tending to chickens, goats, pigs, or cows, and even well before cats were living with us (who, by the way, maintain that this arrangement was entirely their decision, not ours).

Scientists still do not concur about the exact timing, place or circumstances surrounding the creation of dog, but there are several general facts with which most currently agree:

- Domestication, the process by which the ancestral wolf was gradually transformed into the dog, took place sometime between 32,000 and 18,000 years ago.

19

- The most recent evidence suggests that the dog was domesticated more than once, from two different and geographically separated (now extinct) wolf populations that were living on opposite sides of the Eurasian continent. Over time, these two groups of proto-dogs migrated with humans and intermingled.

- Domestication began during a time when people were still living a nomadic lifestyle, periodically moving their camps from place to place. Our more settled way of life did not become established until 12,000 years ago with the invention of agriculture.

- The early stages of domestication of the dog appear to have been unintentional. As wild wolves identified a new ecological niche – the food scraps and garbage that were associated with human campsites - they began to follow human camps and to live on the periphery of temporary settlements to scavenge food.

- The selective pressures on these camp-dwelling wolves favored less timid individuals who had a higher tolerance of humans. Less fearful individuals would experience increased opportunities to feed and reproduce because they stayed longer and fled less readily than more timid animals. These new sub-populations of wolf were also feeding themselves more through scavenging and less through hunting (predation).

- Over generations, selective pressures led to a proto-dog who was naturally tolerant of human presence and began to live permanently near human camps and settlements. This evolving dog was smaller, had a shorter snout and wider skull, and smaller teeth compared with wolves.

Pack Behavior? Changes also occurred in the wolf's *social behavior* during domestication. As early dogs began to live permanently as camp scavengers, the selective pressure for social hierarchies and strict pack order was relaxed as pack hunting behaviors were no longer needed and were replaced by semi-solitary or group scavenging behaviors. Scavengers became more tolerant of the presence of other dogs and the presence of protected nesting sites also reduced the need for cooperative raising of young.

It is theorized that during this branching of the dog and wolf's evolutionary tree, the wild version of wolf remained a pack-living predator, while the evolving dog became specialized in adaptations for living in close proximity to humans. As we will see in later chapters, dogs also evolved a set of social behaviors that enhanced their ability to communicate and cooperate with human caretakers. It is from these semi-domestic scavenger populations that individual dogs are believed to have been selected and purposefully bred by humans for further taming. Eventually (many generations later), selective breeding of these dogs led to the development of different types of working dogs and most recently, the creation of purebred breeds.

Origins of the Dominance Myth: Given this current understanding of the dog's domestication, why is it that Joe and his friends continue to believe that pack order and dominance hierarchies are so important to dogs and should be used in dog training? For this explanation, we have to look more to recent history, going back only about 45 years.

During the 1970's, researchers who were studying wolf behavior focused almost exclusively on a theory called the "hierarchal model of pack behavior." This theory proposes that individuals within a wolf pack are highly concerned with social status and live in a constant struggle for dominance with one another. Because of the dog's close evolutionary relationship to the wolf, it was assumed that dogs would behave similarly.

It became popular to view dogs as pack-living animals who adhered to strictly structured dominance hierarchies – both with their human owners and with other dogs. As a result of this highly popularized (but incorrect) concept, almost any behavior that a dog offered that was not in compliance with an owner's wishes came to earn the label of "dominance". An entire collection of dog training methods grew out of these beliefs, most of which focused on ensuring that that owners established dominant (also referred to as "alpha") status over their dogs. These methods emphasized physical coercion and punishment, and promoted exercises that were believed to be necessary for effectively establishing the owner's dominant status.

Interesting Theory: Too bad it's wrong. There are several errors with this way of thinking. The first lies in the set of false beliefs about wolf behavior that prevailed in the 1970's. Wolf researchers have since reevaluated the appropriateness of using the hierarchy model of social behavior and have found it to be lacking. Despite the widespread belief that wild wolf packs exist in a perpetual state of dominance challenges and bids for enhanced status, the collected evidence shows a glaring *absence* of these rigid types of relationships. There are few reports of wolves seeking higher positions in their pack, fighting over leadership, or physically dominating other wolves through aggression or alpha rolls (Yeah, sorry Joe, it just ain't happening).

Rather, today's wolf experts tell us that the social behavior of wild wolves typically reflect cohesive, well-functioning family units that are built around cooperation rather than conflict. Pack peace is maintained not through aggression and perpetual battling for dominance, but rather through ritualized postures designed to avoid fights and cooperative behaviors such as hunting together, sharing food and raising young together. A parent-family model better describes wolf relationships in packs than does an outdated hierarchy model that focuses on strict social roles and conflict.

This doesn't mean that wolves never display social dominance, however or that the concepts of dominance and submission are completely useless as descriptors of behavior. Wolves (and other animals, including dogs and humans), display social dominance situationally, most often when attempting to defend a valuable resource. It is not the entire concept of dominance and domi-nant/submissive signaling that has been dispelled, but rather the correctness of a simple hierarchical pack structure. That concept is considered obsolete and inaccurate today.

Additionally, our understanding of both learning theory and the cognitive ability of animals has evolved significantly over the years. Attempting to use a simple dominance hierarchy model to explain all things wolf (and dog) has fallen short when consider-ing new evidence that supports the existence of complex thought, planning, perspective taking and even rudimentary el-ements of a "theory of mind" in animals, including wolves and dogs (more about this in Chapter 9).

And finally, we know much more about the social behavior of dogs than we did back in the 1970's. To put it bluntly - *dogs are not wolves*. They do not form packs like wolves (not even at the dog park – Sorry Joe – wrong again), nor do they possess a natu-ral tendency to battle for dominance or a need to constantly challenge humans or other dogs for higher status. Their social lives and relationships are also, just like wolves and other ani-mals, much more complex than a simple concept of dominance hierarchy is capable of describing fully. For example, one of the most striking ways in which dogs differ from wolves is in the dog's ability to understand and learn from human communica-tion signals (more about this later in the book).

The reality is that the social behavior and cognition of the dog has been profoundly influenced by domestication. Today's dog is described by some as a socialized wolf, a variant who is well-adapted to life with humans and has lost the need to exist in a stable (wolf) pack. In groups, feral dogs do not typically hunt co-

23

operatively and only rarely share care of offspring. In homes, the domestic dog's social behavior is directed more towards working with and communicating with humans, not competing with us for some arcane concept of dominance. Similarly, the relationships that dogs share with other dogs in their homes are not analogous to a wolf pack. Rather dogs have social partners (friends really) and acquaintances, just like humans. Importantly, the social groups of dogs, with humans and with other dogs, have characteristics and structures that are adaptive for domestication and for living in close proximity with their human caretakers. These characteristics are all uniquely and amazingly *DOG (not wolf)*.

TALKING TO JOE

Talking to Joe: So, how do we distill all of this down to a series of facts and factoids that will convince Joe that his dog: (a) is not a wolf and (b) does not require dominating? Here are a few talking points for you – modify as needed for your particular Joe (or Josephine).

🐾 Yes, Joe, dogs and wolves are closely related. However, today's wolf is not actually your dog's *ancestor*. Rather dogs and wolves are cousins, similar in many ways to the relationship between you and a chimpanzee, Joe. Just as you would not look at chimpanzee behavior to inform you how to raise your kids (at least I don't think you would), you should avoid focusing on wolf behavior to tell you how to raise and train your dog.

24

🐾 Dogs differ from wolves in some amazing ways. They are more attuned to our facial expressions and communication signals and they are better at cooperating with humans than are wolves. Dogs also often form friendships with other dogs in their home or community, and despite the continued attempts by some to describe it in this manner, dogs do not live in a constant state of dominance-dictated competition with other dogs.

🐾 So, time to chill, Joe. Don't worry so much about your dog's status in your home or whether or not he is attempting to dominate you, your family and the world. (He's not). Rather, focus on all of the amazing traits and talents that your dog has inherited as a dog (not a wolf) and use those characteristics to *train* him to be a good family companion and community member.

🐾 Oh, and Joe, drop the alpha status obsession once and for all, please? It embarrasses all of us, including your dog.

Evidence

Frantz LA, et al. Genomic and archaeological evidence suggest a dual origin of domestic dogs. *Science,* 2016; 352:1228-1231.

Freedman AH, et al. Genomic sequencing highlights the dynamic early history of dogs. *PLOS Genetics,* 2014; 10;e1004016.

Gacsi M, et al. Species-specific differences and similarities in the behavior of hand-raised dog and wolf pups in social situations with humans. *Developmental Psychobiology* 2005; 47:111-122.

Hare B. The domestication of social cognition in dogs. *Science,* 2002; 298:1644.

Jensen P, et al. The genetics of how dogs became our social allies. *Current Directions in Psychological Science* 2016; 25:334-338.

Larsen G. et al. Rethinking dog domestication by integrating genetics, archeology and biogeography. *Proceedings of the National Academy of Sciences,* 2012; 109:8878-8883.

Mech LD. Alpha status, dominance, and division of labor in wolf packs. *Canadian Journal of Zoology* 1999; 77:1196-1203.

Miklosi A, et al. A simple reason for a big difference: Wolves do not look back at humans, but dogs do. *Current Biology,* 2003; 3:763-766.

Range F and Viarnyi Z. Tracking the evolutionary origins of dog-human cooperation: the "Canine Cooperation Hypothesis". *Frontiers in Psychology* 2015; 5:1582.

---

* Note: The "Evidence" section at the end of each chapter is not a comprehensive reference list. Rather, these include citations of studies that were discussed in the chapter and additional readings. For complete bibliographies, see the full list of books and textbooks at the conclusion of this book.

Chapter 2
They are All Designer Breeds

A few years ago, one of AutumnGold's beginner class instructors was helping a young couple with their exuberant Jack Russel Terrier. The couple was delivering a list of complaints about their dog's behavior, which included among other things, digging in the yard, barking and chasing the cat, and not being friendly when meeting new dogs.

After listening intently, Pam (the instructor) asked them: *"So, did you know he was a terrier when you adopted him?"*

Of course, she went on to help the couple and the dog, who became a much loved and decidedly better behaved companion. But, equally important to training him and modifying the behaviors that his owners found objectionable was helping them to realize that their dog was *still (*and always would be) a Jack Russel Terrier.

Herders Gotta Herd: Most people who have spent any amount of time with dogs are aware of clear behavior differences among breeds. Herding dogs like to chase things, retrievers carry stuff, working dogs are prone to guarding, and scent hounds sniff (a lot). The most obvious breed differences relate back to the early selection of dogs to perform various types of work. Many of these behavior patterns represent exaggerations of isolated components of the canid predatory sequence - stalking, chasing, grabbing, shaking, carrying, and finally, dissecting.

For example, the first part of this sequence is intensified in herding dogs, who possess a strong stalk and chase drive. Conversely, sporting breeds such as Golden and Labrador Retrievers are less likely to stalk but are highly motivated to chase, grab and carry as a result of selection for retrieving, and terriers excel at the final portion of the sequence – killing (shaking) and dissecting (or destuffing, if the target happens to be a cherished toy or fancy couch pillow). For trainers and instructors, a complete understanding of the origins and present day expressions of these breed-specific differences are essential to successfully train a wide range of breeds and breed-mixes and to work with owners of different breeds. Let's begin by taking a look at the history of what we consider to be the concept of "purebred" today.

The Early Breeds: Of all of the domesticated species of animals that exist, the dog has been subjected to artificial selection for the longest period of time. Since domestication, it is estimated that over 4000 generations of dogs have been bred for various types of work. Although they often did not look like breeds that we know today, most of these functional groups - hunting, guarding and herding dogs - were already in existence during the Roman period almost 2500 years ago. Following that era, the selective breeding of dogs to meet the functional needs of humans was further refined during two major waves of breeding:

Hunting Dogs for the Nobility: The first of these took place during the late Middle Ages when hunting became an activity associated with aristocracy and was restricted by law to the land-owning nobility. Different types of dogs were developed and bred to hunt various game species. Examples included deerhounds, harriers (beagles), foxhounds, various types of terriers, and later during the period, several types of gundogs. Although the landed gentry paid some attention to pedigrees and prided themselves on the working prowess of their kennel of dogs, selective breeding and breed development focused on working ability and behavior rather than a breed's uniform appearance. Breeding programs also did not yet restrict breeding within a set of animals identified as registered members of a breed, as we experience purebreds today. Rather, the name of a breed simply reflected the function of a loosely related group of dogs who were all used in a similar manner for either hunting, herding, or guarding.

Pure of Blood: The second wave is very recent, starting only 200 years ago during the middle 19ᵗʰ century. This phase represented an entirely new and unprecedented approach to breed development. Dog breeds became increasingly defined by their genetic relatedness and uniformity in appearance, rather than by working ability alone. This change was the product of the growing dog fancy, which was made up of wealthy and socially-privileged dog enthusiasts who placed emphasis on the purity of their dogs' lineages and pedigrees. (Interestingly, this focus paralleled the high value that the aristocracy placed upon their *own* supposedly superior and "pure" lineages, and their tendency to marry within family lines). This new type of breeder began to intensively select for dogs that conformed to a standard appearance described as ideal for the particular breed.

Kennel clubs and breed registries grew out of these practices as a method to establish breed barrier rules. These stipulated that only dogs who were the offspring of a registered dam and sire were recognized as members of a breed and eligible for exhibiting and breeding. This new set of rules ensured that the genetic pool for each breed was reproductively isolated from that of the general dog population, much as the ruling aristocracy of that period isolated themselves reproductively and socially from the working classes. This projection of the values of the upper classes was reflected in the increasing cultural importance that was assigned to dogs' pedigrees and lineages. Breeding related individuals to one another became a common practice that functioned to rapidly create a uniform appearance and to enhance the expression of desirable traits (including many behavior patterns) within a line of dogs.

They are *All* Designer Breeds: Under this paradigm, the creation of a new breed of dog requires four essential elements: (1) a group of founder individuals, (2) reproductive isolation of those dogs from the general population of dogs, (3) generations of inbreeding within the group to stabilize (fix) the physical and behavioral attributes that define the breed, and (4) selection of

29

breeding animals that most closely conform to a prescribed "breed type" in attempts to further perfect the breed.

Each new breed is eventually recognized and accepted by an external purebred registry organization such as the American Kennel Club (AKC) and a stud book is formed. From this point of origin, all future breeding is limited to descendants of the breed's founding dogs who were listed in the stud book. The consequences of this relatively new, (and somewhat bizarre, if you think about it), requirement has become vitally important to the health and behavior of purebred dogs today and cannot be overstated. Because all dogs of a given breed are descendants of only those dogs who were originally included in the breed's stud book, varying degrees of inbreeding have become a fundamental feature of every breed. The degree of relatedness among individuals in each generation varies according to the number and genetic diversity of the original founding dogs in the breed, the vigor with which the prohibition against breeding outside of registered lines has been enforced, and the number of dogs in a given generation that are being used for breeding (and how often). Unfortunately, while this approach to selective breeding initially enhanced the ability of dogs to perform (in the short-term), and resulted in the highly uniform physical appearance of breeds that we recognize today, the imposed genetic isolation has also contributed to the many genetically influenced diseases that we witness with increasing regularity in purebred dogs.

In the United States, the two largest registries are the AKC and the United Kennel Club (UKC). Today, these organizations continue to function as they did when the practice of creating breeds started in the 1800's – they oversee and regulate the acceptance of newly created breeds. The AKC is the larger of the two and currently includes 191 breeds. The very first breeds accepted into the AKC during the late 1800's included, among others, the Bassett Hound, Beagle, Dachshund, Fox Terrier, Greyhound, Newfoundland, Pug and Saint Bernard. Examples of recently accepted breeds are the American Hairless Terrier (2016), Boerboel (2015), Miniature American Shepherd (2015), Spanish Water Dog (2015), Portuguese Podengo Pequeno (2013), American English Coonhound (2011), and the Irish Red & White Setter (2009).

Although the increasingly popular and varied Doodles receive the brunt of criticisms against so-called designer breeds, it is a fact that every single breed (as we know them today) was *designed* by humans from existing dogs in a particular area of the world at a particular point in time. This took place by cross-breeding various breed types to enhance working ability and in some cases by further refining an existing breed-type. For example, the Miniature American Shepherd was designed in the 1960's by selecting for reduced size in Australian Shepherds. The Spanish Water Dog is genetically related to Portuguese Water Dogs and Irish Water Spaniels, and the American English Coonhound can trace its heritage back to Foxhounds and a variety of other coonhound breeds.

Yep, designer breeds, every single one.

If you Want to Race Cars, Don't Buy a Mini Cooper: Since this book is focusing on behavior and training, let's get back to a discussion of differences in behavior among breeds. It is clear that selecting for a specific type of working function impacts both the physical traits of the dog and the behaviors that are necessary to carry out that function. For example, the long slender legs and deep chest of the Greyhound contribute to its ability to run fast and hunt using its eyesight. This breed also possesses a very strong chase instinct, which is considered to be a modification of predatory behavior. (Think race car).

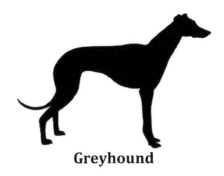

Greyhound

By comparison, the short thick legs of the Basset Hound contribute to this breed's talent as a scent trailer, along with behaviors that enhance an individual's ability to trail - a propensity to keep their nose to the ground when out walking and the inclination to move rather slowly (Mini Cooper).

Bassett Hound

So, depending upon the original function for which a breed or breed-type was developed, different dogs display certain behavior patterns in variable manners or to varying degrees of intensity. The degree to which these behavior patterns are inherited and how sensitive they are to environmental influences such as how a dog is raised and trained, also vary among breeds and individuals. But generally speaking, if your goal is to enjoy a dog sport and have a dog who zips around an Agility course at 90 miles an hour, you may not want to bring home Buffy the Bassett. Conversely, if snuggling on the couch and sharing a bowl of popcorn is more your style, then Buffy may be your dog.

He is a Toller (Not a Mini-Golden): Not only are there pronounced differences among breed-types (i.e. sight hounds vs.

scent hounds vs. herding dogs) in behavior, but there are also subtle differences between breeds that were developed for similar types of work. My husband and I experienced this firsthand with our Toller, Chippy. After more than 20 years of living with and loving Golden Retrievers, Mike and I made the jump to two other breeds. First, Vinny the sweetest Brittany on the planet joined our family. Then, three years later, Chippy, a Nova Scotia Duck Tolling Retriever came home.

Chip

I remember Chip's breeder, Dan Rode, saying to me, "You know, Linda, Tollers are quite different from Goldens, even from the field Goldens who you are used to." He then went on to very accurately describe those differences. And, like all experienced breeders who know their dogs, Dan was spot-on correct. Chippy is 100 percent Toller, not a Golden Retriever (even though people often mistake him for one). While Chip likes new people well enough and absolutely loves to be out and about with us (he has never met a street festival that he has not enjoyed), he prefers to say hello to new people from several feet away and is of the opinion that petting and hugs are reserved for family members only. He also is quite vocal (okay, he barks a lot; they all do), swims like an otter and thinks that sitting at the front of a canoe while I paddle him around the lake is heaven on earth. Oh yeah, and he also barks a lot (have you heard about the "Toller scream"?).

Still, it is not unusual for people who greet us when we are out with our dogs to assume that Chip is a Golden Retriever (albeit a small one with white on his feet). And many of these folks inevitably have their feelings hurt when, unlike our Goldens, Chippy does not approach them for petting. Rather, he stays his distance, happy smile on his face, content to allow his brother and sister to get all of the physical contact from strangers. After all, he is a Toller, not a Golden Retriever. And we love him for every one of his Toller behaviors, idiosyncrasies and weird little traits (if you live with a Toller, you know what I mean).

Just as Chippy is not a Golden, Vinny, our Brittany, is not an English Springer Spaniel, as some people mistake him to be. (Except for hunters – they always know a Brittany when they see one). Nor do Cooper and Alice, our two Goldens, have personalities that are like Labrador Retrievers. Similarly, anyone who lives with an Australian Shepherd can easily list the numerous ways in which Aussies differ from Border Collies and those who share their home with a Rottweiler will be able to tell you how their dog is definitely not a Doberman Pinscher.

So, not only are there behavior (and personality) differences among breed groups, but there are also behavioral distinctions among breeds that were developed for similar types of work. It gets even murkier when we realize that, for some breeds, there are also differences in *types* within the breed itself. For example, differences between field-bred and conformation/pet bred Golden and Labrador Retrievers have been studied in recent years. Generally speaking, dogs of these breeds who are bred for hunting and hunt tests tend to be focused, high energy retrievers (some might call them "intense"), while those bred for the conformation ring and as family companions are generally less intense and somewhat less active (and easier to live with for most families).

34

Behavior Differences among Breed Groups: Although there is limited research that examines true behavior differences (and how strongly or weakly they are inherited) among breeds and breed-types, there are a few generalizations that hold up pretty well under scrutiny and that can be used to help clients and friends (and Joe) as they are trying to decide what breed or breed-type is best for their family and lifestyle:

✓ *Sporting Breeds (Gundogs)*: These breeds were developed to aid hunters by locating, flushing and retrieving game on land and in water. Sporting dogs are energetic and highly active, and require regular vigorous exercise. Many have a natural inclination to retrieve and to swim, and some show a strong tendency to locate and indicate (point) game. These breeds are generally highly trainable and social, though the pointing breeds will tend to be a bit more independent than those developed to retrieve. Most sporting breeds are known to have low aggressive reactivity towards humans and other dogs.

✓ *Hounds*: The two primary types of hound were both developed for hunting, though their skills are widely different. Scent hounds such as Beagles, follow a scent trail to find game, while sight hounds use eyesight and speed to chase and capture quarry. Both types of hound work well ahead of the hunter and as a result, are relatively independent or even aloof in nature. Some of the sight hound breeds, such as the Greyhound and Whippet, are known for their extremely gentle and quiet dispositions.

✓ *Working Breeds:* Dogs classified as working breeds were bred to guard property or livestock, pull sleds, or perform water rescues. Because they were often required to actively protect by warning or even attacking intruders, the working breeds tend to be highly reactive. Many of these breeds will

35

bond strongly to one person or family (though often aloof with strangers), and are highly trainable.

✓ *Terriers:* Terriers were developed to find and kill small rodents and other animals that were considered to be pests. They worked with little or no direction from their handler and were required to immediately kill their prey upon catching it. These two requirements resulted in breeds that have low to medium trainability and very high reactivity. In general, terriers show increased inter-dog aggression as well as a strong predatory response.

✓ *Herding Breeds:* Herding breeds were developed to move livestock, usually in response to their handler's direction. They are considered to be highly trainable and tend to bond strongly to their owners. Because of their need to respond quickly to the movements and changes in the behavior of the herd, herding dogs are also usually highly active and athletic, and possess a strong chase instinct.

✓ *Toy Breeds:* Many, but not all, of these dogs represent miniaturizations of other breeds. In some cases, they retain behaviors similar to that of their larger forefathers. In others, a more subordinate nature was selected along with the neotenized features. The toys were probably the first true companion dogs, and many of these breeds reflect this in their strong predisposition to bonding to humans and for some, retaining puppy-like behaviors.

Within vs. Between Breed Differences: Most of what we currently understand about breed differences in behavior has been gleaned from survey studies with dog owners, pet professionals (such as veterinarians and show judges), and dog breeders. There are a limited number of studies that have directly tested temperament and cognitive differences among dog breeds, and given the logistical constraints, these studies typically test a relatively small numbers of dogs. In 2014, Lindsay Mehrkam and

Clive Wynne published a comprehensive review of the currently available research concerning breed-specific behavior patterns. Some (but not all) of their findings supported the major breed-group distinctions identified by breeders, judges and breed standards (and identified above).

However, they also made an additional conclusion. They found that while studies have reported substantial differences in behavior *among* breed types, they also found significant behavior variations *within* breeds. While some of these differences could be attributed to differential selection practices, such as the field breeding versus show breeding that we discussed previously, other differences may have been due to regional differences among breed lines and environmental effects such as raising, housing and training practices. While these latter factors should not surprise anyone, the researchers noted that research has focused almost exclusively on the effects of genetics (nature) when examining breed differences to the exclusion of considering the behavioral flexibility of dogs and their various responses to differing environmental factors.

It is quite possible (and expected really) that some breed-specific behavior traits are strongly influenced by genetics (excitability and aggression are examples suggested by researchers), while others may be less influenced by a dog's genetic make-up and depend more upon environmental factors (ease of house training and reactivity to unfamiliar dogs may be examples). Therefore, it is important to consider that while a genetic predisposition in a breed may influence an individual's propensity to show a particular behavior, raising and training practices will always influence, to at least some degree, the expression or intensity of that trait. What this means to professional trainers and dog enthusiasts (and Joe) is that, yes, it is helpful to consider a dog's breed or breed-type, but it is also important to consider other factors such as the breed lines, regional differences, and a dog's life experiences which include how she has been raised, trained and currently is living.

What about Mixed-Breeds? We cannot end a discussion of breed differences in behavior without addressing those dogs who currently make up more than 50 percent of owned dogs in the United States - dogs of mixed or unknown heritage. Some of these dogs are purposefully bred cross-breeds – the various Doodle variations come to mind – while others are true Heinz-47 varieties whose genetic make-up can only be guessed at or verified via DNA-testing. And, while there are plenty of arguments on both sides of the never-ending argument regarding *"which is better, a purebred or mix-breed dog"*, that is not my fight to pick in this book. Rather, I am interested in behavior and training. For this book, the question is – is there any evidence for differences between purebred dogs and mixed-breed dogs in terms of their behavior and personality traits?

Generally speaking, when a mixed-breed dog is of known heritage, it is common to attribute his or her behaviors to a mixture of the breeds that are involved. For example, Golden Doodles seem to abound at my training school these days. Personally, I like these dogs. They tend to be highly energetic, playful, and silly social butterflies. Owners often describe their behavior as including traits from each of the two contributing breeds, and indeed that seems to be the case. However, is there really any evidence for this belief? Do mix-breed dogs show behaviors that are a "mix" of the apparent breeds that have contributed to their heritage?

Unfortunately, there are not any studies that have directly compared the behavior of purebred dogs to that of mixed-breed dogs. However, a survey study published in early 2017 collected information about almost 8000 dogs representing 200 breeds (the purebred group) and a similar number of dogs who were identified as mixed-breed. A detailed owner survey was used to collect information regarding the dogs' behaviors and temperaments.

The survey results showed three important demographic differences – mixed-breeds were more likely to be neutered, were acquired at an older age than purebred dogs, and tended to have younger owners. When these differences were taken into account, only slight differences in behavior were observed between mixed-breed and purebred dogs. Mixed-breed dogs were reported by their owners to be less calm, yet slightly more trainable than purebred dogs. Oddly, while they said that their dogs were trainable, owners of mixed-breed dogs also reported a higher number of problem behaviors in their dogs, when compared with purebred dogs.

These less than stunning differences may reflect both the types of people who tend to get mixed-breed versus purebred dogs and environmental differences in the way that dogs are raised and acquired. The most important result of this study was the lack of pronounced differences between mixed-breed and purebred dogs, which suggests that the generally accepted adage that "mixed-breed dogs have fewer [inherited] behavior problems than purebred dogs" is not holding up under scrutiny. Rather, these results emphasize again the importance of environment – how a dog is raised, trained and housed - something that we will be discussing at length in the remainder of this book.

TALKING TO JOE

Talking to Joe: So, what can we tell Joe about purebred dog breeds, cross-breeds and mixed-breeds when he comes to class and asks about the behavior of his Swedish Treehugging Trundlehound? Here are a few suggestions:

🐾 Joe, we know that you love Zippy, your Border Collie dearly.....but, Zip is gonna chase your kids when they race around your yard. So, you have two choices. (1) Train your kids not to run when they are near Zippy, and/or (2) train Zippy to come when called reliably and to "down" on cue (or "leave it")* when he wants to chase. Best case scenario? Enlist your kids to help you to train Zippy to do these things. (Remember, Zippy is a Border Collie; chasing is his thing).

🐾 Hey Joe, I hear that your young Golden Retriever, Dorey, has a lot of energy and likes to carry your shoes around the house. Joe, Dorey is not a bad dog for doing this. Rather, she is a young Golden Retriever. Let's help you to train her to play with her own toys and to respond to a "leave it" cue for those things that are not hers.* Plenty of walks (in lots of new places), games (retrieving is one of the best), and training can all help with her energy level. Oh, and Joe, pick up around your house. That will remove temptations while your girl is learning what are her toys and what are not.

🐾 Joe, we know that you like going to the dog park because you meet other dog owners and enjoy chatting with them as your dogs play together. However, the fact that Lonnie, your West Highland White Terrier, often gets into fights with other dogs at the dog park should tell you something. (Hint: It has to do with Lonnie's sociability with unfamiliar dogs. He ain't so good at it, Joe). You are better served to realize that Lonnie does best if he is introduced to new dogs gradually, under controlled conditions, with care taken to minimize excitement and physical contact. Try taking Lonnie for a walk with a neighbor dog or teaching him fun games to play with you in the yard, instead of taking him to the dog park. (And if you really miss it, just make a visit now and again without Lonnie to chat with your friends).

🐾 And finally, no Joe, even though people tend to think that mixed-breed dogs are going to be better behaved and health-

40

ier, the information that we currently have does not back this up. While mixed-breed dogs are reportedly a bit easier to train, they can also come with more behavior problems than purebred dogs. So, it is a bit of a trade-off, it seems. Bottom line? You are better served to simply get to know your Annie, the terrier-poodle-hound mix, for who she is as an individual. Train her to be a good companion and maintain good health care for her, rather than to focus on who her parents and grandparents may have been. (Though, if you do want to do DNA testing just to find out, certainly go for it!)

*   See Chapter 14, for a discussion of teaching "leave it."

Evidence

Boyko AR, et al. A simple genetic architecture underlies morphological variation in dogs. *PLoS Biology* 2010; 8:e1000451.

Bradshaw JWS, Goodwin D. Determination of behavioural traits of pure-bred dogs using factor analysis and cluster analysis; a comparison of studies in the USA and UK. *Research in Veterinary Science* 1998; 66:73-76.

Lofgren SE, et al. Management and personality in Labrador Retriever dogs. *Applied Animal Behavior Science* 2014; 156:44-53.

Mehrkam LR, Wynne CD. Behavioral differences among breeds of domestic dogs (*Canis lupus familiaris*): Current status of the science. *Applied Animal Behaviour Science* 2014; 155:12-27.

Notari L, Goodwin D. A survey of behavioural characteristics of pure-bred dogs in Italy. *Applied Animal Behaviour Science* 2007; 103:118-130.

Ostrander EA. Genetics and the shape of dogs. *American Scientific* 2007; 95:406-413.

Parker Hg, et al. Genomic analyses reveal the influence of geographic origin, migration, and hybridization on modern dog breed development. *Cell Reports* 2017; 19:697-708.

Serpell JA. Effects of breed, sex and neuter status on trainability in dogs. *Anthrozoos* 2005; 18:196-207.

Serpell JA and Duffy DL. Dog breeds and their behavior. In: *Domestic Dog Cognition and Behavior*, A Horowitz (editor), 2014; Springer-Verlag, Berlin, Germany; pp. 31-57.

Sundman AS, et al. Similar recent selection criteria associated with different behavioural effects in two dog breeds. *Genes, Brain and Behavior* 2016; 15:750-756.

Turcsan B, et al. Trainability and boldness traits differ between dog breed clusters based on conventional breed categories and genetic relatedness. *Applied Animal Behaviour Science* 2011; 132:61-70.

Turcsan B, et al. Owner perceived differences between mixed-breed and purebred dogs. *PLoS One* 2017; 12(2):e0172720.

Wobbler V, et al. Breed differences in domestic dogs' comprehension of human communication signals. *Interaction Studies* 2009; 10:206-224.

Chapter 3
The Use (and Abuse) of Puppy Socialization

Like many dog training schools, AutumnGold, offers a puppy so-cialization class. We call this class "Puppy Preschool and Social Club" and it is available to puppies between the ages of 10 and 16 weeks. Typically we enroll between 6 and 10 pups for each 5-week session.

During a recent orientation, one of our students, Sandy, men-tioned that she was a bit concerned about her rather timid, 11-week-old Border Collie puppy, Bella. Sandy said that her neigh-bor Joe (who happens to know a lot about dogs), informed her that as a puppy Bella needs to be socialized with other dogs so that she learns how to interact with others of her kind. He rec-ommended taking Bella to the local dog park so that she could run freely with a variety of dogs. He instructed Sandy that she should not interfere with any of Bella's dog-to-dog interactions while at the park because part of a dog's socialization involves learning how to "*figure this stuff out*" (Joe is an articulate guy).

Bella enjoyed several play sessions at the dog park with an ado-lescent Aussie and met several friendly adult dogs. However, she also had the misfortune of meeting a dog who was not particu-larly fond of puppies and who reprimanded her aggressively, scaring her badly. On another occasion, a Shepherd mix repeat-edly side-swiped Bella, knocking her to the ground. Sandy re-layed that after three of these tumbles, Bella started to snarl and snap at the dog when he made another pass at her. Lately, Sandy said that Bella did not seem to want to play with the other dogs and would stay close to her, hiding behind her legs and some-times growling and snapping when other dogs approached.

Sandy asked us "*Am I socializing Bella too much?*"

This Word that You Keep Using: That word. *Socialization.* While it has a technical definition and a proper usage, this term has been so over-used (and abused) that many dog owners are confused about what comprises beneficial "socializing" for their pups and what does not and is potentially harmful.

Let's start with a definition. Socialization refers to the process by which a young dog develops species-specific (i.e. canine) social behaviors, learns to identify primary attachment figures (his people and dog family), and forms lasting social relationships. During particular stages of development, puppies are highly sensitive and receptive to learning about their environment, about their littermates and other dogs, and about their human family and friends.

Dogs differ from most other animals in that puppies can be simultaneously socialized to their own species (conspecifics) and to humans. Dogs who have been well socialized to other dogs and to people will incorporate both into their social structure and will tend to direct their communication signals to other dogs and to humans. Additionally, research in recent years has shown that dogs who have been raised in human families become highly capable of understanding and responding to many human communication signals such as pointing, eye contact, and gaze (more about this in Chapter 9).

All good, right? Absolutely. The challenge lies in the proper application of socialization. Let's look at different stages of behavioral development in puppies and what should (and should not) be provided to pups in the name of socialization during each.

Neonates -The First Two Weeks: Newborn puppies are *altricial*. This means that they are born in an immature physiological state and are completely dependent upon their mother for warmth, food, elimination and protection. From birth to two weeks, puppies have limited motor ability and can only crawl for short distances. Their eyes are closed, they cannot hear, and they are unable to regulate their own body temperature. What this means in a practical sense is that the puppy's world consists primarily of the *smell and touch and warmth* of his mother and littermates.

Transition Period – Waking up to the World: The neonatal period is short, lasting the first 10 to 14 days of life. It is immediately followed by the transition period, which represents a period of rapid physiological change as puppies "wake up" to their sensory world. This period begins when a puppy's eyes open at 12 to 14 days. Pups do not have complete visual perception at this age and only begin to see efficiently at around 4 weeks of age. Puppies become a bit more mobile during this week. They are able to stand by day 17 and begin to walk several days later. The transition period ends when puppies' ear canals open and they begin to react to sounds, around three weeks of age.

Puppies will be cared for almost exclusively by their mother during the first three weeks of life (unless of course, they are orphaned, in which case a human or surrogate mother dog must take the place of mom). Although puppies are not yet reacting to many outside stimuli, the breeder (or human caregiver) can provide several positive experiences for pups during these first weeks:

Good **Socialization (First Three Weeks):** Here are a few things that breeders and foster parents can provide during the first three weeks (mom should always be allowed to stay close and supervise):

- Because neonates are very sensitive to smell and touch, gentle handling for a few minutes, several times a day is beneficial for young puppies.

- During the transition period, as puppies begin to react to visual cues and to new smells and sounds, introduction of small, soft toys and other novel objects can help to stimulate puppies' investigative behaviors.

- Provide a clean, warm and draft-free environment for mom and her pups and give mom plenty of freedom to do the job of caring for her puppies.

Bad Socialization: Remaining with their littermates and being cared for by the mother dog is the most important consideration for puppies during these early weeks. Early weaning is a definite No-No. In addition:

- Puppies should not be separated from their littermates or from the mother dog for more than a few minutes at a time and only then for gentle handling or routine care procedures.

- The mother dog should also not be stressed or given cause to worry about her puppies. Do not force her to leave her puppies when she does not wish to go and do not move the litter without cause.

Sensitive Socialization Period: The sensitive (also called "primary) period of socialization occurs when puppies are between 3 and 12 weeks of age. This period represents a time of rapid behavioral change, coinciding with complete maturation of the puppy's central nervous system and special senses. Behaviorally, this is a time in which puppies are highly sensitive to learning to communicate and about the human world that they will be living in. The first half of this period takes place while the pups are still living with their mom and littermates and the second half occurs after the pups have been weaned and are in their new homes. Let's split this period into those two sub-periods and examine how we can best socialize puppies during these stages.

First Half (3 to 8 weeks): After three weeks of age, puppies become increasingly active and curious about their littermates and surroundings. They readily approach and investigate new things and people and show little fear or caution. After five weeks of age, this boldness diminishes somewhat, but active approach continues to prevail over nervousness or fear in most puppies until they are about eight weeks of age. Other important changes during these weeks include:

- **Playtime:** Puppies begin to show interest in their littermates and show rudimentary play behaviors when they are three to four weeks old. Over the next several weeks, play becomes an increasingly large part of their daily activity. Play provides the puppies with the opportunity to practice communication signals, and teaches them valuable lessons about social relationships with other dogs.

- **Mom-time:** The mother dog's interactions are equally important during the first half of the primary socialization period. Puppies continually solicit care and attention from their mother and her responses provide information to them regarding appropriate social behavior. When puppies play too roughly or become too demanding, their mother will discipline using growls, body postures and physical reprimands such as an inhibited muzzle bite. This helps to teach puppies how to interpret signals from other dogs, to inhibit their bites when playing, and to display appropriate submissive postures to an adult dog who is displaying dominant signals.

Weaning: Mother dogs naturally begin the weaning process when puppies are 3 ½ to 4 weeks of age. This is a gradual process that takes place over a period of several weeks. The mother dog gradually allows her pups to nurse only for short periods, and spends increasing periods of time away from her litter. This slow introduction to longer periods of separation teaches puppies self-confidence and allows them to become progressively independent of their mother's care without the need for abrupt or prolonged (stressful) separations. It is important for puppies to remain with their siblings during these weeks, even though mom is spending less and less time with her puppies. Here are a few additional considerations about weaning:

- **Emphasis on the word "gradual":** Natural weaning by the mother dog is characterized by a period of *gradual* lessening of the puppies' attachment to her, as opposed to an artificially introduced or abrupt separation.

- **Not only about food:** Although puppies have usually stopped nursing regularly by six weeks of age, they will show intermittent suckling for several more weeks if they are still with their mother. If allowed, most mother dogs continue to spend time with their puppies and provide a source of comfort, play and discipline until the puppies are seven weeks or older.

- **Communication skills:** As they approach weaning age, puppies continue to develop their social skills and communicative behaviors by interacting with their mother and their siblings. These skills will serve them well in their future relationships with other dogs and with people.

Good Socialization (First Half of the Sensitive Period): During the first portion of the sensitive period, it is important that puppies remain with their litter and their mother *and* that they receive regular socialization with humans. Once they are weaned and living with their forever family, socialization can continue.

- **Human friends:** This is a great time for the breeder and others to spend lots of time interacting and playing with the pups. The breeder of our Toller, Chip, holds regular puppy play parties for friends and their families to come over to play with puppies and their mom. It is great fun for all involved and the pups have the benefit of meeting a wide variety of new people. All interactions should be positive and non-threatening and should never induce fear or avoidance in the pups. The goal it for pups to learn that all types of people are friendly, safe and to be trusted.

49

- *Increase handling:* Pups should receive short periods of individual and daily handling away from their littermates and mother. Handling should be gentle and should never frighten the pup. General grooming procedures and examinations can be included, and it is not too early to introduce the "touch-then-treat" exercises that we discuss later in the book (see Chapter 6).

- *Toys and enrichment:* Puppies become increasingly curious during the sensitive period and enjoy investigating, playing with and gnawing on toys and other objects. As they become more mobile and begin to play with their siblings, pups compete for possession of toys using chase, keep-away, and tug-of-war games. Pups should be given a variety of toys with different textures and should also be exposed to a variety of normal household objects and surfaces.

Bad Socialization: A number of years ago, it became popular to wean puppies at a very early age – sometimes as young as 4 or 5 weeks. Not only is this a risk in terms of a pup's nutritional health, but early weaning can cause excessive timidity and fear and can inhibit a pup's ability to communicate with and form social attachments to other dogs. There is evidence that puppies who are weaned prematurely are at increased risk to develop a range of behavior problems, including destructive behaviors, fearfulness, and separation anxiety. Consider that weaning is a natural and gradual process in which puppies learn to accept separation from their mother (and eventually from their littermates) progressively, over a period of 4 to 5 weeks. If this process occurs abruptly, the puppies are developmentally too young to withstand the stress of sudden isolation and also have not been afforded the time that is needed to feel secure during periods of separation. Puppies do best if the mother dog is allowed to wean them gradually and if they remain with their siblings until they are at least 7 to 8 weeks of age.

Second Half (8 to 12 weeks): The second half of the sensitive period of socialization takes place when most puppies have been adopted into their homes. This is a time of new experiences and rapid learning and is typically the age that most training schools encourage owners to enroll in a puppy class.

Good **Socialization (Second Half of the Sensitive Period):** So, what should we provide to puppies for socialization once they have been weaned and adopted into their forever homes?

- *Plenty of people:* Optimally, puppies should have received frequent and positive human contact while they were still with their litter, and this contact should be expanded to include a wide variety of friendly folks who love puppies and know how to interact gently and kindly with dogs. Care must be always taken to ensure that meeting unfamiliar people is a pleasant and non-threatening experience.

- *New places and experiences:* As soon as a puppy has been immunized adequately, he can be introduced to new places and experiences. Car rides, visits to public areas that are safe for dogs, walks on public paths, trips to dog-friendly stores and cafés, and enrollment in a puppy class are all great opportunities for giving a young dog new and positive experiences with the world.

- *Other dogs:* Just as with unfamiliar people, only dogs who are known to be friendly and gentle with puppies should be allowed to meet and play with a young puppy. If possible, having a regular puppy play group of puppies who are around the same age is ideal. However, despite Joe's advice that puppies should be allowed to "*work things out for themselves*", play sessions should be closely supervised to ensure that all of the puppies who are playing are comfortable, and are showing appropriate play behaviors (i.e. not bullying or intimidating others). Details and some helpful puppy play guidelines are provided in Chapter 12.

- *Keep going:* A dog's socialization should not stop with the sensitive period at 12 weeks nor with the completion of a puppy class. Puppies vary considerably in their need for socialization after 12 weeks of age, but most continue to enjoy and adapt to new experiences throughout the juvenile period.

- *Lifelong learning:* Therefore, while the age of three to 12 weeks is very important for puppy-to-puppy interaction and human handling, it should not be considered a "window" that closes after this age. Rather, socialization (and training) should continue throughout a dog's life to support the development of a well-adapted and friendly companion.

Bad Socialization: So, getting back to Sandy and Bella. While we know that a lack of socialization in young puppies can hinder their future behavior and ability to adapt to new experiences, it is equally true that exposure to frightening stimuli or repeated stressful events at a young age can have long-term harmful effects. At 11 weeks, Bella was still within her sensitive socialization periods and sadly, she had experienced several fear-provoking interactions with unfamiliar dogs. It does not take many of these experiences for a young dog to learn that unfamiliar dogs are unpredictable and not to be trusted. In Bella's case, we recommended no more trips to the dog park and opportunities for "safe" interactions with other puppies and dogs (details about these techniques are provided in Chapter 12). A few additional points about what socialization should *not* be for puppies of this age include:

- *Prevent reprimands by unfamiliar adult dogs:* A puppy should never be introduced to an adult dog whose behavior with puppies is unknown or who has the potential to injure or frighten the puppy (even if the adult dog's owner insists that her dog will simply be "reprimanding", play it safe and decline the interaction).

- *No unsupervised play*: Consider that just as kids on a playground do not always behave appropriately with one another, neither do puppies. Puppies can be "called out of play" to temper the intensity of play sessions (and to give the puppies a break) and excessively rough or aggressive play should always be interrupted. Pushy puppies must never be allowed to bully other pups. The belief that puppies should just be allowed to work everything out on their own is wrong and is potentially harmful – especially to the puppy who is the target of the bully.

- *No force (allow your puppy to say no):* While moderately challenging situations can be a beneficial component of puppy socialization (provided the puppy can succeed and enjoy the experience), flooding a puppy with too many people, exuberant or uncontrolled dogs, or visiting a public event that is too loud and busy can cause fear. Puppies should be allowed as much choice as is feasible when faced with new experiences and should never be forced to interact or participate.

- *Be your puppy's advocate*: Interactions with new people, new dogs, and new places should supervised, enjoyable and should never invoke fear or avoidance. Be your puppy's security and support – someone he can always trust to be there for comfort and who will always have his back.

Juvenile (Adolescent) Period and Adulthood: The juvenile period extends from the end of the socialization period (~ 13 weeks) to sexual or physical maturity (12 to 18 months depending on breed size). A puppy's learning ability is fully developed by this age and he now spends his time refining his existing abilities, increasing coordination, and becoming more exploratory. The puppy's motor skills become more coordinated and adult-like, and his attention span increases.

Continuing Education: Dogs continue to learn and modify their behavior throughout adult life. Although many owners believe that training needs to happen only during the first year of life, dogs (just like people) benefit most from life-long learning. Training can include preventing unwanted behavior problems, teaching enjoyable games and activities, reinforcing good manners in the home and when out in public, and participating in a dog sport such as agility, K-9 Nose Work or canine freestyle. Similarly, life-long socialization and can take the form of regular excursions to parks and new places, accompanying owners on errands and in some cases vacations, and having opportunities to meet and interact with a variety of new and friendly people of all ages. Not only does the concept of "lifelong learning" help to produce a dog who is enjoyable to live with, continued training and engaging in enjoyable activities with dogs is a lot of fun for people as well and strengthens the bond of love that we share with our dogs.

TALKING TO JOE

Talking to Joe: So, how might we advise Sandy to respond when neighbor Joe begins to lecture her about the benefits of taking little Bella to the dog park? And, what should she say when Joe insists that Bella be allowed to "*work it out for herself*" when she is frightened? How can Sandy refute Joe's claims and courteously educate him about puppy socialization?

Here are a few suggestions:

🐾 Joe, I appreciate that you think the dog park is a good place for Bella. While you are completely correct that proper socialization for puppies includes giving them lots of new experiences, I recently learned that it is equally important that puppies are not frightened or exposed to situations in which they don't have an "escape route" to safety. The dog park is just too unpredictable, especially for a puppy as young as Bella. I do appreciate your concern for Bella though, and know you have our best interests in mind. (It's always a good idea to sweeten up Joe with a bit of flattery whilst setting him straight).

🐾 Since we are on the topic, Joe. I know that you thought that driving up to me and Bella on your 500 HP Mario Andretti lawn tractor was a good way to teach Bella about loud noises. Well, you scared the crap out of both of us, Joe. Next time, please turn Mario off and I will allow Bella to approach your lawn toy on her own terms (and will give her plenty of yummy treats in the process).

🐾 Hey Joe – thanks for the offer! I would love to have your little nephews come over and meet Bella. Here are a few handfuls of yummy treats to give them. Let's have them sit in these two chairs on my porch and we will let Bella approach them for the treats. If they wish, they can toss the treats to her gently from a few feet away – that is a fun game for the kids to play with her, don't you think?

🐾 And finally, Joe. Again, appreciate the good intentions. However, I don't think that it is essential that Bella learn to be comfortable around male neighbors who happen to be grilling out at their pool wearing a bright red Speedo bathing suit (and nothing else). Come to think of it, I don't need that type of socialization either, Joe. Thanks for the show though.

Evidence

Appleby DL, Bradshaw JWS, Casey RA. Relationship between aggressive and avoidance behavior by dogs and their experience in the first six months of life. *Veterinary Record* 2002; 150:434-442.

Battagile CL. Periods of early development and the effects of stimulation and social experiences in the canine. *Journal of Veterinary Behavior* 2009; 4:203-210.

Duxbury MM, Jackson JA, Line SW, et al. Evaluation of association between retention in the home and attendance at puppy socialization classes. *Journal of the American Veterinary Medicine Association* 2003; 223:61-66.

Frank D, Minero M, Cannas S, Palestrini C. Puppy behaviours when left home alone: A pilot study. *Applied Animal Behaviour Science* 2007; 104:61–70.

Gassano A, Mariti C, Notari L, et al. Effects of early gentling and early environment on emotional development in puppies. *Applied Animal Behavior Science* 2008; 110:294-304.

Howell TJ, Kind T, Bennett Pc. Puppy parties and beyond: The role of early age socialization practices on adult dog behavior. *Veterinary Medicine: Research and Reports* 2015; 6:143-153.

Hubrecht RC. Enrichment in puppyhood and its effects on later behavior of dogs. *Laboratory Animal Science* 1995; 45:70-75.

Kutsumi A, Nagasawa M, Ohta M, Ohtani N. Importance of puppy training for future behavior of the dog. *Journal of Veterinary Medicine and Science* 2013; 75:141-149.

Pierantoni L, Verga M. Behavioral consequences of premature maternal separation and lack of stimulation during the socialization period in dogs. *Journal of Veterinary Behavior* 2007; 2:84-85.

Seksel K, Mazurski EJ, Taylor A. Puppy socialization programs: short and long term behavioral effects. *Applied Animal Behavioural Science* 1999; 62:335-349.

Chapter 4
Sniff, Listen, Bark

Chippy, my Toller, loves K-9 Nose Work. We started training Nose Work several years ago and now offer it as a class at AutumnGold. Dogs of all breeds, ages, and training backgrounds enroll and they learn to sniff out the scent of cloves, birch and anise. (No Joe, sorry. We do not use that other wacky weed in these classes). What is most noticeable is how much dogs love this activity.

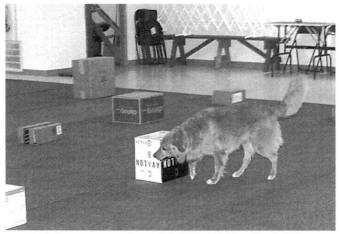

Chippy practices his Nose Work skills

We should not be surprised. All owners know that dogs love to sniff. They sniff a lot of things, a lot of the time. Their noses and sniffing are very important to them. Olfaction is the dog's most cherished (and well developed) special sense. Coming in a close second is hearing; dogs are capable of hearing much higher frequencies of sound than do humans and also excel at locating the source of sounds (it's those swiveling ears).

The dog's highly sensitive nose and ears mean that they perceive the world differently than we do. Walking with our dogs always includes plenty of sniffing and many dogs are incredibly talented at distinguishing the sound of their owner's car or the cookie jar opening from great distances. Visually, humans probably have a step up since dogs do not see the vividly colored world that we enjoy and have a lesser ability to detect detail.

Understanding how the dog sees his world and how this differs from our own perceptions is essential for understanding canine behavior and for effective dog training. In this chapter, we examine what we understand about how the dog sniffs, listens, and barks as he navigates his world.

The Nose: The dog's remarkable smelling talents are due to several unique physical adaptations:

- *Lots of cells*: The dog's nose contains over 220 million olfactory neurons. By comparison, the human nose includes an unimpressive 5 million. This difference contributes to a dog's ability to detect and identify almost impossibly minute concentrations of compounds.

- *Nosey brain*: Two parts of the dog's brain that interpret incoming information from the nose are the olfactory bulb and the olfactory cortex. Both of these areas are highly developed in dogs and are important for how they react to and use the sensory information that the nose provides.

- *Sniff, sniff*: Dogs sniff. We don't. Sniffing involves a disruption of normal breathing patterns and functions to enhance a dog's ability to detect and differentiate smells. As the dog inhales during a sniff, the air is diverted into several flow paths. This partitioning effectively increases the number of sensory cells that inhaled components are exposed to, increasing olfactory sensitivity. During the exhale phase of the sniff, the air leaves via the dog's "side-nostrils", not out the front of the nose as it does with normal breathing. (So **that's** what those slits on the side of Chip's nose are for!). Exhaling through the

59

"side nose" is presumed to prevent the dog's sensory cells from being repeatedly exposed to the same compounds, thus slowing the process of *scent habituation*. (Consider how you no longer can smell "wet dog" after being around it for a while; that's scent habituation).

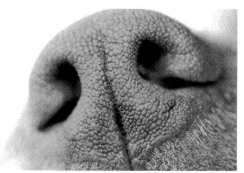

The Remarkable Dog Nose

Together, these adaptations support the dog's extraordinary sense of smell and the talents that come along with it. These include the ability to detect minute amounts of scent, discriminate among a group of different smells and their components, and detect and follow the direction of scent trails. There are many ways in which we have harnessed this canine "super power" in dog training. Dogs can be trained to find illicit drugs, explosives, and land mines for the police and military, to identify the presence of mold, insects and toxins in homes and public buildings, and in recent years, to diagnose the presence of cancerous tumors or changes in blood glucose levels in human patients. On the recreation side of things, anyone who enjoys tracking or K-9 Nose Work with their dog knows that these canine sports are not only interesting and enjoyable for dog enthusiasts, but are great fun for the dogs as well.

Living in an Olfactory World: While humans live in a largely visual world, dogs perceive the world from an olfactory point of view. They pay attention first and foremost to the scents that they come across in their environment, using sniffing as their first line of action when investigating new things. These things may be the deposited smells of other dogs (urine and feces), bits of food left on the training floor, or the body odor of a new friend. Dogs also leave their own scent for other dogs to sniff and to investigate via urine marking behavior.

Let's look at two major types of smell-centric behaviors in detail - marking behavior and social greeting:

Urine marking: Dogs pay close attention to the deposited scents of other dogs and animals. One of the most obvious ways in which they do this is by sniffing the urine and feces deposits of other dogs and by marking with urine. Marking behavior involves frequent and short leg-lifts or squats at numerous sites in which a small volume of urine is deposited at each episode. This differs from normal urination, during which the dog's entire bladder is emptied. Most male dogs use a raised-leg urination display when scent-marking. Some female dogs demonstrate a form of raised-leg urination in which they raise one hind leg while squatting, but most are more likely to just squat more frequently and void small amounts of urine.

When out walking away from home, dogs are often attracted to spots where other dogs have urinated. Although the degree of interest varies among dogs, most spend several moments sniffing these areas intently. Some follow up by over-marking the sniffed area with urine before moving on. Urine marking is not just a "when out walking" behavior in dogs. Some dogs regularly over-mark the urine of a housemate and others will (unfortunately) mark when visiting the home of a dog friend. There is nothing more embarrassing than having your reliably house-trained dog suddenly urinate on a piece of furniture in a (previously welcoming) host's living room. At our training school, it is not unusual for new dogs to suddenly lift a leg on a wall or piece of training equipment. Contrary to the owner's concern, this behavior does not mean that their dog has suddenly lapsed in his housetraining. Rather, this is just normal marking behavior in response to the smell of other dogs in the training building.

Although not as common, feces can also provide a form of scent marking for dogs. The contents of a dog's anal glands are discharged during defecation and contribute pheromones to the feces and around the dog's anal region. Studies have shown that the anal gland secretions of dogs are highly individual in nature, and may provide information about a dog's age, sex, and identity. Dogs also occasionally express their anal glands independently of defecation when they are stressed or frightened. (Many of us have learned this the hard way during a particularly stressful visit with a dog to the vet's office). While out walking, most dogs show an interest in the fecal droppings of other dogs and may over-mark another dog's feces with urine. However, it is not known how important feces are for marking or identifying individuals as "poop marking" seems to come in a distant second to urine for this purpose.

So, what exactly does urine marking and sniffing the marks of other dogs *mean* to our dogs? Historically, urine marking was interpreted as a type of communication meant to deter other individuals of the same species from entering the marked territory. However, this *"drive off competitors"* theory has not held up under scrutiny. There is no evidence that urine deposits left by one dog functions to repel or change the path of other dogs (even in feral dogs). Because both male and female dogs investigate the urine marks of other dogs and over-mark, it is now believed that urine marking provides information about the depositing dog's identity and frequented territory, but does *not* act as a barrier or warning signal for others to stay away. Urine marks are a canine calling-card, if you will.

Marking behavior may also have a stress-reducing benefit for dogs. Because urine marking deposits an individual's scent and often adds it to the milieu of scents in an area, it is theorized that making an area smell "more like me" enhances feelings of security in a dog who may be in an area that is suddenly filled with the smells of unfamiliar dogs. For this reason, it is important to distinguish between dogs who are urine marking versus those who are not completely house trained or are lapsing in their training. Owners should not look at this as a lapse in house training, but rather as a dog who may be feeling a bit insecure about the unfamiliar dogs whose scent he is detecting and so adds in some of his own to reduce that anxiety and add his own smell to the mix.

Sniffs when greeting: Olfaction is an integral component of the dog's social behavior and is of particular importance when dogs are greeting other dogs and people. The pattern of sniffing that is observed when a dog greets another friendly dog tends to be highly consistent and ritualized. Initially, dogs sniff each other's mouth or face, and this is followed by sniffing the groin (inguinal) region.

First, We Face Sniff

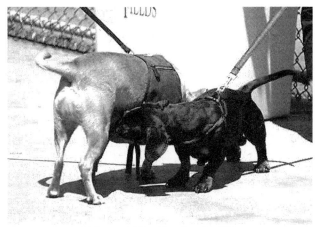

Then, We Groin Sniff

When greeting a new person, dogs often sniff a hand, pant leg (or other body part) first, prior to allowing the person to touch or pet them. Most people will naturally offer a hand for a dog to sniff before attempting to touch or pet the dog. While this is acceptable to many dogs, some prefer to sniff while the person is turned to the side (laterally), is crouching, or even turned away. Regardless, allowing dogs to "get in a sniff" first, is imperative to normal and friendly greeting behaviors for dogs. (We look at greeting behaviors in dogs in more detail in the following chapter).

The Ears: Like their sense of smell, the dog's auditory sense is well developed and highly sensitive. Dogs are capable of detecting sounds of high frequencies, well above what we can hear. While the human ear can detect sounds that are up to 20,000 cycles per second (cps), dogs can detect sounds as high as 45,000 cps. What this means practically speaking is that dogs are capable of hearing and responding to sounds that we are completely oblivious to. It is probable that this capability evolved to aid in the detection and capture of small prey species, such as mice, that use high frequency sounds to communicate. Dogs also have mobile ears. Not only do their ears swivel to help them to locate sound – each ear is also capable of moving independently! Finally, the structure of dogs' ears enables them to hear over a great distance, about four time further than humans are able to hear.

The Voice (Bark, Bark): Dogs produce a wide range of utterances and use vocal communication frequently (sometimes more frequently than their owners would like - more about this in Chapter 14). Research has shown that dogs' vocalizations are highly contextual. This means that they can convey different messages depending on the particular situation in which they are used. The most common canine vocalizations that we all know include whines, growls, howls, grunts, and of course the ubiquitous bark.

Grunts are often heard during greeting or as a sign of contentment or relaxation. Puppies typically grunt while they are eating or sleeping, but many adult dogs retain this (pretty adorable) vocalization throughout their lives. Growls are used to signal defensive or offensive aggression, resource guarding, or in a modified form, playfulness. Whines and whimpers signal hunger, discomfort, stress, fear or loneliness. Some dogs also whine when they are seeking attention or during greeting. For many owners, deciphering *"what the whine means"* can be a challenge simply because dogs whine in such a wide variety of situations. Howling is a frequent wolf and coyote vocalization but is relatively rare in dogs. It is believed that all dogs are capable of howling, but many never do so. Wild canids use the howl to seek contact with other pack members when separated or to assemble prior to hunting or travel. Dogs may howl when they are isolated or in response to an unusual sound, such as sirens, airplanes flying overhead, or even certain types of music.

Perhaps one of the most interesting dog vocalizations is the bark. The domestic dog is unique among canids in its extensive use of barking. Although wolves bark, they usually exhibit only one or two short barks followed by silence. Repetitive barking appears to be unique to the domestic dog. It has been suggested that during domestication, repetitive barking was desirable because it provided a method of signaling alarm or the approach of intruders. Others have suggested that repetitive barking is a neotenized behavior, representing vestiges of puppy and adolescent vocalizations that now persist into adulthood.

Regardless of its evolutionary basis, the dog's bark is here to stay. And dogs sure do use it a lot - they bark in defense of territory, when announcing the presence of another dog or person, when playing, when excited, when isolated, when frustrated, or when seeking attention. Barking is an example of a communicative signal that conveys a warning or change in situation, but one that is also highly variable and context-specific. Interestingly, humans have been shown to be quite talented at deciphering the meanings of a dog's bark, even when they do not know the context and often times when they do not even know the dog! This ability is more well-developed in dog professionals and owners but most people tested can easily tell the difference between the barks of a dog who is stressed or afraid and those of a dog who is playing or defending territory.

While there is less evidence regarding how *dogs* interpret the barks of other dogs, a series of studies produced in the last few years found that dogs are quite able to identify their friends simply by the sound of their bark and, like people, can differentiate between types of barks quite successfully. Even though repetitive barking can often be annoying and a problem behavior that needs to be modified, barking is an important form of communication that both dogs and people understand and respond to.

The Eyes: Many dog owners have heard that dogs are color-blind and interpret this information to mean that dogs see the world in black-and-white and shades of grey. While not technically correct, it is true that the dog has significantly more limited ability to see color when compared with humans (and other primates). This difference is due primarily to different concentrations of photoreceptor (light sensitive) cells in the dog's eye.

The retina of all mammals contains two types of photoreceptors, called cones and rods. Cones are responsible for color perception and for detecting detail. Rods detect motion and aid in vision in low light intensity. Dogs have fewer cone cells and more rod cells in their retinas compared with that of the human eye. The reduced number of cones results in dogs having *dichromatic* color vision rather than *trichromatic*, like humans. This means that rather than seeing blues, yellows and reds (and their combinations) as we do, dogs see only two of these three colors, blues and yellows (and their combinations). So, dogs do see color – they just see fewer primary colors than we do.

The larger proportion of rods in the dog's retina means that dogs see much better at night and are also better adapted to detect and track movement, especially under conditions of dim light. In addition to these advantages, the dog's eye has a second adaptation that aids in dim light vision. The tapetum lucidum is a unique anatomical feature of the dog's eye composed of a layer of reflective cells located immediately behind the retina. This area functions to reflect scattered light back onto the photoreceptive cells of the retina, increasing the eye's light-gathering capability by about 40 percent. The tapetum is responsible for the "red eyes" that are seen when a light is shown straight into a dog's eyes, or when pictures are taken with a flash camera. However, this enhanced ability to capture reflected light is also associated with increased scattering of light waves, which reduces the ability of dogs to see the details of images.

Because of the placement of their eyes on the skull, most dogs also have good lateral vision. The further to the side of the head that the eyes are placed, the greater is the visual field of view. The total field of view for the average dog is about 60 to 70 degrees greater than that of humans. While this increased field of vision is advantageous for scanning the horizon and for detecting movement, it is offset by decreased binocular vision. This deficit contributes to the dog's lesser ability to focus on objects that are at close range or to judge distance (depth perception).

The Dog's World: Taken together, the dog's highly sensitive nose, finely-tuned ears, range of vocalizations and visual distinctions lead to a different perceptual world for dogs than the one in which we reside. While humans tend to rely upon our visual perceptions to inform us, dogs rely on their noses and ears first, with vision taking a distant third. As an example, let's return to K-9 Nose Work training. When I hide the scent tin in one of a series of 40 boxes strewn about the training room floor, I use *vision* to select a box and then to remind myself where the clove-scented box is hidden. (*Okay, it's in the white box with the bright blue label with a tear on the left side).* Chippy, on the other hand, enters the room, races around all of the boxes, using his sense of *smell* to locate the hidden clover-smelling cotton swab. He suddenly stops short and drops into a down in front of the correct box. Where I need vision to inform me, Chippy needs and uses his amazing canine nose. As always with Nose Work and with dogs, I am amazed and humbled.

TALKING TO JOE

Talking to Joe: Joe may arrive at your training school (or at your door) armed with a list of theories about the dog's abilities to smell, hear and see. Some of these may be true, some may contain bits of fact and bits of fiction, and some may be pure myth. Here are a few tips to educate the Joes in *your* world regarding how dogs perceive *their* world.

🐾 Joe, I overheard you mention that dogs can "smell fear". Well, to date, no one has identified a specific odor of fear (although human sweat may come close). Still, although we have no evidence that dogs can smell actual fear in humans (or any oth-

68

er animal), there is recent evidence showing that dogs react differently to the sweat of people who are fearful versus the sweat of people who are happy. This comes pretty darn close to smelling fear! Dogs are also masters at paying attention to and understanding an entire host of body language signals in humans. Together, these smells and signs may help dogs to sense when a person is nervous, anxious, or afraid versus confident and friendly.

🐾 And, the color-blind thing, Joe. It was once thought that dogs could see only in black and white (and shades of gray), kinda like your favorite old TV shows. Many people still think this is the case. However, dogs do see color, just in a more limited range of hues compared with people. Dogs see blues and yellows, but not reds, greens, or oranges. So, that red plaid shirt that you like to wear with your orange striped shorts, Joe? Your dog Sammy thinks those look just fine together.

🐾 Hey neighbor Joe, I see you are blowing one of those silent dog whistles. Did Jet escape from your fence again? So, how is that whistle working for you? (Note: It is probably wise to refrain from pointing out that Jet is nowhere to be seen). You know, Joe, despite some slick marketing claims, there are no magical qualities to a silent dog whistle. It is simply producing a high frequency sound that Jet can hear and (mercifully) that we cannot. In terms of training, this means that if you want Jet to respond to the silent whistle by coming to its sound, then you must *train* him to come when called in response to it. It's not an automatic response that dogs are born with. If you would like some help with that, we have a Rollicking Recalls class starting next week at my training school that would be perfect for you and Jet!

🐾 While we are on the topic of dog whistles, let's dispel one more myth. Silent dog whistles (or their electronic equivalents which also produce the same type of high-frequency sounds) do NOT solve problem behaviors in dogs such as excessive barking, aggressive behavior, digging, or any other undesirable behavior. That sound that you keep making with your whistle will have absolutely no effect (other than to annoy all of the dogs in the neighborhood) unless your dog is trained to respond to it. Attempts to use a silent signal to punish unwanted behavior can quickly backfire because the sound it produces may be so irritating that it could provoke a dog to bark more, or if he is really smart, to run away from that grating sound. (Seeing how hard you are blowing on that thing, I am really glad that I cannot hear it, Joe).

Evidence

Farago T, et al. This bone is mine: Affective and referential aspects of dog growls. *Animal Behaviour* 2010; 79:917-921.

Feddersen-Petersen DU. Vocalization of European wolves (*Canis lupus lupus*) and various dog breeds (*Canis familiaris*). *Archives fur Tierzucht* 2000; 43:387-398.

Horowitz A, Hecht J, Dedrick A: Smelling more or less: Investigating the olfactory experience of the domestic dog, *Learning and Motivation* 2013; 44:201-217.

Johnen D, Heuwieser W, Fischer-Tenhagen C. Canine scent detection - Fact or fiction? *Applied Animal Behaviour Science* 2013; 148:201-208.

Kogan LR, Schoenfeld-Tacher R, Simon AA. Behavioral effects of auditory stimulation on kenneled dogs. *Journal of Veterinary Behavior* 2012; 7:268-275.

Molnar C, Pongracz P, Farage T, Doka A, Miklosi A. Dogs discriminate between barks: The effect of context and identity of the caller. *Behavioural Processes* 2009; 82:198-201.

Pongracz P, Szabo E, Kis A, Peter A, Miklosi A. More than noise? Field investigations of intraspecific acoustic communication in dogs (Canis familiaris). *Applied Animal Behavioural Science* 2014: 159:62-68.

Pongracz P, Molnar C, Miklosi A. Barking in family dogs: An ethological approach. *The Veterinary Journal* 2010; 183:141-147.

Pongracz P, Molnar C, Miklosi A. Acoustic parameters of dog barks carry emotional information for humans. *Animal Behaviour Science* 2006; 100:228-240.

Pongracz P, Molnar C, Miklosi A, Csanyi V. Human listeners are able to classify dog barks recorded in different situations. *Journal of Comparative Psychology* 2005; 119:228-240.

Prato-Previde E, Marshall-Pescini S, Valsecchi P: Is your choice my choice? The owner's effect on pet dogs' (Canis *lupus familiaris*) performance in a food choice task. *Animal Cognition 2008; 11:*167-174.

Raglus TI, Groef BD, Marston LC. Can bark counter collars and owner surveys help identify factors that relate to nuisance barking? A pilot study. *Journal of Veterinary Behavior* 2015; 10:204-209.

Wells DL, Graham L, Hepper PG. The influence of auditory stimulation on the behavior of dogs housed in a rescue shelter. *Animal Welfare* 2002; 11:385-393.

Chapter 5
The Whole Picture – Understanding Dog

At AutumnGold, we use a three-page behavior profile form to screen dogs for entry into group classes. The form includes standard demographic information (age, sex, neuter status, where the dog was acquired, etc.), plus a series of questions about the dog's behavior at home and when in public. At the end of the form, prospective students can circle a number of problem behaviors that their dog is showing and can add their own remarks. When we receive forms that indicate problem aggression or excessive fear, I call the owner to discuss the behavior and to set up private, in-home lessons if necessary.

It is not uncommon for clients to circle *"aggressive to other dogs in the home"* or *"aggressive to people"* on this form. However, when I call to chat with them, I sometimes learn that the behavior that their dog is demonstrating is simply play behavior (albeit often rough play) or vestiges of puppy nipping and mouthing. Similarly, we frequently encounter owners who refer to their dogs as *"a bit timid"* with new dogs, only to find that their dog becomes almost catatonically fearful when she leaves the home or sees an unfamiliar dog.

So, what is going on? Why do owners who are devoted to their dogs and are motivated enough to enroll with us in a training class, frequently misinterpret their dog's behavior? Part of the problem may be related to persistent myths about canine body language. Some examples of these are *"A wagging tail means a friendly dog"*, *"A growling dog is going to bite"*, *"Dogs feel threatened by eye contact"* and one of my personal favorites *"Dogs who jump up when greeting are being dominant."* A second contributing factor may be lack of attention to the non-verbal communication signals of dogs. Because humans rely heavily upon verbal communication and language to communicate, it is theorized that people are often unpracticed at perceiving the non-verbal signals of others - both human and canine. Some dog owners may not pay attention to the signals that their dog is sending via facial expressions and body postures that communicate how he is feeling and is about to do.

Dogs use a range of complex and varied visual signals when communicating with others. These signs include variations in eye contact, facial expression and body posture. The direction of a dog's gaze, carriage of her head, set of her ears, retraction of her lips, position of her tail and placement of her feet combine to tell a story about how she is feeling. Equally important is the context within which these visual signals occur and the identity and behavior of the receiver of the signals - is the approaching individual a known and friendly dog, an unfamiliar dog, a welcomed owner, or a potentially threatening stranger? Is the dog in an environment that he knows well and has visited often or is he entering a new space where there are numerous uncertainties?

Understanding canine body language and communication includes the *whole picture* – all of the visual (and often subtle) signals that the dog is displaying plus consideration of the situation that he or she is responding to.

What do People *Need* to Know? There are several excellent books by other authors that provide detailed reviews of canine body language (see the "Books" section at the end of this book for recommendations). It is not necessary that I attempt to repeat the information provided in those comprehensive books. Rather, the intent of *this* book is to help trainers and other pet professionals to educate the average dog owner (Joe and his pals) about what exactly it is that dogs are saying to them in a given context.

While there is much that we could teach to our students about canine body language, the essential skill that is needed by everyone, including non-owners, is the ability to recognize dogs who are friendly versus those who are fearful or potentially aggressive. Because many students also have more than one dog or allow their dog to play frequently with neighbor dogs, it is also helpful for owners to understand a bit about dog-to-dog interactions and play. In a nutshell, most dog owners are interested in the answers to these four questions:

🐾 Is this dog friendly (to me, to other dogs)?

🐾 Is this dog afraid (of me, of my dog)?

🐾 Might this dog become aggressive and bite (me or my dog)?

🐾 Is this normal play behavior (with me, with other dogs)?

Let's start with the easiest of the four – recognizing a friendly dog.

Are You Friendly? The important components of a dog's facial expression include her eyes, ears, and mouth. As Sophie shows on the following page, a dog who is friendly and interested in greeting will have relaxed ears (appropriate for ear type), retracted lips (corners of the mouth are pulled back) and a relaxed and open mouth. This happy face is often referred to as a "greeting grin." Her face will show no facial tension and she will either be giving direct eye contact (without a hard stare) or more commonly, short periods of offering eye contact and then looking away.

Friendly Face (Sophie)

The body posture of a friendly dog is relaxed (i.e. not stiff) and the dog will have a neutral body carriage (neither leaning forward intensely or shrinking away). As Stanley shows below, a confident and friendly dog will hold his head level with or above the topline of his back and the tail is out or slightly up (and often wagging).

Friendly and Confident (Stanley)

If the dog is less confident or is showing submission, her greeting posture changes slightly to signal appeasement (Duchess, below). The tail is lowered but is still wagging, ears are down and shifted backwards (but usually are not pinned back), and the dog's body posture is slightly lowered (but not cowering). Some dogs may also lift a front paw, which is considered an appeasing gesture. The dog may also lick (tongue flick) and her eyes may be partially shut with a "squinting" appearance.

Friendly and Appeasing (Duchess)

Finally, dogs who are very excited during greeting but are still showing deference often "wiggle" their hind ends as they greet. This is sometimes referred to as active submission. A dog showing this level of appeasement will usually avoid eye contact altogether, but will still approach, usually with a lowered head and tail down. The tail is wagging, and she may even have a "groveling" appearance, a look that some owners misconstrue as "guilt" (sorry Joe; that is not what it is; more about this later). Some dogs roll onto their backs when greeting, either as a signal of passive submission or as a learned behavior to solicit a belly rub and attention. All of these postures are normal canine greeting behaviors that convey a friendly, non-threatening dog who is interested in interacting.

The importance of sniff: Friendly dogs begin each greeting encounter with a sniff. Interestingly, there is evidence that dogs gravitate to different human body parts for their hello sniff, depending whether the person they are interacting with is a friend versus someone unfamiliar. They focus on sniffing the person's hands or face when greeting their owner or a friend and focus on the anogenital region (the groin) of people who they do not know. (Anyone who has been embarrassed by their dogs inquisitive and intrusive nose with visiting guests knows exactly what I am talking about). Regardless, all owners (and anyone who likes dogs, really) should be taught to *"accept the sniff"* by holding out a hand, turning laterally (sideways) to avoid towering over the dog, and allowing the dog to approach first for that all important greeting sniff.

Dogs who jump up to greet: A common dog myth that needs to be put to rest once and for all is the belief that dogs who jump up while greeting are asserting dominance. This is false. A dog who jumps up to greet is usually just a friendly, exuberant dog who has never been taught *not* to jump up while greeting. In many cases, the dog has also unintentionally been reinforced for jumping up. For example, Max's owner, Brian (next page), clearly enjoys greeting Max in this manner. As a result, Max jumps up not only when he is saying hello to Brian, but whenever he meets someone new. Max is a friendly dog and his jumping up has been repeatedly reinforced with good stuff – contact, petting and attention. So sorry Joe, Max is not being dominant, just friendly. To solve this, when it is identified as a problem behavior, we teach Max to offer sit or offer another alternate behavior for greeting (see Chapter 14 for details).

Jumping Up to Greet (Brian and Max)

Dog-friendly dogs (and the sniff): Friendly (non-threatening) greeting behavior between two dogs includes body postures that are similar to those seen when dogs communicate friendliness to people. When both dogs are comfortable, their body postures are relaxed, corners of the mouth are pulled back (that smile again), ears are pivoted back or forward (but relaxed), eyes or slightly squinted or directed to the side to avoid direct stares and tails are gently wagging. Although one dog may be more confident than the other (who is often showing appeasement gestures), this does not signal a threat in the absence of other signs. As we discussed in Chapter 4, the sniff is an integral component of dog-to-dog greeting. Greeting sniffs between dogs are directed towards faces (Gabby and Sally, following page), or sides and groins (Carter and Harpo). After sniffing, the greeting either ends peacefully or one dog invites the other to play.

Face Sniffing during Greeting (Gabby and Sally)

Groin Sniffing during Greeting (Carter and Harpo)

Are You Afraid? Accurately recognizing fear in dogs is an important skill set to have. Dogs vary tremendously in the types of situations and interactions that cause them to be fearful. Understanding when their dog is feeling nervous or afraid will help owners to recognize these situations and find ways to reduce potential triggers of stress for their dog. For trainers, helping our

80

clients to be sensitive to signs of stress and fear in their dogs promotes the development of empathy and understanding as well as encourages humane training.

A dog who is nervous or fearful stands or lies rigidly and is not relaxed. His body posture is lowered, his tail is tucked tightly and his eyes are wide and rounded with dilated pupils (see Jeb, below). His mouth will be either closed tightly or he may be panting. Some, but not all dogs also have piloerection (raised hackles). Although a nervous dog's ears may be directed forward when he initially alerts, fearful dogs usually keep their ears pivoted back and down. Finally, because a fearful dog's primary desire is to escape, his body posture is often directed backward rather than forward and he may make an effort to run away or hide.

Fearful Body Posture (Jeb)

A dog who is non-reactive (i.e. will not become aggressive) and who is extremely fearful may lie down, with his head lowered and turned away, in a posture that is often referred to as "freez-

81

ing." Some dogs may show displacement behaviors when they are stressed, which can include yawning, a tongue flick, licking, or sniffing the ground. Conversely, a dog who is more reactive and perceives himself to be cornered and unable to escape may become defensively aggressive.

Might You Bite? Body postures that convey the potential for aggression can be divided into two general categories, offensive threat and defensive threat. Offensive threat refers to a confident dog who is displaying threat signals when he is in control of a valued resource such as a toy or food bowl, or when he is responding to a perceived challenge to territory or social status. The dog will stand tall on his toes, raise his head, lean forward, and elevate his tail. As an interaction becomes more aggressive, piloerection will develop along the dog's shoulders and back and his facial expression will change. The dog's lips will be retracted vertically into a snarl, sometimes called a "C" lip position and the dog may growl deeply (see Riley, below).

Offensive Threat (Riley)

If the offensive threat display is directed toward another dog, the threatening dog may attempt to place a forepaw over the shoulders of the second dog. If the second dog shows deference (reduced body posture, avoiding eye contact), the interaction may end peaceably. However, if the second dog responds with direct eye contact or growls, a fight may ensue. When a dog showing offensive threat is guarding a valued resource such as a bone or toy, the dog will freeze over the object and direct his eye contact (a hard stare) toward the encroaching person or dog. If the intruder continues to approach, an aggressive air snap or actual bite will usually occur as the dog attempts to prevent access to the resource.

In contrast to offensive threat, a dog will show a defensive threat posture when he is fearful but perceives that there is no escape route available. Defensive aggression can also become a preemptive response in dogs who have learned to distrust approaching people or unfamiliar dogs. In these cases, the dog's body posture often becomes a mixture of defensive and offensive signals or shifts to completely offensive, as the dog learns over time that aggression is an effective means of driving the threat away.

The body posture of a dog who is defensive includes pinned back ears and retracted lips, which shows all of the side molars and premolars. The dog may growl or bark as he gazes toward the stimulus. Some dogs show a characteristic "whale eye", with the head averted slightly as the dog still attempts to watch the stimulus that is causing fear. This posture causes the white of the eye to become easily visible (see Jack, next page).

Defensive Threat (Jack)

Some trainers describe the defensive dog's body posture as depicting a state of ambivalence, since the dog is both feeling fear (and wants to flee) and that he has to defend himself. This state of conflict is said to be displayed when the dog shows the lowered body posture of fear, while his facial expression and snarls warn of an impending snap or bite dog (see Cody, below).

Defensive Threat (Cody)

Are You Playing? At AutumnGold we have an informal group of trainers and dog friends who get together regularly to train, go for group dog walks, and give our dogs free time to play together (with supervision). During play time, we take care that the dogs who are loose know one another well, are comfortable together and demonstrate appropriate play manners. We include plenty of "calling out of play" and pauses to keep things safe and tension free. One of the most enjoyable things about these sessions is that they give us a chance to watch our dogs having fun together and to observe the many ways in which dogs communicate with each other during play.

There is also a substantial body of science on the topic of play behaviors. Researchers have long been interested in the expression and functions of animal play in a variety of species, including dogs. Several scientists, such as Marc Bekoff, Nicola Rooney, John Bradshaw and Alexandra Horowitz have published work in recent years examining play behavior in puppies and adult dogs. We have learned several important things about dog play from their research.

Alice and Colbie Enjoy a Play Session at AutumnGold

First, like many other social species, dogs exhibit a set of highly ritualized cues that communicate to their play partner that their intention is to play. Clear signals are important because many of the behaviors that occur during play mimic those typically used during aggressive encounters and predation (hunting). Therefore, a signal that communicates *we are playing now – this is not real*" is important for play partners so that they can prevent misinterpretations and fights.

Perhaps the most well-recognized communicative play posture in dogs is the play bow. Humans and dogs alike recognize this posture and respond to it appropriately. A play bow is used when dogs invite another dog or a person to play, as a way to synchronize (match) play behaviors, and to restart play after a pause. The dog lowers his forequarters slightly while leaving the back legs extended and the rump raised (see Lily and Mr. Bean, below). The inviting dog may initially raise a front paw in an intention movement or paw at the face (dog) or leg (human) partner. If the slight forward movement and pawing does not have the desired effect, the dog may then progress to a full play bow. This is often followed by either a pounce forward or running away in an invitation to chase. The play partner usually interprets a play bow as an invitation to begin or continue play and will respond with a similar bow or begin a chase to instigate a "catch-me" game.

Play Bow (Lily and Mr. Bean)

Both puppies and adult dogs use play solicitation postures to signal friendly intentions. Interestingly, recent studies of how dogs and their owners interact have found that one of the most common body postures that humans use to entice their dogs to play is a simulation of the canine play bow. Most of the dogs in the study interpreted this posture as invitation to approach and to make contact with the person for play or petting.

Dogs demonstrate a wide variety of play styles and enjoy various combinations of object play (tug, teasing), physical play (wrestling, body slamming, mounting), and chase games. There are some general breed-specific play styles. For example, retrieving breeds tend to be very oral (mouthy) and physical (wrestling, body slamming), herding breeds usually enjoy chasing and being chased, and many working breeds focus on possession games such as tug or keep-away. However, play style ultimately depends upon an individual dog's personality, socialization history and relationship with his or her play partner. Rough and tumble play that includes wrestling, mounting, and play biting is common between dogs who live together or are well-acquainted friends who trust each other (see Cooper and Vinny, below). Conversely, chase and keep-away games, with less direct body contact, are more often observed between dogs who are less well-acquainted and are gradually getting to know each other.

Wrestling Play between Housemates (Cooper and Vinny)

87

In addition to the play bow, dogs use several other body language signals to communicate play intentions. These include the open-mouthed play-face, intention (teasing) gestures with a paw or toy, and jumping away as an invitation to chase. Mouth-wrestling (Cooper and Alice, below), is also a common play behavior, especially between dogs who know each other well.

Mouth-wrestling (Cooper and Alice)

Play, normal greeting or something else? Owners are often uncertain regarding what constitutes normal and acceptable play, what is too rough and increases risk of injuries, and what is too intense and in danger of leading to aggression. We hear of these concerns both when client's dogs are playing with another dog and when the dog is playing with family members (especially children). In our classes, we teach owners to pay attention to a set of specific body language and vocalization cues that can be used as markers for inappropriate play and other types of interactions, such as dog-to-dog greeting and territorial responses.

Vocalizations are one of the most important cues that owners should attend to during play. Many dogs vocalize while playing - they bark and yip when chasing and play-growl when wrestling or playing tug. The pitch (frequency) of play barks is rapid and the tone is high (think puppy yips). Similarly, play growls are higher in tone than are aggressively-motivated growls (and will also be accompanied by play body signals). Dogs who are becoming over-stimulated or aggressively aroused during play will change both the pitch and the tone of their vocalizations. Barks may stop altogether (or become lower in tone), while deep-throated growling will replace play growls. When helping clients to learn how to recognize these changes in tone, tell them to think about the different way that they speak when playing with an infant versus when they are verbally reprimanding a surly teenager. High pitched/high frequency = happy interactions; low pitched/lower frequency = unhappy (potentially aggressive) interactions.

The three S's: Body language also tells owners when their dog is playing versus becoming overly stimulated, fearful or aggressive. At AutumnGold, we teach the three most important cues as "*The Three S's*" - Stillness, Stiffness and Staring. A dog who is feeling apprehensive, either when greeting another dog or if play becomes frightening, will no longer have a relaxed, loose body posture. Rather, he will stop moving as freely and may become completely still. Stillness, when viewed in contrast to the happy young dog wiggling his butt to say hello or offering a play bow, becomes an obvious cue that something is not quite right and the dog is feeling uncomfortable. Stiffness is one step further along the discomfort scale. A dog who is becomes stiff while greeting another dog or when guarding a toy during play is signaling extreme discomfort or possessiveness and has the potential to become aggressive. The third S is staring. Owners typically think of this cue as occurring only when the dog is showing a hard stare directly into the eyes of another dog or person. However, in the majority of cases, dogs who are still and stiff and staring will be gazing straight ahead (seemingly at nothing). While some will stare at the approaching dog or person, many do not. Staring straight ahead, when accompanied by stillness and stiffness, is a sign of a dog who is on either the offensive or defensive, is no longer playing or greeting happily, and needs to be helped out of the situation to prevent escalation.

What to do? The most important recommendation we can make to our clients and dog owners is to avoid situations in which the three S's appear in dogs. Use proper greeting techniques when introducing new people and dogs. Introduce dogs on play dates gradually and in pairs or small groups. One of the best ways to allow dogs to get to know each other gradually is simply taking them for on-lead walks together. Owners can begin with one dog leading and the other following (allowing short-duration sniffs), and then switching the lead dog. As the dogs become comfortable with each other, the owners can walk in parallel, with a human between the dogs. Eventually, dog friends walk easily together and may be given opportunity to play together.

During off-lead play between dogs, the play should be interrupted frequently by calling dogs out of play and taking pause breaks. For puppies, these breaks can include reinforcing calm behaviors and short petting sessions with the owner (see Chapter 12) and for adult dogs, owners can reinforce a short down/stay on a mat. It is most important for owners to learn to interrupt play *before* it escalates into rough play or bullying behavior, *not* in response to the unwanted and potentially dangerous behaviors (see preemptive redirection in Chapter 14 for details).

Context Matters: Every dog interaction must be considered in context. When greeting a person, is the approaching individual someone known to the dog or a complete stranger? Is the dog at home, in his yard, or out walking in the neighborhood? Is the dog well-socialized to new people and situations or does he generally become nervous when in new situations? Similar factors should be considered during dog-to-dog interactions. Have the dogs met previously? If not, are they both generally friendly and playful with other dogs? If so, what are their respective play styles? Does one or both guard toys? Does either or both dogs like to play rough? To chase? The big picture includes body language signs and situational factors, many of which are highly dependent upon the dog's personality and history. Here is an example.

Take a look at the dog below. How would you interpret this facial expression?

Now look at the complete photo (following page), which provides more context. This photo was a play session between my Toller, Chippy (the dog above) and one of my Goldens, Cooper. And of course, the type of vocalizations was important. This play session included plenty of high pitched play growls and yips. In isolation, Chippy's face looked almost classically like a dog who was displaying offensive threat, perhaps to guard territory or a favorite bone. However, when taken in context (along with vocalizations and other body cues), this interaciton was clearly very different than what Chip's snarly face alone suggested.

Big picture – Body language, vocalizations, situational context, knowledge of the individual dog or dogs. All are important and vital for understanding (and training) dogs.

TALKING TO JOE

Talking to Joe: So, Joe has a new dog, Maggie. Perhaps Maggie is a social butterfly who loves (and leaps upon) every new person and dog who she meets. Alternatively, Maggie might be a bit nervous when she meets new people and may prefer not to have her space invaded by an unfamiliar dog. Here are a few quick tips that you can use to help Joe learn to pay attention to Maggie's body language as she communicates how she is feeling:

🐾 Hey Joe, nice to see you and Maggie in class with us. I see that you wrote on your profile that Maggie loves people, but I noticed that Maggie is crouched low, has her hackles up and woofed when I come up to greet. These are signs that Maggie is a bit nervous right now. The good news is that Maggie did relax and said hello to me when I crouched, turned sideways, and tossed yummy treats to her. If you can encourage your neighbors to say hello to Maggie using this approach, Joe, it will help her to meet new people without feeling nervous.

🐾 Jumping up is common in young dogs, Joe. They do this because they want to get close to us for petting and sometimes for a bit of face-licking. Despite what you may have read on the internet, jumping up is not a sign of dominance in Maggie. The fact that she jumps up on you to greet does not mean that she is plotting a power coup in your home. Rather, it is a sign of affection and excitement. Dogs will continue to jump up to greet if they have not been actively trained to something else, such as a sit-for-greeting, something that we are going to teach you how to do in class!

🐾 Your daughter Susan mentioned that Maggie seems to be afraid of her new boyfriend. Susan suspects it is because of his purple Mohawk, clanking body piercings, and booming voice. (She also said that it is because Maggie knows that you do not like the boyfriend, but I will stay out of that conversation). Susan related that her boyfriend repeatedly attempts to pet Maggie but Maggie barks and backs away from him. Susan thought that this meant Maggie wanted to play, so the boyfriend has been throwing toys to her (it is not working). The boyfriend needs to learn that a nervous dog does not *want* to be petted or to play and that Maggie needs to be allowed to greet on her own terms (if at all).

🐾 And Joe, remember the three S's: Stillness, Stiffness and Staring. If Maggie shows these body cues when she is greeting another dog, they are signs that she is highly uncomfortable (in her case, fearful) and may feel forced to snap or bite. Help her out by avoiding situations in which you know she will not handle well. In this class (and later in this book), we will

93

teach you how to introduce Maggie gradually and safely to new dogs, new people and new activities.

Evidence

Byosiere SE, Espinosa J, Smuts B. Investigating the function of play bows in adult pet dogs (Canis lupus familiaris). *Behavioural Processes* 2016; 125:106-113.

Bekoff M. Play signals as punctuation: The structure of social play in canids. *Behaviour* 1995; 132:5-6.

Casey RA, Loftus B, Bolster C, et al. Human directed aggression in domestic dogs (Canis familiaris): Occurrence in different contexts and risk factors. *Applied Animal Behavior Science* 2014; 152:52-63.

Doring D, Roscher A, Scheipl F, et al. Fear-related behavior in dogs in veterinary practice. *The Veterinary Journal* 2009; 182:38-43.

Farago T, Pongracz P, Miklosi A, et al. Dogs' expectations about signalers' body size by virtue of their growls. *PLos One* 2010; 5:15175.

Hecht J, Miklosi A, Gacsi M. Behavioral assessment and owner perceptions of behaviors associated with guilty in dogs. *Applied Animal Behavior Science* 2012; 139:134-142.

Horowitz A. Disambiguating the "guilty look": Salient prompts to a familiar dog behavior. *Behavioural Processes* 2009; 81:447-452.

Jacobs JA, Pearl DL, Coe JB, Widowski TM, Niel L. Ability of owners to identify resource guarding behavior in the domestic dog. *Applied Animal Behaviour Science* 2017; In Press.

Mariti C, Gazzano A, Moore JL, Baragli P, Chelli L, Sighieri C. (2012) Perception of dogs' stress by their owners. *Journal of Veterinary Behavior* 7:213-219.

Ostojic L, Tkalcic M, Clayton N. Are owners' reports of their dogs' "guilty look" influenced by the dogs' action and evidence of the misdeed? *Behavioural Processes* 2015; 111:97-100.

Wan M, Bolger N, Champagne FA. (2012) Human perception of fear in dogs varies according to experience with dogs. *PLoS ONE* 7(12): e51775. doi: 10.1371/journal.pone.0051775

Part 2 – How Dogs Learn

Chapter 6
This is Classic

We use a training exercise in our classes at AutumnGold that teaches dogs to tolerate, and (hopefully) enjoy, handling and grooming. We call the exercise "Touch-then-Treat" to give owners an easy mnemonic to remember. This phrase also describes the exact sequence of events in the exercise.

Touch-then-Treat begins with the owner reaching out to handle their dog's collar. After one second of contact, they remove a treat from their pouch with the opposite hand and give it to the dog. After several repetitions, the owner notices that their dog begins to anticipate the delivery of a treat each time that they reach for his collar. The dog is learning that "touch collar" reliably predicts a yummy treat. Once students have the timing well-established with the collar, we move on to other areas of the dog's body – using the touch-then-treat sequence with handling ears, feet, and mouths, and eventually for gentle restraint. As repetitions increase and more body parts are targeted, students find that their dog happily anticipates being touched by moving towards them, rather than avoiding handling.

Touch-then-Treat Handling of Paw

This is classical conditioning, first described and studied by the Russian physiologist, Ivan Pavlov.

Father of Classical Conditioning: When most people hear the name "Pavlov", they think of bells ringing and dogs drooling. Pavlov, who did his research in the late 19th century, is credited with identifying the principles of classical conditioning. Specifically, he showed that a neutral (meaningless) stimulus could become meaningful to a dog when followed by something that elicited a natural response. In his experiments with dogs, when the sound of a ringing bell was consistently followed by the presentation of food, the sound of the bell alone began to trigger the dog's natural response to seeing food - salivation (drooling).

Classical conditioning is all about associations between events (technically called stimuli). There are five basic elements involved during this type of learning. These are:

- **Neutral Stimulus (NS):** A neutral stimulus is a meaningless event that initially elicits no response from the dog. Prior to being paired with the presentation of food, the bell sound (BING!) was a neutral stimulus in Pavlov's experiments. Other than perhaps causing a startle response, the bell held no other meaning to the dogs, nor did it *predict* anything to them.

- **Unconditioned Stimulus (US):** This term refers to an event that is naturally meaningful to a dog without the need for prior conditioning. For Pavlov's scenario, the unconditioned stimulus was the presentation of food.

- **Unconditioned Response (UR):** Similar to an unconditioned stimulus, an unconditioned response is an emotional or physiological response in the dog that occurs spontaneously in response to an unconditioned stimulus. In this example, the unconditioned response is salivation. Dogs naturally salivate in response to the presentation of food, without prior conditioning.

- **Conditioned Stimulus (CS):** The consistent pairing of the two stimuli, with the neutral stimulus *preceding* the unconditioned stimulus (i.e. bell ring precedes presentation of food), leads to a change in the meaning of the neutral stimulus to the dog. Because the neutral stimulus consistently *precedes* and *predicts* the unconditioned stimulus, it begins to elicit the same response that is elicited by the unconditioned stimulus. Once this learning has taken place, the neutral stimulus (bell ring) has been converted to a conditioned stimulus for the dog.

- **Conditioned Response (CR):** Classical conditioning has occurred when the dog begins to show the same or a very similar response to the neutral stimulus that was initially elicited only by the unconditioned stimulus. This is called a stimulus-stimulus association and forms the basic principle of classical conditioning. When this association has been established, we refer to the dog's response (salivation) to the conditioned stimulus (bell ring) as a conditioned response. The flow chart below shows the development of this association.

Sound of Bell ➡ **Presentation of Food** ➡ **Salivation**
  (NS)*   *(US)*   *(UR)*

After Frequent Repetitions

Sound of Bell   ➡   ➡   **Salivation**
    (CS)   *(CR)*

---

*NS = Neutral stimulus; US = Unconditioned stimulus; UR = Unconditioned response; CS = Conditioned stimulus; CR = Conditioned response

Timing Plus Reliability: The two conditions that are essential for effective classical learning are referred to as *contiguity* (the two events are closely paired in time and place) and *contingency* (the neutral stimulus is reliably followed by the unconditioned stimulus).

Contiguity: The neutral stimulus must be presented immediately before and, if possible, overlapping with, the unconditioned stimulus. This facilitates the development of a strong and enduring connection between the two events and the transformation of the neutral stimulus into a conditioned stimulus. Conversely, if the conditioned stimulus is presented after the unconditioned stimulus (if the bell rang after the food was presented), learning proceeds slowly, if at all. From the dog's point of view, there is no need to pay attention to the bell because it has no predictive value if presented after the food!

Contingency: Similarly, the contingency rule tells us that the neutral stimulus must be followed by the unconditioned stimulus every occasion in which it is presented in order for an association to be established. If Pavlov entered the room 10 times a day and the bell rang each time, but he fed the dogs during just one of those 10 visits, nine out of 10 bell rings would not be followed by the presentation of food. In this situation, the dogs would be much less likely to learn that the ringing bell always predicted food (because, well, it did not). While they may eventually learn this association, it would be hampered by the inconsistent relationship of the two events.

There are many examples of real-life classical learning in dogs. Here is one that my dogs demonstrate every day when they hear my husband's car approaching the driveway (following page). This example satisfies both the contingency and continuity requirements for classical learning:

Sound of Car ➡ Mike Comes Home!! ➡ Excitement
    (NS)*   *(US)*   *(UR)*

After Frequent (Daily) Repetitions

Sound of Car ➡ ➡ Excitement
     (CS)   *(CR)*

*NS = Neutral stimulus; US = Unconditioned stimulus; UR = Unconditioned response; CS = Conditioned stimulus; CR = Conditioned response

Consider What Matters: In addition to contiguity and contingency, the value that a particular unconditioned stimulus has for a dog directly influences his or her tendency to pay attention to other events that may be predictive. Though it may sound obvious, dogs are highly likely to become classically conditioned to events that matter to them and are unlikely to learn about associations between events that are of no interest or concern to them. An owner picking up a shampoo bottle will quickly become classically conditioned to predict bath time, because the presence of that particular bottle reliably predicts time in the tub, an experience that most dogs are not fond of. Dogs who learn this also often become very adept at disappearing as soon as the bottle appears. Dogs pay attention to shampoo bottles because baths matter to them. Another example is the dog who shows appeasement gestures or outright disappears when his owner approaches the drawer that holds the nail clippers.

Conversely, the same dog is unlikely to associate her owner picking up a bottle of glass cleaner immediately prior to cleaning nose prints off of the living room window because "wiping off nose prints" is neither of concern nor of interest to the dog. So, even though all sorts of predictive stimuli are present in a dog's world, just like humans, dogs only attend to (and learn about) connections that lead to either something pleasurable (food, husband returning home) or to something that is unpleasant (bath time, nails getting trimmed).

Most of the classically conditioned associations that we see in dogs involve emotional responses such as pleasure or fear and are respondent in nature. Respondent behaviors are those that are relatively innate and are in large part involuntary (i.e. dogs do not *choose* to feel fear – more about this later). The most common respondent behaviors that we are familiar with in dogs (and which are often the subject of classically conditioned behavior problems) include those expressed when a dog is fearful, anxious, excited or happy.

Training with Classical Conditioning: Classical conditioning is useful in dog training in two different contexts. The first and most obvious involves the deliberate pairing of neutral and unconditioned stimuli to promote pleasurable and desired responses in dogs, as in Touch-then-Treat. We can expand this exercise to numerous additional interactions with dogs – here are a few examples:

- *I LOVE my brush!* Many young dogs resist brushing and grooming because the feel of the brush is unfamiliar to them or because they dislike having to remain still for grooming. We can use the pleasurable emotions associated with food treats and anticipation of eating (the unconditioned stimulus) to condition the brush as a pleasant stimulus, signifying something to look forward to rather than something to avoid. The brush (a neutral stimulus) appears and is followed immediately by plenty of yummy food treats. This sequence is repeated several times until the dog's reaction to the brush is positive and excited (i.e. he anticipates food treats). At this point, the brush has been transformed from a neutral stimulus to a conditioned stimulus that predicts something pleasurable.

- **I HATE my brush!** This type of training differs from the previous example because the dog has an established reaction (opinion, if you like) about his brush – he hates it. This can happen if a dog has a long and unruly coat that easily mats and has caused brushing to be uncomfortable (Doodles come to mind), or because the dog is infrequently brushed and associates the brush with unwanted restraint. In scenarios in which we are attempting to *change* established classical associations, the technical term for training is *counter-conditioning*. For dogs and their brushes - if the dog had previously developed a fear or dislike of the brush, counter-conditioning could be used to gradually change a negative association into a more positive association. (I discuss this difference and the use of counter conditioning in detail in Chapter 11).

- **I LOVE the car!** Dogs who are unfamiliar with car rides (and have not yet developed any opinion about them one way or the other), can learn that car trips predict pleasant things quite easily (barring any inherent motion sickness issues, of course). Pairing a short ride (neutral stimulus) with the pleasantness of a walk in the park or a visit with friends easily sets up car rides as a conditioned stimulus. When initially established, car rides should be of short duration to ensure that a clear connection is made by the dog *"Oh! I get into this odd machine, it rumbles about a bit, and YAY! I am at the park! I love the car"*! It should go without saying (but I will say it anyway) that owners who only plop their pup into the car for rides to the veterinary clinic or so infrequently that the dog is frightened by the sheer novelty of the car may find that the car is quickly established as an aversive conditioned stimulus – one that predicts anxiety and fear rather than pleasure.

- **Pick your pleasure:** The pattern should now be clear. By carefully selecting events in our dogs lives that we wish to establish as pleasant for them (or at least, not frightening or anxiety-producing), we can go a long way towards these goals with classical conditioning. Classical conditioning can be used as training insurance that regular and simple events such as visiting a new park, meeting new people, allowing various forms of handling, and being introduced to a new dog friend can all be turned into pleasurable activities. But remember that the pendulum can readily swing in the opposite direction – a pup who is rushed by other dogs on his first visit to the park, is frightened by a stranger who approaches too quickly or has repeated episodes of new dogs bowling him over will also learn (classically) that unfamiliar people, new dogs, and even visits to the park can be predictors of unpleasantness and anxiety.

Classical Conditioning and Cue Words: The second way in which we use classical conditioning in dog training is less obvious. It involves how dogs learn the specific words or hand gestures that we use as cues (traditionally called "commands"). As an example let's use teaching a dog to eliminate on cue when taken outdoors.

In this case, the unconditioned stimuli include internal signs and external events that trigger elimination. External stimuli include events such as eating, waking up after a nap, and puppy behaviors that reflect the need to eliminate such as circling and sniffing are area that was previously used for elimination. The neutral stimuli are taking the dog outside to a specific spot and using a cue word such as, *"Hurry Up"* or *"Go Potty"* (or *"Make Popcorn"* for that matter; the words themselves do not matter to the dog). The cue should be consistent and should be repeated several times as the dog is circling or sniffing an area of the yard that is used for elimination. If the new verbal cue is consistently paired with elimination, it can eventually be used to encourage a dog to eliminate in a specific area or at particular times during the day.

"Go Potty" ➡ Puppy circling, sniffing ➡ Elimination
    (NS)*   (US)   (UR)

After Frequent Repetitions

"Go Potty"   ➡   ➡   Elimination (in yard)
    (CS)   (CR)

*NS = Neutral stimulus; US = Unconditioned stimulus; UR = Unconditioned response; CS = Conditioned stimulus; CR = Conditioned response

Other examples are the cue words or gestures that we use when training new (operant) behaviors (next chapter). An example is teaching a young dog to come when she is called. One component to teaching dogs to come involves pairing an unconditioned stimulus (presence of food) and unconditioned response (dog approaching to consume the food) with a neutral stimulus (the cue words *"Chippy Come!"*). If the verbal cue is presented consistently and immediately prior to the presentation of food, classical conditioning results. Chippy associates the cue (*"Come!"*) with an opportunity to eat, with another behavior - coming toward me – in the middle. We use this approach to introduce "coming when called" in our puppy and beginner classes at AutumnGold, prior to starting the operant portion (dog offering the behavior voluntarily) of this training. As we will see in Chapter 8, this example demonstrates the connection between classical conditioning and operant conditioning in many learning situations.

A Classic Example – The Guilty Look: It begins the same way each time. The owner relates a detailed account of her dog Roscoe raiding the kitchen garbage bin when no one is home. After describing (in unnecessary detail) the mess that she returned to find, the owner adds the *coup de grace* – she is becoming particularly infuriated by these episodes because (wait for it).......she is certain that Roscoe *"knows he has done something wrong."*

She knows this because......."*Roscoe always looks guilty when she confronts him about what he did."*

Ugh.

Like many trainers, I repeatedly have to explain to owners that what they are witnessing in these circumstances is their dog communicating signs of appeasement, submission, and sadly, in some cases, fear. And, also like many other trainers, I often feel as though I am beating my head against the proverbial wall.

So, let's examine the classical learning nature of "the guilty look" along with the evidence that what owners are actually witnessing in their dogs is not guilt. (And for good measure, we will include some tips for talking to neighbor Joe about this at the end of the chapter).

Classical Conditioning and the Guilty Look: It's pretty simple, actually. Dogs learn to react to their owner's body language and verbal cues that predict impending punishment. Here is the classically learned sequence of events for the typical "guilty looking" dog:

1. Owner away from home. Roscoe does *not* get into the garbage because he is tired from his morning walk and snoozes. Owner returns home and greets Roscoe happily. Roscoe responds with happy greeting behaviors. All is well in Roscoe's world.

2. Owner away. Roscoe *does* get into the garbage because it was raining this morning, he did not get his daily walk and the sound of rain predicts (classically) thunder, which makes Roscoe a bit unsettled and anxious. Roscoe raids the garbage, then takes a nap. Owner returns home and sees the mess. In-

stead of a happy and loving reunion, she greets Roscoe with anger and punishment. She shows Roscoe the mess and scolds him. Roscoe responds with appeasement, anxiety and fear. Roscoe's world is not well at all.

3. Repeat # 1 and # 2 a few times.

4. Roscoe learns these two (classical) associations:

Owner + No Mess ➡ Happy Greeting ➡ Happy Roscoe
(NS)*   *(US)*   *(UR)*

After Repetitions

Owner + No Mess   ➡ ➡   Happy Roscoe
(CS)   *(CR)*

---

*NS = Neutral stimulus; US = Unconditioned stimulus; UR = Unconditioned response; CS = Conditioned stimulus; CR = Conditioned response

AND

Owner + Mess ➡ Scolding ➡Fear/Appeasing Roscoe
(NS)*   *(US)*   *(UR)*

After Repetitions

Owner + Mess   ➡ ➡   Fear/Appeasing Roscoe
(CS)   *(CR)*

---

*NS = Neutral stimulus; US = Unconditioned stimulus; UR = Unconditioned response; CS = Conditioned stimulus; CR = Conditioned response

The body language of fear in dogs (see photos in the previous chapter) does NOT signify guilt. Period. (Geez, Joe, let this myth go once and for all, man). Rather, Roscoe is simply responding directly to the conditioned stimulus (CS) of the presence of a mess plus the presence of his owner, with an expectation of punishment. Unfortunately for dogs, the myth of the guilty look can lead to emotional abuse and mistreatment. Roscoe is not showing guilt, nor is he saying he's sorry. He is just trying to get his owner to refrain from punishing him.

We have evidence of this: A series of studies conducted by Alexandra Horowitz's Dog Cognition Lab at Barnard College in New York City showed unequivocally that the "guilty look" people claim to see in their dogs is attributable to whether or not the owner expects to see this look. Dogs responded to their owners *expectations*, regardless of whether or not the dog had actually done something wrong. For example, if the owner believed that the dog had stolen a forbidden piece of food, their dog was highly likely to exhibit appeasement or fear, even when the dog had not actually taken the food. Similarly, dogs were not more likely to show a guilty look after disobeying if the owner thought that they had *not* stolen food. This series of studies showed that dogs who show signs of appeasement, submission or fear (aka the guilty look) upon greeting their owners will do so regardless of whether or not they misbehaved in the owner's absence. It is the owner's behavior and use of scolding and reprimands that were the most significant predictors of anxious greeting behavior in dogs.

TALKING TO JOE

Talking to Joe: So, how do we handle neighbor Joe, (who happens to know a lot about dogs), who continues to insist that dogs "*know when they are guilty.*" Keep in mind that Joe's eyes will begin to roll back in his head if you begin to spout facts about learning theory, classical conditioning and stimulus-response connections. Here are a few tips to help you out:

🐾 Hey Joe, I noticed when your kids were leaving for school this morning that your dog Benny escaped from the front gate (again). It seems that Benny has learned quite nicely that two small children carrying their lunch boxes and back-packs approaching the gate predicts an opportunity for getting out of the gate for a romp. Here is a suggestion. Try modifying that association by giving your kids a bunch of yummy dog treats before they leave the house. As they approach the gate, they can stop, ask Benny to sit, and give him lots of treats. Then, as they leave, they can toss a few treats backwards (away from the gate) and ask Benny to "wait." As Benny is enjoying his treats (and searching for a few more), they can leave for school without having to compete with Benny as he rushes the gate. (We teach more of this stuff at our classes and encourage entire families to come and train, if you are interested Joe)!

🐾 While we are on the topic of Benny, not to be nosey, Joe, but I also noticed that Benny lurches away from you when you reach for his collar. I know you were trying to catch him, but chances are that a few repetitions of Benny losing his freedom (and the fun that goes with it) immediately after you grab his collar has taught him to avoid you when you reach for him. This is just a simple association, and one that you can prevent by having your kids play a game with Benny called "Touch-then-Treat." Ask your kids to sit with Benny and practice repetitions of reaching for Benny's collar, and then giving him a yummy treat. Benny will start to enjoy having his collar grabbed rather than avoiding it. (Plus, it gives your kids something fun to do with Benny – a win-win, for sure!)

🐾 Walk-time excitement is another one of these "conditioned behaviors", you know. Benny has learned that the appear-

110

ance of his leash predicts great fun – a walk in the neighbor-hood! If you would like to insert some control into your daily walk routine, try picking up the lead, asking for a sit from Benny, and giving him lots of yummy treats, then put the leash away. Repeat multiple times (again – great game for your kids). While Benny will still become excited about his leash and his walks, you can probably get a bit more control over your boy using this technique.

* Ditto for mealtime (bowl predicts food), bath-time (shampoo bottle predicts bath), car rides ("time for a ride, Benny?" pre-dict fun times in the car), and pulling out the nail clippers (predicts discomfort of nail trimming). It is good to know what these connections are Joe, so that you can modify those that need changing and strengthen those that you like.

* And last but not least. You need to drop the belief that Benny acts guilty when he misbehaves, Joe. The look that you equate with guilt in Benny is not remorse. Benny has learned to as-sociate your tense body language and your anger with im-pending punishment and he also has learned that this hap-pens when there is a mess around, even if he did not make that mess (honestly, Joe, ask your kids sometime who was to blame). Benny is not showing guilt. Rather, he is trying to convince you not to be mad at him and is anxious. Lay off the guilt trip, Joe and we can help you to prevent unwanted be-haviors in Benny through training.

111

Evidence

Hecht J, Miklosi A, Gacsi M. Behavioral assessment and owner perceptions of behaviors associated with guilty in dogs. *Applied Animal Behavior Science* 2012; 139:134-142.

Horowitz A. Disambiguating the "guilty look": Salient prompts to a familiar dog behavior. *Behavioural Processes* 2009; 81:447-452.

Ley J, Coleman GJ, Holmes R, Hemsworth PH. Assessing fear of novel and startling stimuli in domestic dogs. *Applied Animal Behavior Science* 2007; 104: 71–84.

Ogata N, et al. Objective measurement of fear-associated learning in dogs. *Journal of Veterinary Behavior* 2006; 1:55-61.

Ostojic L, Tkalcic M, Clayton N. Are owners' reports of their dogs' "guilty look" influenced by the dogs' action and evidence of the misdeed? *Behavioural Processes* 2015; 111:97-100.

Yin S. Classical conditioning: Learning by association. *Compendium of Continuing Veterinary Education, Small Animal Practice* 2006; June; 472–476.

Chapter 7
Consequences Matter

We begin each orientation night at AutumnGold with a popular game to demonstrate the concept of consequence-based training. First, I ask our new group of students to select one behavior from a set of four: sit, down, spin, or bow. This session, our youngest Golden, Ally, joined me as the demonstrator dog. The students selected "bow" as their behavior.

I removed Ally's lead and stood very still. Ally (knowing that it was "game time") began to offer various bits of behavior in anticipation of their potential consequences. She offered spin first, because it is a favorite trick for her. She enjoys spinning and it also has a strong reinforcement history (i.e. we have practiced it a lot). I ignored her spin and continued to stand quietly. She then offered a down (throwing in a little bark for some pizzazz). Still no response from me. Finally, she gave a tentative bow. I immediately said "*Good Girl*" and tossed her a treat.

"*Bingo!*" said Ally! She started to offer more renditions of "bow" and fewer spins or other selections, as she realized that "bow" was the behavior that was *working* – it was the behavior whose consequences were something that she enjoyed, praise and a treat. To test the rules, she threw in a "down"; no response from me (no consequences). This provided her with a bit more information. She offered "bow" again – "*Good Girl – Treat!*" From this point on, it was all bows. I threw in her cue word ("*Take a Bow*") and Ta Da, we demonstrated the power of using positive consequences to train dogs!

Best Training Tool We've Got: At the risk of hyperbole, operant conditioning that focuses on the use of positive reinforcement, also called reward-based training, is the best training tool that dog trainers have. This training approach has taken off like a house on fire over the last 25 years not only because it works so well (it does), but also because it is easy to learn, is humane and kind, and because it helps to build strong and loving bonds with our dogs.

Really, what's not to like?

So, what is operant conditioning and how is it used in dog training? The term operant conditioning originates from the concept that animals are continually *"operating on"* their environment, and alter their behavior in response to consequences. As Ally did with "bow", a dog is likely to repeat behaviors that have pleasurable consequences. We say that these behaviors are *reinforced*. Reinforced behaviors increase in frequency. Conversely, animals tend to avoid repeating behaviors that have aversive consequences. We say that these behaviors have been *punished*. Behaviors that are punished decrease in frequency. It gets just a bit more complicated than those two scenarios however, because the stimuli (events) that result in reinforcement or punishment can be either positive or negative.

- *Reinforcement/Punishment:* These terms refer to how consequences influence future behavior. Reinforcement leads to an increase in the targeted behavior; punishment leads to a decrease in the targeted behavior.

- *Positive/Negative:* There is often confusion about these two terms because it is natural to assume that they refer to emotional responses (good/bad) rather than to math (+/-). *Think math, not emotions.* Positive (+) refers to adding in a stimulus while negative (-) refers to subtracting (removing) a stimulus. The stimulus may be either pleasurable/desirable to the dog (food treats, praise, petting) or unpleasant/painful for the dog (harsh voice, collar corrections). Among dog trainers, unpleasant stimuli are commonly referred to as "aversives."

The combination of these factors results in four types of consequences that can occur. BF Skinner, one of the first scientists to study operant conditioning, called these the four *quadrants.*

The Four Quadrants: These are (1) Positive reinforcement, (2) Negative reinforcement, (3) Positive punishment and (4) Negative punishment.

Positive reinforcement: Positive reinforcement occurs when a behavior results in the attainment of something that the dog finds to be pleasant and desirable. For example, I teach all of my dogs to offer "eye contact" on cue (below). As a young puppy, Cooper quickly learned that glancing up and into my eyes and holding eye contact had the consequences of a treat. In another example, when Coop sits next to me as I type at my computer, he has learned that nudging my elbow with his nose results in my hand dropping down from the keyboard as I absently pet his lovely, soft head. (Cooper is a smart cookie). In the first case, we say that Cooper's eye contact has been *positively reinforced* by a food treat and in the second, Cooper's "nose-nudging behavior" has been positively reinforced with petting. In each of these examples, Cooper is very likely to *increase* the frequency that he offers these behaviors as he learns that they both result in desirable consequences for him.

Cooper Offering Eye Contact

115

Negative reinforcement: Negative reinforcement occurs when a behavior results in the prevention (avoidance) or termination (escape) of something that a dog finds to be unpleasant or painful. A naturally-occurring example of this is when Chippy, my Toller lies in his favorite sun spot on the couch and starts to feel too warm (a rather rare occurrence for Chippy, but it does happen now and again). As he feels increasingly uncomfortable, Chip rises and moves to a shady spot. The unpleasant feeling of being overheated is ended (or avoided) by changing position. In this case, we say that Chip's behavior of moving to a shady spot has been *negatively reinforced*. The frequency of moving to a shady spot when overheated will *increase* in the future as a result of being negatively reinforced. Unfortunately, traditional dog training methods have relied upon the use of negative reinforcement for many desired behaviors in dogs. Luckily for dogs (and for us), progressive training methods minimize the use of negative reinforcement and focus primarily on using positive reinforcement – more about this in Chapter 8.

Positive punishment: Positive punishment occurs when a behavior produces an aversive (unpleasant, painful) consequence. A dog puts his feet up onto the kitchen cupboards and encounters a motion-sensitive canister that emits an unpleasant blast of air. The dog removes his paws to avoid the air blast. An aversive stimulus (air blast) has been *added* (+) to cause a decrease in the target behavior. In this example, jumping onto the kitchen counter has been *positively punished*. The frequency of "putting paws on the counter" *decreases* as a result of being positively punished.

Negative punishment: Finally, behaviors that result in the prevention or termination of a pleasant stimulus are being *negatively punished*. A young puppy is playing with his owner and starts to nip. The owner stops play (takes away/subtracts the pleasant interaction of playing) and (theoretically) the puppy stops nipping. In this commonly cited scenario, nipping has been negatively punished. If the owner consistently plays with the puppy

116

only if the puppy plays gently, then "playing gently" is being positively reinforced (assuming this is an effective approach – more about this in Chapter 12).

The chart below shows the four quadrants and the relationships between pleasurable and aversive consequences and their ability to both increase (reinforce) and decrease (punish) targeted behaviors.

TYPE OF STIMULUS	BEHAVIORAL CHANGE	
	INCREASE FREQUENCY	*DECREASE FREQUENCY*
DESIRABLE	*Positive Reinforcement (add stimulus)*	*Negative Punishment (remove stimulus)*
AVERSIVE	*Negative Reinforcement (remove stimulus)*	*Positive Punishment (add stimulus)*

Applying Consequences in Dog Training: Each of the four quadrants can be used to change behavior. Here is how each would be applied in training a dog to sit and stay in position (hereafter sit/stay):

1. *Positive reinforcement (+R):* The dog is sitting. The trainer provides quiet praise, gentle petting, and food treats to the dog during the time that the dog remains in the desired position (sitting). In this example, the behavior of remaining in a sit position is being *positively reinforced*; increasing in frequency. (*Positive* = food being added; *Reinforced* = Sit/stay increases to attain food)

2. *Negative reinforcement (-R):* The dog is sitting. The trainer stands quietly, saying nothing, and waits until the dog moves out of position or attempts to lie down. If the dog moves, collar jerks or harsh verbal reprimands (NO!) are given until the dog stops attempting to move and remains sitting. In this ex-

ample, the sit/stay is being *negatively reinforced*; increasing in frequency. (*Negative* = collar corrections removed; *Reinforced* =Sit/stay increases to avoid aversives).

3. ***Positive punishment (+P):*** The dog is sitting. The trainer stands quietly, saying nothing, and waits until the dog moves out of position or attempts to lie down. If the dog moves, collar jerks or harsh verbal reprimands (NO!) are given until the dog stops attempting to move and remains sitting. Moving out of position is being *positively punished*; decreasing in frequency. (*Positive* = aversive stimulus is added; *Punished* = moving out of position decreases to avoid aversives).

4. ***Negative punishment (-P):*** The dog is sitting. The trainer provides quiet praise, gentle petting, and food treats to the dog during the time that the dog remains in the desired position. If the dog attempts to move, the trainer immediately stops all interactions, praise, and food treats. In this example, moving out of position is being *negatively punished*; decreasing in frequency. (*Negative* = food/praise are removed; *Punished* = moving out of position decreases to avoid losing access to food/praise).

Positive Reinforcement/Negative Punishment: The sit/stay example illustrates the connection between reinforcement and punishment in practical training situations. When one behavior is being positively reinforced, alternative behaviors are (usually) simultaneously being negatively punished. In this example, sit/stay results in desirable consequences (treats, praise and petting) while alternate behaviors that the dog could offer, such as moving out of position or lying down, result in the withdrawal of the desirable consequences (treats/praise stop). More subtly, when a dog offers the behavior that is desired, other behaviors become "off-limits" in the sense that opportunities for positive reinforcement for those behaviors are not available.

Because of this connection, negative punishment must always be used judiciously and with caution. I provide training examples of this in Section 3, but I think that it is essential to fully understand this basic and very important rule about negative punishment:

- Withholding desirable consequences from all behaviors other than the target behavior is *only effective* (and should only be used) when the dog is capable of offering the desired behavior at a frequency that is high enough to earn enough positive reinforcement to encourage learning.

Using our sit/stay example; the dog must initially have multiple opportunities to be positively reinforced for sit/stay (even for a second or less) so that he has the opportunity to learn that the targeted behavior – the behavior that earns positive reinforcement (treats, praise) - *is* the sit/stay. Only when the dog understands that it is that *particular* behavior – this sitting and staying thing – that results in the good stuff, will *withholding* the good stuff support further learning – to stay without moving or for longer periods.

If this is not the case (for example, if the dog has no idea that sit/stay is the targeted behavior), removing the good stuff (negative punishment) when the dog moves out of position will not result in learning because the dog will not know which behavior to offer to go back to getting the good stuff. In this (unfortunately) common training mistake, the dog becomes frustrated and stressed simply because he does not understand the rules that are in play – which behavior he should be offering to get positively reinforced.

The Bottom Line? Training situations must always be designed to allow ample opportunities for the dog to earn positive reinforcement and at the same time minimize "mistakes" that have the consequences of negative punishment. This approach allows the dog to maximize desirable consequences and minimize aversive consequences, even when those consequences appear rela-

119

tively mild to the trainer. (We will apply this concept to specific training scenarios in Section 3).

The Other Two Quadrants: Positive punishment and negative reinforcement are also intricately linked. In the example we used, moving out of a sit/stay was punished with collar corrections and verbal reprimands, while sitting and staying was negatively reinforced because the dog learned to avoid all of that unpleasantness by freezing in place (staying).

The repeated use of negative reinforcement and positive punishment results in a dog who may stay in position but who is also stressed and anxious. This occurs because any behavior that does not comply with a "sit/stay" results in unpleasant and even painful consequences for the dog. A sit/stay can be achieved, but at the expense of instilling anxiety or fear as the dog learns that the only way to avoid aversive consequences is to freeze in place. I will return to this issue in the following chapter.

Positive Punishment on its Own: In some situations, positive punishment is used to stop an undesirable behavior without being paired with negative reinforcement. For example, positive punishment might be used to stop a dog from raiding the garbage. A noxious smelling substance is applied to the outer surface of the waste bin. When the dog smells or tastes the area, the behavior of disturbing the trash is positively punished by an aversive stimulus (the noxious tasting substance). The dog is less likely to offer the behavior of raiding the garbage in the future (i.e. garbage can raiding has been punished; decreasing in frequency). In this example, the owner is not concerned with increasing any other behavior – he just wants "garbage raiding" behavior to decrease. The dog may do any number of things after leaving the garbage alone – walk away, lie down, leave the room or play with a toy.

While some may consider this to be simply a matter of semantics, it is an important difference to recognize because negative reinforcement (targeting a very specific behavior) results in the dog being subjected to a much higher frequency of aversives and the emotional toll that these can take, compared with situations in which a single, unwanted behavior is being punished and the dog has multiple alternative options for avoiding the aversive stimulus.

Emotions Matter: It is true that dogs can be trained using any one or a combination of the four operant conditioning quadrants. For example, I could train Cooper to walk on a loose-lead at my side by using an aversive stimulus (jerks on his collar) to negatively reinforce loose-lead heeling <u>OR</u> I could use desirable consequences (treats, praise, friendly eye contact) to positively reinforce the same behavior (below).

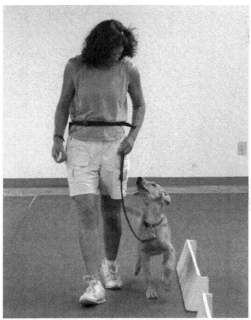

Cooper learns to walk on a loose lead using +R

Each of these two training approaches is accompanied by an emotional response in the dog. There is simply no denying (though some scientists and trainers still attempt to do so) that dogs are harmed by aversive stimuli – they become frightened, stressed and anxious when repeatedly subjected to unpleasant or painful consequences such as collar corrections, verbal reprimands, or physical punishment. While not as dramatic, the use of negative punishment, removing something that a dogs finds to be desirable and pleasant, can also lead to the unpleasant emotions of frustration and anxiety.

For these reasons (and others discussed in Chapter 8), ***the four types of consequences should <u>not</u> be viewed as equally effective or valuable for use in dog training.***

Simply eliciting a behavioral response is not the desired outcome of most trainers and dog owners, nor is it a value of my training center or of this book. The aversive stimuli that are used with negative reinforcement and positive punishment have harmful effects on dogs and on our relationships with them. The next chapter examines the details (and evidence) of why we should "choose kindly" for our dogs.

For now, let's see how we can teach neighbor Joe about these basic rules of operant conditioning.

TALKING TO JOE

Talking to Joe: You have recently learned (from neighbor Sue) that neighbor Joe (who happens to know a lot about dogs) has been training his dog Duffy to not jump up when he greets. It seems that Duffy, a very exuberant, young Labrador Retriever, enjoys greeting by planting his front feet squarely on the shoulders of visitors. Apparently, Joe saw a YouTube video instructing owners to raise a leg and "knee" the dog in the chest to train the dog to greet more politely.* (Yeah, your job is cut out for you on this one).

Here is an approach for teaching Joe about consequence-based dog training with his dog Duffy:

🐾 Hi Joe! Hope you do not mind that I stopped by to say hello to you and Duffy. I heard from neighbor Sue about her recent visit when she stopped by to borrow an egg. Sue mentioned that you instructed her to reprimand Duffy for jumping up on her. (Oh, yeah, Sue is doing okay. Thanks for asking. The doctor says she will be out of the shoulder sling in just 4 or 5 weeks).

🐾 Anyway, about this "kneeing" method that you are using to teach Duffy to greet more politely. You know, Joe, Duffy is a friendly and happy (and um, untrained) dog who jumps because he loves people and because he has not been taught to *not* jump up on them. While kneeing Duffy in the chest seems to work (it does knock him off), it does not give Duffy any real information about what it is that you would *like* him to do when he greets, Joe.

🐾 Consider, just for a minute, how this would be for you, in a similar situation, Joe........ (cue dreamy music here).......

---

*Kneeing in the chest positively punishes jumping up.

🐾 Imagine Joe, that you have an upcoming vacation trip to a foreign country, one in which you do not know the language and have little knowledge of local customs. To prepare, you enroll in a class that will teach you about the region and its customs. Your goals are simple – you want to be able to order a beer at a restaurant and to find the public bathrooms.

🐾 On the first day of class, the instructor tells you that the people in this country greet using a traditional handshake that is unfamiliar to most Americans. In fact, he tells you that our handshake is considered an insult in this country and so you should refrain from greeting in that way. You are best served to learn their traditional handshake and use that to say hello. (You know where this is going, don't you Joe. You are a smart guy).

🐾 Your instructor continues, explaining that he has two ways of teaching this greeting gesture to his students. You are free to choose which you prefer and simply need to select one of two available classrooms:

🐾 **Classroom A**: You enter this room to find that the desk chairs are electronically wired so that a mild but quite unpleasant electric shock can be sent to each chair by the instructor. After you select your seat, the instructor approaches and asks you to greet him using the country's traditional gesture. If you greet with the correct custom, the instructor tells you that you are right, practices with you a few times, and you are allowed to leave and progress on to the next segment of the course (asking where bathrooms are located). However, if you respond incorrectly, you receive an immediate electric shock from your chair. After recovering, you are required to try again. The instructor does not give you any help. If you get it wrong, well you know what happens Joe. The instructor remains standing in front of your chair, asking you to greet and will refrain from shocking you once you greet him correctly.* When you finally get it right, you are allowed to move forward in the course.

🐾 **Classroom B:** In this room, you will see an enormous bowl of fancy chocolates sitting on the front desk. You find a seat (no hot wires in this room) and the instructor approaches and asks you to greet him using the country's traditional gesture. If you greet with the correct custom, the instructor tells you that you are correct and gives you one of the fancy chocolates. He practices this with you a few times, giving you a chocolate for each correct response. You are allowed to leave and progress on to the next segment. If you greet incorrectly, the instructor quietly demonstrates the gesture for you and gives you a chocolate if you get part or all of the gesture right. If you are incorrect, he says nothing, demonstrates it again (maybe a bit more simply this time for you, Joe) and you try again. The instructor remains standing in front of your chair, asking you to greet and helping you until you can greet correctly and reinforcing each correct try with a chocolate.**

🐾 So, tell me Joe, where will you be sitting? Classroom A or Classroom B? Which approach do you think Duffy would choose for learning to greet properly, if you asked him?

---

* Answering correctly is being negatively reinforced.
** Answering correctly is being positively reinforced.

Joe, the belief that negative reinforcement and punishment is effective and necessary for dogs to learn is a myth. Just like people, the use of physical reprimands and scolding with dogs does not give them the information that they need to learn desired behaviors. While hitting Duffy in the chest with your knee knocks him (or Sue) to the ground, it does not teach him to sit for greeting and can upset him, scare him, or even injure him. It may also cause Duffy to be afraid of visitors and avoid them. So, avoid this form of training, stick with me Joe, and I will teach you a better way!

Evidence

Bentosela, M, Jakovcevic A, Elgier AM, Mustaca AE, Papini MR. Incentive contrast in domestic dogs (*Canis familiaris*). *Journal of Comparative Psychology* 2009; 123:125-130.

Borchelt PL and Voith VL. Punishment. In: *Readings in Companion Animal Behavior*, (VL Voith and PL Borchelt, editors), Veterinary Learning Systems, Trenton, NJ, 1996; pp. 72–80.

Burch MR, Bailey JS. *How Dogs Learn*. Howell Book House, New York, 1999; 188 pp.

Donaldson J. *Culture Clash: A Revolutionary New Way of Understanding the Relationship between Humans and Domestic Dogs.* James and Kenneth Publishers, Oakland, CA, 1996; 221 pp.

Gabrielsen AM. Training technologies: Science, humans and dogs in the age of positive dog training. *Nordic Journal of Science and Technology Studies* 2017; 5:5-16.

Lindsay SR. *Handbook of Applied Dog Behavior and Training; Volume 1: Adaptation and Learning.* Iowa State University Press, Ames, Iowa, 410 pp, 2000.

Pearce WD, Cheney CD. *Behavior Analysis and Learning. 3rd edition*, Lawrence Erlbaum Associates, Inc. Mahwah, NJ, 388 pp., 2004.

Pryor K. *Don't Shoot the Dog*. Bantam Books, New York, New York, 187 pp, 1984.

Pryor K. *Karen Pryor on Behavior*. Sunshine Books, North Bend, Washington, 244 pp, 1995.

Reid P. *Excel-Erated Learning: Explaining How Dogs Learn and How Best to Teach Them.* James and Kenneth Publishing, Oakland, California, 172 pp, 1996.

Schilder MBH, van der Borg JAM. Training dogs with help of the shock collar: short and long term behavioral effects. *Applied Animal Behavior Science,* 2004; 85:319–334.

Skinner, BF. How to teach animals. *Scientific American* 1951; 185:26-29.

Chapter 8
Treats, Please! Choosing Kindly

I introduced the previous chapter with a story about starting each orientation class at AutumnGold with a version of the training game. While I emphasized that our students are usually impressed by these demonstrations and immediately catch on to the power of positive reinforcement, I would be remiss to not mention that we do see the occasional "frownie-face" in the audience during these demonstrations.

What I am referring to is the human version of this:

That face, human form, tells us that the student expressing it is not convinced and is usually taking umbrage with the use of food treats to train dogs. Mr. or Ms. Frownie-face invariably raises a hand to utter some version of the following:

"I don't want to use food with my dog to train him because I want him to work for me out of love [or respect, or because I am alpha, or because I am King Tut, ruler of the world]"

Okay, maybe I made that last bit up. But you get the picture.

While we get the frownie-face and the resistance that accompanies it less frequently than in the past (*thank you positive trainers!*), we still see it now and again. So, in this chapter we explore evidence for staying, as much as possible, within the positive reinforcement (+R) quadrant of Skinner's four consequences. I also will provide a means for communicating this information to the doubting Joes, Josephines and Frownie-faces of the world when you encounter them as clients, in classes, or as your neighbors.

Training in the +R Quadrant: I don't think it is an outrageous claim to assert that the vast majority of people do not want to harm their dogs, either physically or emotionally, in order to train them. Unfortunately, a substantial number of dog owners continue to think that using punishment is the only effective and reliable way to train dogs. These beliefs may arise from continued reliance upon "dog-as-wolf" myths that tell owners they must establish dominance over their dogs, or upon the view that using positive reinforcers in training is synonymous with bribing. (These beliefs are false, as Joe finds out at the end of this chapter). For now though, let's look at what we know to be *true* about the aversive control of behavior, commonly referred to as "correction-based" training, versus training methods that focus primarily on positive reinforcement, commonly referred to as "reward-based" training.

Correction-Based Training: Aversive training methods, even if "balanced" with positive reinforcement, rely upon a dog's natural desire to avoid pain and discomfort. The dog pulls forward into his leash; a collar jerk occurs; the dog moves back into a loose-lead heel position to avoid the discomfort. If a consequence is not sufficiently unpleasant, the dog has no reason to change his behavior to avoid it and learning does not occur. Therefore, *by its very definition*, a training approach that relies partially or fully on aversive consequences involves causing some level of discomfort or pain to the dog.

In addition to the discomfort that this approach relies upon, there are emotional costs. The basic emotions associated with pain and discomfort in dogs (as in humans) are fear and anxiety. Although proponents of correction-based methods argue that anxiety and fear can be minimized by using the mildest intensity of an aversive that is necessary, there is no evidence that such a level exists. Rather, all of the studies that have examined the use of aversives to control behavior in dogs have reported signs of stress and/or fear as direct results of these training methods (see following section for details).

A third problem with reliance upon aversives in dog training is that the exact nature of a dog's response is not always predictable. Although some dogs move away from an aversive stimulus if there is an escape route available (for example, a dog stops pulling into a corrective collar), others may freeze in place, panic, attempt to run away, or become aggressive. As a result, the risk is that the response of the dog is not always what was intended by the trainer. This is a common problem because applying an aversive only provides the dog with information about *what NOT to do*, but does not provide information about *what TO do*. Essentially, the dog is forced to learn through the process of elimination. Negative reinforcement relies on the dog's ability to select the desired behavior that will allow her to escape or avoid the aversive. Because a variety of behaviors are often equally successful in avoiding an unpleasant consequence - for example, running away or showing aggression - the behavior that is elicited each time a correction is applied may not be the behavior that the trainer was expecting to see.

Finally, because stress is often introduced with the use of negative reinforcement and punishment, the use of correction-based training as a humane approach to training is questionable. In addition to the potential for intentional or unintentional abuse, aversives that are associated with the owner have the potential for damaging the relationship between the dog and his owner. The overuse of aversives or using corrections that are too harsh can cause generalized fear and avoidance as the dog may learn that one behavior that will allow him to avoid discomfort and fear is to simply avoid being near his owner. No one wants this. Why take the chance when there are better ways?

Reward-based Training: There are three major reasons to choose a training approach that emphasizes the use of positive reinforcement:

- *It works:* Relying on positive reinforcement as your primary training approach is effective and efficient. It works, really, really well. A major reason for this is that positive consequences can provide very specific information to the dog about the exact behavior that the trainer is targeting. Using the sit/stay example from Chapter 7, food treats and praise are provided *only* while the dog is sitting, and are simply withheld if the dog moves or changes his position. Most dogs rapidly associate the targeted behavior (sitting and staying) with the positive consequences (praise, petting, food treats). Contrast this to using aversive consequences in the same training situation. Collar jerks and yelling "NO" inform the dog about incorrect behavior (moving out of position), but provide no information about the behavior that is desired (sit-stay). In this same manner, unlike negative reinforcement, positive reinforcement lends itself well to successive approximation (shaping), a training technique that I discuss in detail in Section 3.

- *It results in a happy, relaxed dog:* Second, an emphasis upon pleasurable consequences during training promotes emotional states such as pleasure, contentment, and enjoyment in dogs. This can be directly compared with the varying levels of stress, fear, or distress that are associated with reliance upon aversives. Because learning new tasks is not associated with aversive stimuli, the dog is relaxed and comfortable during training and is more likely to attempt new behaviors. A dog who has learned that "guessing wrong" simply goes un-

132

rewarded and is not punished is much more likely to try new behaviors than is a dog who has a history of receiving aversive consequences for any incorrect behaviors that she attempted.

❖ *We have evidence for it benefits:* In recent years, researchers from a range of academic institutions have studied the effects of different training approaches on dogs' behavior, emotional states and ability to learn. These studies have used a variety of methodologies, including directly measuring training responses, videotaping dogs in homes, and owner surveys. Here is a summary of some of the evidence that they have collected (full citations are included in the evidence section at the end of the chapter):

✓ Behavior problems in dogs were positively correlated with reliance upon correction-based training methods but not with reward-based training methods. Owners who used reward-based training reported overall better obedience in their dogs when compared with those who used primarily negative reinforcement and punishment to train (Hiby, 2004).

✓ German Shepherds trained for guard dog work using an e-collar (shock collar) showed lowered body postures, high pitched yelping, avoidance behaviors, and redirected aggression – all signs of fear and pain. These signs were not seen in dogs who were not shocked during training. This study also showed that dogs trained with shock learned to associate the presence of their owner with impending shocks, even outside of the training context (Schilder and van der Borg, 2004).

✓ Dogs owned by people who stated that they used a high proportion of punishment when training were significantly less playful and were less likely to enjoy interacting with visitors to the home compared with dogs of owners who reported that they trained using primarily reward-based methods (Rooney and Cowan, 2011).

✓ A comparison of dogs trained at a school that used primarily reward-based methods to dogs trained at a school that used primarily correction-based methods found that dogs who were trained with negative reinforcement showed significantly more stress signs and were less likely to offer spontaneous eye contact with their owners than were dogs trained with reward-based methods (Deldalle and Gaunet, 2014).

✓ A group of pet dogs were trained to come when called by either (A) trainers using an electronic (shock) collar; (B) the same trainers but without an e-collar (C) trainers who used primarily reward-based training methods. While all three groups successfully taught the dogs to come when called, dogs trained with e-collars were more tense, yawned and vocalized more frequently, and explored their environment less than dogs trained using +R. These behaviors were interpreted as signs of stress and anxiety in the dogs trained with an e-collar (Cooper et al, 2014).

✓ Several studies have reported increased prevalence and risk of aggression-related behavior problems in dogs trained with aversive methods, when compared with dogs trained using reward-based methods (Herron et al., 2009; Arhant et al, 2010; Casey et al, 2014).

Should be an Easy Call, Eh? For the remainder of this chapter (and book), I am going to focus on the use of reward-based training methods (aka positive reinforcement) as a training approach because:

1. It works well.

2. It has desirable emotional and relationship benefits for our dogs and for us and is not associated with causing pain, anxiety or stress in dogs.

3. We have evidence for 1 and 2.

At my training school, AutumnGold, we attempt to stay within the +R quadrant as much as is practical. We use negative punishment (-P) on a limited basis (I am not personally a big fan of negative punishment so use it rarely; more about this in Section 3). We avoid the use of negative reinforcement (-R) and positive punishment. We also focus on management of a dog's environment and daily life to prevent unwanted behaviors and encourage good manners. The application of these methods is discussed in detail throughout Section 3. For now, though, let's take a closer look at the rewards that we use in operant conditioning; specifically, the types of reinforcers that we select to use in dog training to positively reinforce desired behaviors. These can be divided into two major categories; primary reinforcers and conditioned (or secondary) reinforcers.

Primary Reinforcers: Primary reinforcers are stimuli that are naturally pleasurable to dogs and require no prior conditioning (learning) to be effective. These are the same as the unconditioned stimuli that we discussed in Chapter 6; now they are being used as reinforcers. Primary reinforcers are items that your dog inherently enjoys and wants more of. The most potent primary reinforcers for dogs include yummy food treats, social interactions such as petting, praise and friendly eye contact, and opportunities for play and exercise. Conversely, primary aversive stimuli are any event that causes discomfort, pain, anxiety, or fear and which the dog naturally wishes to avoid. These would include collar corrections, verbal reprimands, e-collar shocks, and physical punishment such as swatting or hitting.

The dog decides: Although sounding somewhat circular, by definition, a *reinforcer is something that reinforces a behavior* (causes it to increase in frequency). In dog training, we provide reinforcement for desired behaviors by presenting *pre-selected* consequences (reinforcers) to our dogs. If a targeted behavior does not increase in frequency in response to the pleasurable consequence that we selected, then that consequence was *not* a reinforcer for that dog in that situation. The value that something holds for the dog determines its effectiveness as a positive reinforcer. It is the dog who decides what these things are, not us.

For example, I happen to enjoy eating baby carrots as a snack. If I tried to use these as a food reinforcer for Ally, they would never do the trick. Ally likes carrots well enough and will eat one or two if offered (she is a Golden Retriever after all; she eats anything). However, raw carrots are not a favorite food for her and it would be rather silly for me to attempt to use them as a reinforcer for her training. Rather, the treats that Ally does enjoy include several types of soft training treats, a meat-roll (cured meat) form of dog treat, and when I am feeling domestic, homemade tuna treats.

This rule does not only have to do with the type of food treats that we choose for our dogs. For example, most dogs enjoy petting and social interaction, and this type of interaction is, for many dogs, a strong positive reinforcer in a variety of training situations. However, my Toller, Chippy, has always been a busy boy and typically only wishes to be petted at the end of the day during his cuddle time on the couch. If we are out and about hiking or training, touch and petting are not potent reinforcers for Chip. Rather, with Chip, I stick with a variety of food treats and opportunities to retrieve – both things that he loves during training.

High value versus low value treats: Many trainers selectively use what we call "high-value treats" for some behaviors and "low-value treats" for others. These are ranked according to the dog's response to and enjoyment of different forms and flavors of food reinforcers. For example, with my dogs (who generally will eat everything), I use dry kibble as low-value, various brands of soft-moist treats as moderate-value, and meat roll and homemade dog treats as high-value reinforcers. Most trainers who pay attention to differently valued reinforcers use high-value treats when training a difficult or complex behavior. Typically, we pair high-value treats with the behavior that is most difficult or the part of a sequence that the dog is least motivated to offer (more about this in Section 3).

Some evidence: However, other than subjectively observing the level of our dog's pleasure at receiving different types of treats, do we have any *evidence* that treats vary in their influence upon learning? While limited, there are some data for this. When researchers trained dogs to offer eye contact using either a high-value treat (dried liver pieces), or a low-value treat (dry kibble pieces), all of the dogs learned "gazing behavior." However, the dogs trained using the high-value treat maintained eye contact longer durations than did dogs trained using low-value treats. Additionally, when the trainers proceeded to reinforce only with dry kibble, dogs who were downshifted from liver to kibble rapidly *decreased their gaze duration.* Although this was a small study, it suggests that learning efficiency is influenced by the *value* of the positive reinforcer that is used and that dogs are affected by changes in anticipated reinforcer value. Dogs trained with high-value treats showed a stronger response (longer duration of gaze), but also demonstrated signs of extinction when suddenly switched to a low-value treat and even rejected the reinforcer!

This evidence tells us that, yes, using a variety of treat types can be helpful, and that ranking treats – using high value treats for new or more difficult behaviors may enhance learning. However, the results also suggest that we might want to pay close attention to downshifting from high to lower value treats during training sessions. Dogs may not only notice the switch, but it can affect the stability of a previously trained behavior, at least when that behavior has been only recently learned and is not yet reliable. We will revisit "treat ranking" in Chapter 10. For now, keep in mind that all food treats may not be created equal!

Must We Use Food? Getting back to Mr. Frownie-face. One of the objections that some dog owners have to reward-based methods is not the use of pleasurable consequences per se, but rather an objection to the use of *food treats* as a primary reinforcer. These are the folks who protest that they prefer that their dog "work for love" and so are willing to use praise and petting to positively reinforce desired behaviors in their dogs, but draw the line at using food.

The good news is that dogs, being the social and unique creatures who they are, respond well to many different types of positive reinforcement. Of these, food treats are considered to be one of the most, if not *the* most, powerful and universal primary reinforcer that we use in dog training. This is true because, simply, food works really well. However, dogs also respond to petting, verbal praise, and an opportunity to play tug, a retrieving game, or even a chance to play with a best dog buddy. And, we definitely should (and do) use those to reinforce desired behaviors. But, are they as effective as food treats? Again, not much evidence, but what there is tells us that we should keep those food treats at the top of our training tool box.

Some evidence: Researchers at the University of Japan trained a group of dogs to maintain position in a sit/stay and to come when called, using either soft moist dog treats, gentle petting, or verbal praise to positively reinforce the targeted behaviors. All of the dogs learned the two behaviors, but fewer training sessions were needed when food treats were used as the positive reinforcer, compared with praise or petting. Dogs also responded more rapidly to "coming when called" when food treats were used. These results show that, as expected, food treats, petting and praise are all effective primary reinforcers for dogs. Using food had benefits over praise and petting in that it enhanced learning and reduced response time. So, no, Joe, you do not *have* to use food treats, but your training will progress more rapidly and your dog will probably learn more efficiently if you do.

Food treats (of various values), petting and praise are all potent primary reinforcers for dogs. While a trainer can certainly train with reward-based methods and not use food, to do so would be throwing away a highly potent and effective positive reinforcer for our dogs. Why would you want to do that?

Conditioned (Secondary) Reinforcers: There is one more class of reinforcer that we must consider when using reward-based training methods. These are called "conditioned or secondary reinforcers." These are conditioned stimuli (defined in Chapter 6) that are now being used as reinforcers. They are stimuli that are either completely neutral or that have weak naturally reinforcing properties. These are deliberately paired with a primary reinforcer and once properly conditioned, take on the reinforcing power of the primary reinforcer. For example, if I say *"Good!"* to Ally and immediately follow this utterance with a food treat, this can establish a predictive (classical) relationship between the word *"Good!"* and the presentation of a food treat. When using a word as a conditioned reinforcer, most trainers choose a monosyllabic word such as *"Good"* or *"Yes!"* and pronounce it using a distinct emphasis (more about this later).

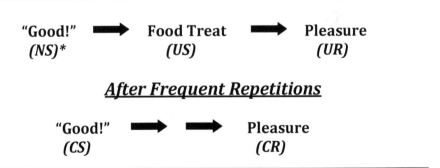

"Good!" ➡ Food Treat ➡ Pleasure
(NS)*   (US)   (UR)

After Frequent Repetitions

"Good!" ➡ ➡ Pleasure
(CS)   (CR)

*NS = Neutral stimulus; US = Unconditioned stimulus; UR = Unconditioned response; CS = Conditioned stimulus; CR = Conditioned response

More commonly today, many dog trainers, including myself, use a *clicker* as a conditioned reinforcer. This is by far the most powerful and frequently used conditioned reinforcer employed by dog trainers. In my opinion, it is a training tool that has revolutionized dog training over the last 20 years.

Clicker Training: Clicker training refers to using the sound of "click" made by a small, handheld device called a "cricket" with the delivery of a food treat immediately following the click. After several repetitions of this pairing (Click-Treat; hereafter CT), in which the click sound reliably *predicts* the treat, the sound comes to possess the same properties as the presentation of the treat itself - *a pleasurable emotional response.*

A Clicker (or Cricket)

Clicker training packs an enormously powerful positive punch because it allows trainers to precisely target tiny bits of behavior at the exact moment they are occurring and communicates that the primary reinforcer (treat) will be arriving soon. The click sound, the conditioned reinforcer, becomes analogous to saying to the dog:

"That's it!! That thing that you are doing right this instant is what will earn you the yummy treat that is coming shortly! You are SO very smart!"

A second advantage of using a clicker for training, a benefit that it shares with all reward-based training, is that it shifts a substantial proportion of control and choice to the dog. This empowerment leads to a dog who loves to learn new things and is eager to *"find out what's clickin' in each training session."* (More about this in Section 3).

Operant and Classical Conditioning Together: Although classical and operant conditioning are often discussed as if they are separate and distinct ways in which dogs learn, in actuality the two types of conditioning are intricately linked. Clicker training provides a great example of these connections because using a click as a conditioned reinforcer to teach dogs new behaviors encompasses both classical and operant learning:

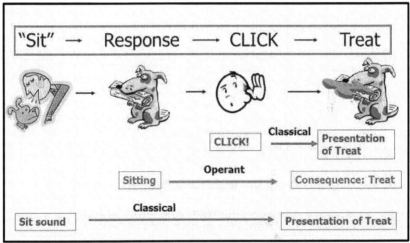

The Connection between Classical & Operant Conditioning

- **Classical:** Click (neutral stimulus) consistently precedes and predicts Treat (unconditioned stimulus). After several repetitions, the Click takes on the properties of the treat and is now said to be a conditioned stimulus. Trainers typically refer to it as a "conditioned reinforcer" because the CT is used as a consequence (positive reinforcer).

- **Operant:** Dog offers a behavior (sit), which results in the presentation of CT (positive reinforcement). Dog says *"Yum! Sitting results in a treat! I like treats. I will increase the frequency that I offer a sit!"*

- **Classical:** This last one is really cool, because it provides additional evidence for why our dogs SO enjoy reward-based training and in particular, clicker training. The voice cue "*Sit*" is added to the training process when the dog has begun to offer sit for CT. The trainer then will only CT when the dog offers the behavior in response to the voice cue (and no other time that the dog sits).

  Over time, as the dog attains proficiency (offers sit reliably in response to the cue), the cue "*Sit*" becomes a classically conditioned stimulus because it reliably precedes and predicts an opportunity for CT to the dog (with the operant sit behavior thrown in the middle). This means that the cues that the trainer uses with trained behaviors become *imbued* with the same characteristics as the click sound; the *voice cues themselves become something that the dog enjoys and looks forward to, because they are always paired with an opportunity to earn a CT*. (I love this stuff!).

Hopefully, this chapter has convinced you to focus primarily on reward-based training methods with your own dogs and, if applicable, in your training programs and with your clients. We also examined different types of primary and conditioned reinforcers and how they are selected and used in reward-based training. Before we move on to the final chapter in this section, which examines social cognition and learning, let's revisit Mr. Frownie-face and Joe and their various objections to using food treats to train their dogs.

Talking to Joe: So, what to do when you have a Mr. or Ms. Frownie-Face in training class, as a private client, or as a neighbor Joe (who happens to know a lot about dogs)? Here are a few tips for responding when Joe tells you,

"I don't want to use food treats when I train because......"

❖ *".....using food is a bribe and I do not want to bribe my dog to behave"* **Answer:** Well, Joe, you are confusing bribery with reinforcement. Bribery refers to giving your dog something he wants *before* he offers a desired behavior, while reinforcement occurs immediately *after* your dog offers the desired behavior. It's all in the timing, Joe. Here's an example. If I show a large dog biscuit to Cooper and then call him to me, he will of course see the biscuit and then come over to receive it. That is a bribe (or a lure). While it might help to initiate the behavior of "coming when called", if I continue to use that sequence – show biscuit then call Cooper - he will learn to come when called *only* if he sees the biscuit. (Hint. We do not want that). Alternatively, calling Cooper and *then* giving him a biscuit (*after* the targeted behavior) reinforces the behavior. This is not bribery, but rather it is payment for a desired behavior. The difference is that when we use reinforcement, we teach dogs to respond to the cue without the need to show them the biscuit first.

143

❧ *"......I don't want to start using food because then my dog will only listen to me if I have a food treat in my hand."* **Answer:** This is the same as the previous answer Joe. Your dog will learn to respond to your cues only when you have food in your hand if you *trained him that way* (i.e. with a bribe rather than with reinforcement). The correct use of operant conditioning and proper timing of reinforcement prevent the problem that you are so worried about.

❧ *"......I want my dog to behave because he sees me as his leader and alpha in his pack"* **Answer:** Sorry Joe, your dog is not trying to be in charge of your family, your home or the universe. Nor is he challenging your status when he jumps up, runs away, digs in the yard, counter-surfs or barks at the fence. He is doing these things because they are reinforcing for him (i.e. they work) and because you have not yet taught him better behavior. It's not about dominance, Joe. It's about training.

❧ *"......Using food and praise and petting is overly-permissive and spoils dogs."* **Answer:** Well, Joe, do you think that getting your paycheck at the end of each week means that your employer is overly-permissive with you? When your wife thanks you for taking the car to have the oil changed, do you consider her praise to be spoiling you? Much like you receive positive reinforcement for good behavior at work (pay) and at home (praise, love), your dog earns his positive reinforcement by offering behaviors that you like and select to reinforce. You are not being overly-permissive because you only reinforce desirable dog behaviors and you prevent (through various means) behaviors in your dog that are undesirable. Your dog will not be spoiled, Joe. He will be trained.

❧ *"......I don't want to just ignore bad behavior; I want to DO something about it to stop it."* **Answer:** No worries here Joe. Positively reinforcing desired behaviors is just one tool in your training box, albeit, one of your most important tools. We have other methods that can prevent and reduce unwanted behaviors in dogs while you still use reward-based training for those desired behaviors. And, we agree with you that simply ignoring unwanted behaviors is not enough (and actually is often ineffective). Stick with us, Joe - more about this to come.

Evidence

Arhant C, et al. Behavior of smaller and larger dogs: Effects of training methods, inconsistency of owner behaviour and level of engagement in activities with the dog. *Applied Animal Behaviour Science* 2010; 123:131-142.

Bentosela M, et al. Incentive contrast in domestic dogs (*Canis familiaris*). *Journal of Comparative Psychology* 2009; 123:125-130.

Blackwell EJ, et al. The use of electronic collars for training domestic dogs: estimated prevalence, reasons and risk factors for use, and owner perceived success as compared to other training methods. *BMC Veterinary Research* 2012; 8:93.

Blackwell, EJ, et al. The relationship between training methods and the occurrence of behavior problems as reported by owners in a population of domestic dogs. *Journal of Veterinary Behavior; Clinical Applications and Research* 2008; 3:207-217.

Casey RA, et al. Human directed aggression in domestic dogs (Canis familiaris): occurrence in different contexts and risk factors. *Applied Animal Behaviour Science* 2014; 152:52-63.

Cooper JJ, et al. The welfare consequences and efficacy of training pet dogs with remote electronic training collars in comparison to reward-based training. *PloS One* 2014; 9:e102722.

Deldalle S and Gaunet F. Effects of two training methods on stress-related behaviors of the dog (Canis familiaris) and on the dog-owner relationship. *Journal of Veterinary Behavior: Clinical Applications and Research* 2014; 9:58-65.

Fukuzawa M and Hayashi N: Comparison of 3 different reinforcements of learning in dogs (*Canis familiaris*). Journal of Veterinary Behavior 2013; 8:221-224.

Gabrielsen AM. Training technologies. *Nordic Journal of Science and Technology Studies* 2017; 5:5-16.

Herron ME, Shofer FS and Reisner IR. Survey of the use and outcome of confrontational and non-confrontational training methods in client-owned dogs showing undesired behaviors. *Applied Animal Behavioural Science* 2009; 117:47-54.

Hiby EF, Rooney NJ and Bradshaw JWS. Dog training methods: Their use, effectiveness and interaction with behaviour and welfare. *Animal Welfare* 2004; 13:63-69.

Pescini-Marshall S, et al. Does training make you smarter? The effect of training on dogs' performance (*Canis familiaris*) in a problem solving task. *Behavioural Processes* 2008; 78:449-454

Rooney NJ and Cowan S. Training methods and owner–dog interactions: Links with dog behaviour and learning ability. *Applied Animal Behaviour Science* 2011; 132:169-177.

Schilder MBH and van der Borg JM. Training dogs with the help of the shock collar: short and long term behavioral effects. *Applied Animal Behavior Science* 2004; 85:319-334.

Ziv G. The effects of using aversive training methods on dogs – A review. *Journal of Veterinary Behavior* 2017; 19:50-60.

Chapter 9
The Cognitive Canine

Eye contact is one of the first things that I teach to my dogs and is a basic exercise that we include in our training classes at AutumnGold. It is an easy behavior to train and in class it provides rapid and positive results to owners who may be frustrated with their young dog's lack of attention. Like most trainers, we teach "watch" operantly – a quick glance into the trainer's eyes gets a "Good!" (or click) and a treat. Very quickly, the dog learns that the consequence for friendly eye contact is pleasurable and subsequently starts to offer eye contact more frequently. We then put the behavior on cue ("Watch") and ask for more duration (holding eye contact). From a training point of view, a dog's gaze into our eyes follows the simple operant rule of *positively reinforced behaviors increase in frequency.*

That's all there is to it, right?

Cooper offering "eye contact" to me on cue

No. There is more. The eye contact that Cooper and I share is much more than a simple "cue-response" (trained) behavior. Rather, Coop, like many other dogs, uses human eye contact and gaze to communicate, gain information, and make decisions – all *cognitive* skills that dogs are now known to possess.

The last 15 years have witnessed an explosion of research examining numerous facets of canine cognition. As a group, cognitive scientists study a range of mental functions in humans and other species. These include (but are not limited to) reasoning, problem-solving, conceptual learning, decision-making, communication, memory, emotions, and perceptions. Their studies with dogs have focused on the dogs' ability to understand human gestures, emotions and communication, whether dogs are able to take the perspective of another individual, whether or not dogs demonstrate empathy, and their skills at learning to solve a problem by observing another dog or person.

The generally accepted conclusion of these studies has been that dogs are cognitively unique among social animals because of their remarkable ability to detect and understand *human* communication signals, attentional states and emotions. While other social animals possess innate abilities to learn the social signals of their own species, the dog is the first (and only, apparently) species to demonstrate enhanced abilities to pay attention to and rapidly learn the communication cues of *another* species (us). This talent influences the bond that they so readily develop with people as well as the ease with which dogs learn new behaviors. So, let's take a look at what we now know about our dog's inner mind and how our understanding of the cognitive canine may influence some of our training practices.

Pointing: Dogs are highly sensitive to human communication signals such as body language, tone of voice, and various forms of directional cues. Human pointing gestures have been used as a research litmus test for measuring dogs' ability to understand human directional cues, one of the underpinnings of the dog's unique cognitive talents. Responding correctly to a pointing gesture is considered to be a form of inferential reasoning. The dog sees a gesture, infers its meaning, and reacts appropriately – *"There is something over there that may interest me; I had better take a look."* While the early studies focused on pointing with our hands, it quickly became evident that dogs, being the masters of body language that they are, also understand other types of directional cues from humans. They react to the position of our bodies, to head turns, to the use of our legs and feet, and, perhaps most subtly, to where (and at what) we are gazing.

To investigate these abilities further, researchers have compared pointing comprehension among various groups of dogs: dogs versus wolves, dogs in homes versus dogs living in shelters, and puppies versus adult dogs. Pointing talent has been tested using different types of pointing (hand, body position, and head movements) and when the pointing person is either familiar or unfamiliar to the dog. A few general conclusions of these comparisons are:

- *Puppies (9 to 24 weeks) can do it:* And they do it best if the pointing person first makes eye contact with them. These studies provide evidence that dogs are born with an innate predisposition to attend to human communication signals.

- *Living with people improves performance:* Adult dogs usually perform better than puppies; well-socialized dogs perform better than shelter dogs, and highly trained dogs perform better than dogs with little training. This means that while dogs are naturally inclined to pay attention to our cues, learning is an important (and possibly essential) component for improving these abilities.

- *Arms work best:* Dogs are most successful when the pointing appendage is a person's arm, extended towards the correct selection (usually a food choice). They are less consistently correct with more subtle cues such as body positioning or pointing with a foot. However, some individual dogs excel at the most subtle of cues (we all know one of these dogs).

- *Visual communication matters*: When owners make eye contact with their dog first, signaling intention, dogs respond more successfully to pointing than when eye contact is not made first. This effect is seen in pre-weaned puppies (who have had no opportunity to learn about the meaning of eye contact with people) and in adult dogs.

Although there are a number of nuanced points (literally) to be made, there is no longer any doubt.

Dogs are good at this pointing stuff.

We point to something and they will look there. They come to this naturally by paying attention to our body language, our movements, and our eyes, but living with people and learning, as would be expected, strongly influences a dog's talent at reading his or her owner's directional cues.

Eye Contact and Gaze: Dogs also initiate eye contact with people and respond to visual communication signals. We are well matched in this respect because humans, of course, use eye contact to communicate all of the time. Similarly, anyone who lives with multiple dogs knows that when one dog's attention is suddenly drawn to a morsel of food on the ground (or something more smelly), other dogs quickly pick up on these cues and gather round to look. Dogs notice and follow the gaze of their owners to gain information. Most dogs readily follow direction when we are looking toward something that holds high value to them – for example a piece of food on the floor or a wall hook holding their lead.

However, when food choice is not involved, dogs vary considerably in their inclination to spontaneously follow our gaze. Interestingly, research studies of gaze-following in dogs have found

151

that some dogs naturally and consistently excel at this (and learn something from it) while others repeatedly fail this test. Take a moment and give it a try with your own dog. First get his attention. Once he is interacting with you, gaze towards something located several feet away, such as a doorway, a piece of furniture or an object on the floor. Does your dog follow your gaze? Or, does he continue to gaze adoringly up into your eyes? If he follows your gaze to find out what you are looking toward, count him as one of the approximately 50 percent of dogs who show this behavior, which is considered to be a form of referential learning.

But, what about the rest of the dogs? Why might some dogs either never develop or lose the ability to understand gaze as a form of pointing gesture? This is especially puzzling since following the gaze of another dog is such a strong communication signal among dogs. One answer may be related to the amount of training that a dog has received. A study conducted at the Clever Dog Lab in Vienna, Austria found that teaching dogs to offer eye contact interfered with their ability to use gaze as a directional cue from their owners. Dogs who were trained to offer and hold eye contact were *less* likely to follow their owner's gaze towards a distant object than dogs who were not trained to offer this behavior. As the amount of formal training increased, the tendency of the dogs to naturally follow their owner's gaze decreased. (Yikes).

In my view, as a dog trainer, the important implication of this evidence is what it tells us about our ability to inhibit, albeit with the very best of intentions, one of our dog's natural social behaviors – to follow visual directional cues. This made me think a bit more carefully about when and how often I ask for default eye contact with my own dogs. If one agrees that social cognition, the ability to understand and respond to the social cues of others, is an important part of a dog's life quality (I do), then we should make conscious decisions regarding the types of training that contribute to or detract from our dogs' natural social behavior.

I am certainly not advocating an end to training eye contact. For me, it remains an important behavior to teach to dogs because eye contact contributes to strong communicative bonds and facilitates learning. One cannot really teach new behaviors, after all, if we fail to have our dog's attention. Rather, I would suggest that we consciously strive for a balance between those training activities that require our dog's undivided attention and those in which we encourage dogs to use their cognitive skills and work independently to problem solve.

Looking for Help: Understanding gaze as a directional cue is not the only way that dogs use eye contact with us. Many dogs approach and initiate eye contact with their owner when they are asking for something (a walk, food, petting or a game of fetch) and in some cases, when asking for a bit of help. These apparent requests for assistance are of interest because it seems that this is one of the ways in which dogs differ from wolves. One of the earliest studies of canine social cognition compared the response of dogs and wolves when presented with an unsolvable task. In this test, the dog is first allowed to solve a food puzzle in which a bit of food in a container can be accessed by manipulating the container. After several successful trials, the nefarious researcher, unbeknownst to the dog, steps in and alters the puzzle, making the task now impossible to solve. So, the method that the dog used to previously obtain the food is now futile. (I know, very frustrating. Bad researcher).

When presented with this situation, most dogs work at the puzzle for a few minutes and then turn to look back at their owner, presumably as a request for aid. In contrast, wolves rarely look back at humans. This initial research showing that *wolves do not look back at humans, but dogs do* served as a jumping-off point for a flood of innovative research regarding the dog's social cognition skills.

Since then, additional studies have shown that a number of factors can influence an individual dog's tendency to look to their

153

owner for help when faced with a frustrating task. Some of these are a dog's living situation (homes vs. shelters), the type of relationship that the dog has with people, and once again, of interest for this book - the degree and type of training that the dog has experienced:

- **_Training enhances problem-solving (usually):_** When dogs are focused on a solvable task such as learning to open a food-box with their paw or muzzle, those who have a history of formal training are _less_ likely to look to their owner as they work at the task than are dogs who have experienced little or no formal training. This suggests that training enhances dogs' ability to work independently and solve problems.

- **_A bit of help here, please?_** Conversely, when the task presented to the dogs is NOT solvable, things suddenly change up a bit. When frustrated and faced with a puzzle that they simply cannot get to work, the specific type of training that a dog has received influences their response:

  ✓ Agility dogs and water rescue dogs, both types of training that require dogs to respond reliably to their handler's cues were _most_ likely to look to their owners for help.

  ✓ Search and Rescue dogs and dogs who had recently finished their training as guide dogs generally continued to work at the puzzle and were _less_ likely to look to their owner for help (or looked for shorter durations).

  ✓ Working guide dogs who had been living in homes for a year or more were more likely to turn to look for help. Unlike their younger counterparts, these guide dogs behaved more like untrained dogs in that they would turn and seek help when presented with a difficult problem.

What these studies collectively suggest is that the life experience of training generally promotes increased confidence and independence in dogs when they are presented with novel tasks that are solvable. However, when dogs are experiencing a failure to succeed at a new task (and possibly are becoming frustrated), the type of training that they have experienced influences their inclination to look to their owners for help.

Dogs who have been trained to work closely with a human partner and to depend upon their cues are more likely to look to their people for help. Conversely, dogs who have been trained at tasks in which they work independently are less likely to ask. Most interesting perhaps is the evidence that a dog's living situation may trump his or her training history. It is possible that living in close proximity with human caretakers and experiencing daily interaction and communication may be more important than training in terms of encouraging our dogs to ask for a little help.

Learning by Observing: It is generally accepted that social learning plays an important role in the lives of dogs. Observing the behavior of others helps dogs to learn about their environment, modifies their responses to new situations, and can teach them new behaviors and solutions to problems. Social learning differs significantly from associative forms of learning such as classical and operant conditioning because the dog is not directly *experiencing* an action or its consequences. Rather, he is simply watching another individual perform a behavior and subsequently offers a form of that behavior. There are several types of social learning that reflect different degrees of cognitive complexity. Much of the debate among those who study social learning revolves around what information the dog is actually using and the complexity with which that information is processed cognitively. For the purposes of this book, I am interested in how social learning might occur between dogs in training situations.

Interestingly, much of the cognitive research with dogs has focused on their ability to learn by observing *human* demonstrators, rather than other dogs. Dogs have been shown to be quite skilled at solving food puzzles and following a detour path around a fence after watching a person perform the task correctly. They do this best when the demonstrator is a person who they know well such as their owner or a friend. Other factors such as the dog's age, living situation and prior training experiences influence success as well.

Conversely, studies that have examined the dog's ability to learn socially from other *dogs* are fewer in number. There is some evidence that, just as with human demonstrators, dogs show improved performance and problem-solving ability after watching a demonstrator dog successfully complete a detour or puzzle task. One of the earliest experiments reported that puppies who were allowed to observe their mother working at a scent detection task went on to become more successful as scent dogs in adult life. Another found that pre-weaned puppies could learn to grasp a ribbon and pull a packet of food into their pen after watching another puppy learn the task through trial and error.

So, what about *both* – human and dog? Can dogs learn a new task by watching another dog being trained by their owner?

The reason that I am interested in this is that at AutumnGold, it is not unusual for us to enroll students who live with and train more than one dog. A common question that these clients have is how to arrange their training sessions to allow them to train one dog while the other dog "waits his or her turn." In most of these cases, the student laments that the dog who is not chosen for training becomes upset, does not enjoy being isolated or confined, and may even show some separation stress or frustration with the overall unfairness (in their opinion) of the entire situation.

Over the years, my personal solution to this problem has been to teach each of our dogs to stay on a pause table located off of the training floor while they await their turn to train. Although it can be challenging to teach, I like this arrangement because it is convenient and saves me from having to return to the house multiple times to get a different dog. It is also fun for the dogs because they generally receive more training time and also get to play together after the session.

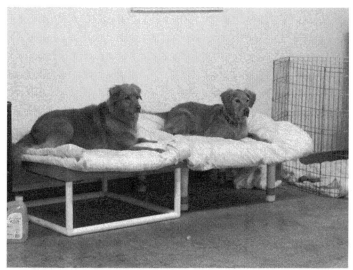

Chippy and Cooper wait their turns to train

So, is there evidence that dogs who watch another dog being trained with their owner learn to perform a new behavior more quickly? Will Cooper learn to "take a bow" more rapidly if he has watched Chippy perform this behavior with me first? Although research is limited, it appears that he might!

A study conducted at the University of Naples in Italy showed that dogs who had watched another dog jump up onto an obstacle and sit/stay on cue by their owner were more likely to successfully perform the same exercise after watching, compared with dogs who did not observe the training. Specifically, 62.5 % of the observing dogs were successful compared with 23.5 % of the non-observing dogs. Neither a dog's sex nor his/her level of prior training experience influenced the probability that they would perform the new task successfully. Age was somewhat important, as older dogs tended to be more successful than younger dogs.

On one level, these results are not surprising. Anecdotes abound among dog folks regarding our dogs' abilities to learn from one another through observation. Ask anyone who lives with more than one dog and they will relate numerous examples of their dogs sharing information (and not always in a good way). For as long as I can remember our dogs have learned to "wait" at the door and in the car by watching each other. While I do train this cue, our young dogs learn to wait very rapidly when they notice that the entire family is frozen in its tracks. Similarly, because we hike a lot with our dogs, one dog finding something yummy or smelly on the trail is quickly observed and acted upon by the others. Still, these examples may arguably fall relatively low on the social learning scale in terms of cognitive complexity.

What is exciting about this new information is that it demonstrates that a dog who has the opportunity to observe another dog who is performing a trained exercise and is not physically participating in any way, benefits from that observation. I would venture that this type of learning would be most influential when the dogs are highly motivated to engage in the task and perhaps when they know each other well. For example, teaching something that is target-oriented, such as jumping up onto an obstacle or retrieving a toy, may be more successful than training a static exercise such as a down/stay. This difference is reflected in the results of another study reporting that untrained dogs did not perform well in learning a positional behavior (lying down on cue) after watching another dog perform it. While dogs are often naturally interested in examining and engaging with new objects, most are decidedly less motivated to spontaneously offer a static behavior such as a sit/stay or down/stay.

These results make me consider the relative ease with which my youngest dogs, Alice and Cooper, have learned platform positions, retrieving tricks such as "put your toys in a basket" and goouts to a target. Both regularly watch and get excited as the other is being trained in these behaviors. (And, not to put too fine a point on it, I rarely see that level of interest or excitement when I am training sit/stays and down/stays). While I have no control group for my own anecdotal experiences, these results suggest to me that having all of my dogs present and attending during a training session may have benefits that go beyond convenience. Watching the other dogs learn new things may help my observing dogs to learn more rapidly, at least in those exercises that interest and engage them.

Empathy: It is without dispute that dogs, like many other species, experience a range of basic emotions and express these behaviorally. These include fear, anxiety, pleasure, playfulness, joy (happiness) and probably jealousy. (I would also add silliness to these, but then, I live with a Toller). They also have an impressive ability to comprehend and respond to human emotions, as expressed by our body language, facial expressions and vocalizations. These reactions are assumed to reflect some level of an emotion that rests higher on the cognitive scale – empathy.

Empathy refers to the ability to feel and respond to what another individual is feeling. At its most basic, empathy refers to the ability to share the emotions of another individual. However, there is debate over whether or not the expression of empathy must involve the capacity to take the perspective of the other, a level of cognition that requires at least a rudimentary "theory of mind" (we discuss this in more detail in the next section of this chapter).

One approach to resolving this debate has been to classify empathy into several types, each requiring different levels of cognitive complexity. The lowest level is called *emotional contagion* and refers to simply being affected by and sharing another's emotional state. There is substantial evidence that dogs show this level of empathy with their owners. The next step up, *sympathetic concern* is expressed through comforting behaviors. Chimpanzees, some species of birds, *and dogs* all have been shown to demonstrate comforting behaviors towards others in distress. Once again, this has been studied most extensively between dogs and humans. At the peak of the cognitive scale is *empathic perspective,* which requires the capacity to understand and appraise a situation from the other individual's perspective. An example of this is prosocial helping, a talent that some dogs have indeed been found to be capable of when they are made aware of their owner's goal. Although not studied as extensively, there is also evidence that dogs show empathy to the other dogs in their lives, specifically to their dog friends and housemates.

For example, when dogs listened to the distress calls of either an unfamiliar dog or their housemate, they all reacted to the distress calls, regardless of whether the dog was their housemate or an unknown dog. Upon hearing the distressed barking, dogs moved towards the source of the sound, gazing intently. Some dogs became visibly upset and cortisol (stress hormone) levels increased. When the distressed calls were a recording of the dog's housemate, dogs showed intense examination and affiliative (loving) behaviors towards their partner when reunited. Dogs did not show these intense greetings during the reunion if they had listened to the distressed whining of an unfamiliar dog.

This study, the first to directly measure dogs' empathic response to other dogs, provides evidence that dogs are capable of the first level of empathy, emotional contagion. The dogs were clearly affected by and shared the distressed emotional state of a dog who they could hear but not see. The study also showed us that dogs recognize and respond to the distress of a friend more intensely than they do to the distress of a dog who they do not know and that they show strong affiliative behaviors towards their friend upon being reunited. These behaviors suggest that not only do dogs recognize the vocalizations of their friends (which has been demonstrated in other studies) but that they express the second level of empathy - sympathetic concern – showing comfort. While we do not know for certain that dogs show the highest level of empathy, empathic perspective, we do have some evidence for perspective-taking behaviors in dogs in other situations.

Perspective-Taking: Chippy, my Toller, is a terrible food thief. (Of course, the use of the word *terrible* is one of perspective. Given his impressive success rate, Chippy would argue that he is actually a very *good* food thief).

Like many other expert food thieves, Chip is quite careful in his pilfering decisions. He will only steal when we are not in the room or when we are being inattentive. The parsimonious (simplest) explanation of this is a behavioristic one; Chip learned early in life that taking forbidden tidbits was successful when a human was not in the room and was unsuccessful if someone was present and attentive to him. In other words, like many dogs who excel at food thievery, Chip learned what "works."

Chippy does like cake

However, while a behavioristic explanation covers most aspects of selective stealing behavior in dogs, there is evidence that, at

161

least for some dogs, there may be a bit more going on here. Once again, we turn to gaze. Dogs alter their behavior in response to whether a person is actively looking at them versus if the person is distracted. For example, in separate studies, dogs were more apt to steal a piece of food from an inattentive person and would preferentially beg from an attentive person. However, these differences can *still* be explained without a need for higher cognitive processing. A dog could learn over time that human gaze and attentiveness reliably predict certain outcomes, such as positive interactions and opportunities to beg for food. Similarly, inattentiveness might reliably predict opportunities to steal a tidbit (or two or five).

Conversely, it is also possible that, just like humans, dogs use a person's gaze to determine what that individual does or does not *know*. This type of learning is considered to be a higher level of cognitive processing because it requires perspective-taking, meaning that the dog is able to view a situation through the perspective of the person and then makes decisions based upon what that individual is aware of (or not). The significance of this type of thinking is that it reveals at least a rudimentary *"theory of mind"* - the ability to consider what another individual knows or may be thinking. Theory of mind is considered a mental function that falls relatively high on the cognitive scale – and is certainly indicative of more going on than simply associative learning.

So, while it is established that dogs are sensitive to the cues that human eye contact and gaze provide, it has not been clear whether they can use this information to determine what the person may or may not *know*.

Enter, once again, the cognitive scientists:

- **The Toy Study**: One approach to teasing out "theory of mind" evidence is to control what a dog observes about what a person may or may not be able to see. In "the toy study" dogs sat behind a barrier that allowed them to see two toys but which

162

blocked the owner's view of one of the toys. When asked to retrieve, the dogs preferentially retrieved the toy that the owner could also see. This suggests that the dogs were aware that their owners could *not know* that there was a toy located out of their view, and so retrieved the toy that they (presumably) assumed that the owner was requesting.

- ***The Food Thievery Study:*** Chippy likes this set of experiments. Situations were set up in which dogs had the opportunity to steal a bit of prohibited food. In all of the conditions, the owner showed the dog a hotdog sitting on a plate and cued the dog to "leave it". In the first situation, the owner remained with the dog (and the food) in a well-lit room. The majority of dogs did not steal. No big surprise there. In the second scenario, the owner remained in the room with the dog, but the room was completely dark. A bunch of dogs went for it and took the food (score!). Then things got a bit more complicated. In scene 3, the *food* was in the dark but the rest of the room was illuminated. This meant that the owners could not see the food even though they were still in the room with the dogs. In this situation, many dogs grabbed the food and also pounced on it much faster than when the owner could see it. (*I'll just weasel on over to the food and snort it up.......heh heh.....she can't see it and will never know.....I am such a clever dog....*). Chippy would love these dogs. This suggests that it is not just a person's *presence or attentiveness* that becomes a cue whether or not to steal, but that dogs may also consider what they think we can or cannot *see* when making a decision about what to do.

Without a doubt, gaze and eye contact are highly important to dogs. They use eye contact in various forms to communicate with us and with other animals. We know that many dogs naturally follow our gaze to distant objects (i.e. as a form of pointing) and that dogs will seek our eye contact when looking for a bit of help. And now we know that dogs, like humans and several other social species, can be aware of what a person may or may not be

163

able to see and, on some level, are capable of taking that person's perspective into consideration. While "learning what works" is probably still the strongest underlying form of learning in play with our food-stealing dogs, we must also consider these higher levels of cognitive thought when Chippy, once again, pilfers that piece of cake.

Are Dogs Self-Aware? Do they recognize themselves as individuals, distinct from others? Although rather tricky topics of study, animal self-recognition, self-awareness and consciousness have been examined by scientists for decades. Animal consciousness is neither a new idea, nor is it a radical way of thinking. Lucky for us, we no longer live in the age of Descartes when animals other than those of the human variety were viewed as non-thinking automatons who lacked both consciousness and the ability to feel emotions. (Though, personally I can think of a few humans who may fit that description).

Evidence for at least a rudimentary sense of self-awareness is available in a wide range of non-human animal species. A leading theory of the evolutionary benefits of this trait is that the ability to distinguish self from other helps social animals to recognize their place within their social group, to cooperate successfully with others, and to identify individuals who are outside of their group. As we have seen in this chapter, dogs, also members of a highly social species, are now known to have much more complex inner lives than we once gave them credit for. Having a sense of self as distinct from others is an additional cognitive faculty that dogs may possess given their highly social nature and the functional benefits of self-recognition and self-awareness.

The classic test used to study self-recognition has been the mirror self-recognition test. Using this method, an animal examines her image in a mirror after an area of her body has been surreptitiously marked with a spot of dye. The animal's reaction to this alteration is observed and if the subject uses the mirror to exam-

164

ine the spot on her body, this attention is interpreted as evidence for recognizing the image in the mirror as oneself rather than simply an image of a like-looking animal with a funny spot on her head. Species that regularly pass the mirror test include the great apes (chimpanzees, bonobos, and orangutans), dolphins, a single elephant, and even some bird species, such as the Magpie. Oh yeah, and most humans pass, as long as they are older than 2-years of age.

Do Dogs Pass the Mirror Test?

Dogs however, have routinely failed this test. I know, you are now almost certainly muttering, "*Well of course, dogs do not use vision as their primary special sense - they use olfaction - their noses.*" This difference is significant of course, since dogs believe what their nose tells them first and foremost, compared with primate species such as ourselves, who perceive the world primarily through vision. Additionally, because of anatomical and social differences, dogs do not regularly self-groom in the same manner that primates do, so are not as apt to care about an unexpected spot that suddenly shows up on the top of their head. For those who study dogs, clearly, another type of test was needed. Enter the dog pee researchers from Barnard College in New York City.

The canine mirror test: Dogs regularly investigate the urine scent of other dogs. There is evidence that they spend more time investigating the urine markings of other dogs and less time sniffing their own urine, which suggests that dogs distinguish their own scent from that of others. Using this knowledge, Dr. Alexandra Horowitz and her team devised a new type of mirror test for dogs - this one based upon their primary sense - smell.

They reasoned that just as a chimpanzee notices the sudden change in appearance when a spot of dye shows up on her head, if dogs recognize their own scent, then they too should be surprised to find an unexpected change in that smell and attend to it (sniff it) for a longer period of time. She devised an experiment that asked, using their sense of smell, *"Do dogs recognize themselves?"*

Dogs were presented with three vials of dog urine - one contained water only (decoy sample), one contained the subject dog's urine (self), and the third contained either (1) the dog's adulterated urine (marker self), (2) the urine of an unfamiliar dog (other), or (3) the scent of the adulteration substance alone (marker). Similar to mirror tests, the researchers expected dogs to pay *more* attention to a scent of themselves that was unexpectedly altered compared with their reaction to their unaltered urine scent. Here is what they found:

- ***Who's this guy?*** As earlier research has shown, dogs spent more time investigating the urine of an unfamiliar dog compared with the time that they spent sniffing their own urine. *("Hmm.... Smells like I was here earlier......whoa.....hello....who is this new dude who peed here too?)*

- ***Does this smell funny to you?*** The dogs spend significantly more time investigating the canisters that contained their altered urine scent compared with how long they investigated their unadulterated urine. *("Wowza. This is weird. Did I eat* *something odd last night? Maybe I am getting a cold? What the heck IS that smell on me???")*

Although certainly more work needs to be done, the results of this creative study suggest that dogs may possess one of the cognitive traits, *self-recognition*, that humans have historically co-opted for our species and our species alone. In the past, we have worked diligently to make clear cognitive distinctions between human animals (us) and non-human animals (everyone else). A wide range of traits have been used for this purpose, many of which have fallen like a house of cards as they are discovered to exist in other animals, including dogs. Examples include the expression of emotions, perspective taking, ability to reason, and the demonstration of empathy and altruism.

We also know that humans do not hold exclusive rights to the expression of self-awareness and consciousness and are not the only species capable of complex thought, internal representations of the world, planning, intention and deception. Yes, we do have language and we are capable of "meta-thinking" (thinking about thinking), but many types of cognition and complex thought have been demonstrated to exist in a host of other animals, including dogs. So what is the big deal? Is there really anything to argue about here? Well, yeah, as a dog trainer (a clicker trainer, I must emphasize), I think that there is an important point to be made. It has to do with the tension that exists between the two sciences that influence dog training: behaviorism and social cognition.

The Dog Fight – Behaviorism vs. Social Cognition: The first three chapters of Section 2 of this book, Chapters 6, 7, and 8, focus on the well-established tenets of behaviorism. The science of behaviorism, as established by JB Watson, Edward Thorndike and most famously, BF Skinner, rests upon the premise that all of the behaviors that a dog (or rat or pig or human) shows are a product of their respective consequences. Those behaviors that result in pleasurable consequences will increase and those that result in unpleasant consequences will decrease. Behaviorism "purists" claim that while internal mental states such as emotions, intentions, memories and perspective-taking may exist, they are functionally irrelevant to modifying a dog's behavior because we can only influence the end result – the observed behavior. Behaviorism focuses *only* on behaviors that can be observed and upon factors in a dog's environment that are either reinforcing or punishing. With dog training, these are the factors that we typically manipulate through management of a dog's environment or by applying reinforcers or punishers as part of a training program (more about this in Section 3).

The scientists who study canine social cognition agree that behaviorism and its two primary types of associative learning (classical and operant) are an important way in which dogs learn. Most of them also agree that these are highly useful and successful methods for dog training and behavior modification. However, the scientists who study social cognition in dogs argue that classical and operant conditioning represent just two of the numerous ways in which dogs learn. They suggest that trainers, behaviorists and other dog professionals may err by focusing too singularly upon behaviorism while ignoring the internal mental lives of dogs. They believe (and have evidence, as we have seen) that dogs are not always just learning through association (trial and error) but rather that they are highly cognitive – and specifically, socially cognitive, and learn a great deal by being uniquely attuned to the humans and other dogs in their lives. While Skinner argued that we can understand animal behavior without understanding the animal mind, a cognitive approach assumes we cannot truly understand dogs without a comprehensive understanding of how their minds work. Such an understanding should not only make us better trainers, but more sensitive and caring owners as well.

So, what is this fight all about? Well, it appears that we have a firm behaviorism camp on one side; this camp can be further divided into strictly reward-based trainers and those trainers who use a combination of rewards and aversives (and who self-identify as "balanced" trainers). The other camp consists primarily of a group of cognitive scientists who, while not outright rejecting behaviorism, do not agree with several of its tenets and do not see operant and classical conditioning as the best way to train dogs. Arguments between the two groups – referred to in the vernacular as "*quadrant queens*" vs. "*cognitive kings*" - typically take place only on social media and various websites, and can (as these things do) become rather heated and polarizing.

Ain't Got a Dog in this Fight: So, what does the evidence actually tell us and how should we use this information to assist with training dogs without taking sides in this, um, little dog fight? We know for certain that classical and operant conditioning are evidence-based forms of learning in animals. We also know that training methods that are based upon the rules of behaviorism are highly effective with dogs (especially, as we saw in Chapter 8, when we stay within the +R quadrant). There is also no doubt at this point that dogs have complex mental lives and that many of these skills center on their unique ability to attend to human communication cues and gestures.

So what is the big deal? Is there really anything to argue about here? Well, yeah, as a dog trainer (a clicker trainer, I must emphasize), I think that there is an important point to be made. It is this. Behaviorism alone can no longer be enough. The science of behaviorism and its application in dog training can no longer adequately capture and address all that is dog. Sorry to all of you purists out there, but there it is. (And remember, I am a clicker trainer).

I ain't got a dog in this fight because, really, there should be no fight in the first place. Although dogs respond well to the tenets of behaviorism (just as humans do), the fact that we successfully use operant and classical conditioning to train dogs should not be confused for evidence that dogs are *lacking* in a host of mental skills that fall higher on the cognitive complexity scale. Be-

169

haviorism and social cognition are not mutually exclusive sciences (though to listen to some trainers and some scientists, you would think they were disciplines existing on different planets).

Behaviorism has its clear benefits - mainly it works great when applied as a training technique. However, given the boatloads of research published by cognitive scientists that demonstrate the mental complexity of the domestic dog, trainers cannot discount evidence showing that dogs pay attention to the social cues of humans and of other dogs, that they possess some level of perspective taking, that they regularly learn through the observation of others, that they can recognize one another and understand intent by the sound of their barks, and that they recognize one another and themselves through smell. It is time to embrace both of these important and enlightening bodies of science. We should support and use behaviorism because it provides simple and elegant rules for training that work, and we must also encourage studies of canine cognition because they continue to teach us more about the internal lives, experiences and perceptions of our canine best friends. This information may also, as it had for me and teaching "watch" to my dogs, lead us to modify some of the training approaches that we have previously believed to be indisputable.

TALKING TO JOE

Talking to Joe: The Joe problem that we run into with canine cognition is not so much about what Joe *doesn't* know, but rather a problem of Joe thinking he knows too much (yeah, I know, this happens a fair amount with the Joes of the world). In this case it is about Joe over-interpreting what we know to be true about canine cognition rather than underestimating dogs. Here are a few tips for helping Joe to appreciate, but not misconstrue, the cognitive talents of his amazingly talented dog, Stanley.

🐾 Hey Joe, you have been complaining that Stanley sneaks into the kitchen and steals food whenever you are talking on the phone. You say that you do not understand why he continues to do this when he knows it is wrong. Well Joe, chances are that Stanley has learned to steal food when you are not in the room because it "works" (i.e. the consequences are desirable for him – he gets a snack). He also may be quite attuned to your attentional state, Joe, and use your inattention as a sign of clear sailing for a stolen snack. What he does *not* have is a sense of what is morally "right or wrong" – we just do not have evidence that supports that. Regardless, I imagine that you prefer that Stanley not eat your lunch. We can give you some training tips for this in class (and later in this book), Joe.

🐾 I know you and Stanley enjoy watching Lassie movies to-gether, Joe. I agree, that Lassie is one amazing dog. Each and every time Timmy falls into that well, Lassie is on the job, running home to get help and to let everyone know that Timmy is in trouble again (what is it with that kid and deep holes, anyway)? You do know, Joe, that Lassie is not capable of communicating the exact circumstances of Timmy's pre-dicament, don't you? However, dogs are pretty empathic be-ings and certainly do react to the emotional states of others (in this case, probably Timmy's embarrassment at being in the well again). Many dogs, like Lassie, are quite capable of asking for help from their people. I bet that Stan could do this if you were unfortunate enough to fall down into a well.

🐾 Wow, Stanley sure does have intense eye contact with you, Joe. He is a lovely boy indeed and clearly loves you. What's that? Hmmm.....not sure I really agree that Stanley is reading your mind when he stares at you like that Joe. Rather, Stan is communicating with eye contact, just as we do when we gaze at other people. He *is* reading your emotions (not your mind) and if you look away he may follow your gaze to see what you are looking at and to determine if it is something he should react to. However, not sure he is psychic to the degree that he knows that you are willing him to go into the kitchen, and bring you a beer. But, give it a good try, Joe. All the power to you.

🐾 Hey Joe, I just saw your neighbor's kid, Little Stevie, playing with Stanley in your backyard. He was throwing a ball for Stan. Well, kind of. He kept doing that horrible teasing thing where he would swing his arm and pretend to throw the ball but........not throw the ball. Then, he would laugh. Stanley on the other hand, was not having fun. Anyway Joe, in addition to being an awful way to play with a dog, faking hand motions could actually interfere with the ways that Stanley naturally communicates with you. I noticed that Stanley readily follows your hand whenever you point at something for him. This is one of the many body language gestures that dogs naturally use with their humans to communicate. I would hate to see that ruined for you and Stanley because of some bratty kid's teasing Stan with a ball. Tell him to stop that, Joe. And, teach him instead how to play more respectfully with your sweet dog Stanley.

Evidence

Adler LL, Adler HE: Ontogeny of observational learning in the dog (Canis familiaris). *Developmental Psychology* 1977; 10:267-280.

Call J, et al. Domestic dogs (Canis familiaris) are sensitive to the attentional state of humans. *Journal of Comparative Psychology* 2003; 117:257-263.

D'Aniello B, et al. What's the point? Golden and Labrador retrievers living in kennels do not understand human pointing gestures. *Animal Cognition* 2017; May 15. doi: 10.1007/s10071-017-1098-2.

D'Aniello B, et al. Gazing toward humans: A study on water rescue dogs using the impossible task paradigm. *Behavioural Processes* 2015: 110:68-73.

Gacsi M, et al. Are readers of our face readers of our minds? Dogs (Canis familiaris) show situation-dependent recognition of human's attention. *Animal Cognition* 2004; 7:144-153.

Hare B and Tomasello M. Human-like social skills in dogs? *Trends in Cognitive Science* 2005; 9:439-444.

Horowitz A. Smelling themselves: Dogs investigate their own odours longer when modified in an "olfactory mirror" test. *Behavioural Processes*, 2017; 143:17-24.

Huber A, et al. Investigating emotional contagion in dogs (*Canis familiaris*) to emotional sounds of humans and conspecifics. *Animal Cognition* 2017' 20:703-715.

Kaminski J, et al. M. Domestic dogs are sensitive to a human's perspective. *Behaviour* 2009; 146:979-998.

Kaminski J, Pitsch A, Tomasello M. Dogs steal in the dark. *Animal Cognition* 2013; 16:385-394.

Kubinyi E, et al. Dogs (*Canis familiaris*) learn from their owners via observation in a manipulation task. *J Comparative Psychology* 2003; 117:156-165.

Kubinyi E, Pongracz P, Miklosi A. Dog as a model for studying conspecific and heterospecific social learning. *Journal of Veterinary Behavior* 2009; 4:31-41.

Marshall-Pescini S, et al. Does training make you smarter? The effects of training on dogs' performance (*Canis familiaris*) in a problem-solving task. *Behavioural Processes* 2008; 78:449-454.

Marshall-Pescini S, et al. Agility and search and rescue training differently affect pet dogs' behavior in socio-cognitive task. *Behavioural Processes* 2009; 81:416-422.

Merola I, et al. Social referencing: Water rescue trained dogs are less affected than pet dogs by the stranger's message. *Applied Animal Behavior Science* 2013; 147:132-138.

Miklósi A, et al. A Simple Reason for a Big Difference: Wolves Do Not Look Back at Humans, but Dogs Do. *Current Biology* 2003; 13:763-766.

Pongracz P, et al. Social learning in dogs; the effect of a human demonstrator on the performance of dogs in a detour task. *Animal Behaviour* 2001; 62:1109-1117.

Pongracz P, et al. Verbal attention getting as a key factor in social learning between dog (Canis familiaris) and human. *Journal of Comparative Psychology* 2004; 118:375-383.

Pongracz P, et al. The pet dogs' ability for learning from a human demonstrator in a detour task is independent from the breed and age. *Applied Animal Behaviour Science* 2005; 90:309-323.

Quervel-Chaumette M, et al. Investigating empathy-like responding to conspecifics' distress in pet dogs. *PLOS-One* 2016; 11 (4):e0152920.

Scandurra A, et al. Conspecific observational learning by adult dogs in a training context. *Applied Animal Behaviour Science* 2016; 174:116-120.

Slabbert JM and Rasa OAE: Observational learning of an acquired maternal behaviour pattern by working dog pups: An alternative training method? *Applied Animal Behaviour Science* 1997; 53:309-316.

Silva K, Bessa J, Sousa L. Auditory contagious yawning in domestic dogs (Canis familiaris): first evidence for social modulation. *Animal Cognition* 2012; 15:721-724.

Silva K, Bessa J, deSousa L. Familiarity-connected or stress-based contagious yawning in domestic dogs (Canis familiaris)? Some additional data. *Animal Cognition* 2013; 16:1007-1009.

Wallis LJ, et al. Training for eye contact modulates gaze following in dogs. *Animal Behavior* 2015; 106:27-35.

Part 3 – Dog Smart Training

Chapter 10
Training Practices

We teach a variety of classes at AutumnGold. One of my personal favorites is Canine Freestyle, teaching dogs various body movements and tricks that are eventually set to music. Although I have two left feet and a tin ear, our instructor for these classes, Amanda, is both a talented freestyle trainer and an experienced instructor. Amanda often uses her young dog Colbie to demonstrate the freestyle exercises that she teaches. One exercise that is particularly impressive involves Colbie moving *backwards*, completely circling Amanda. Amanda has trained Colbie to do this in response to both a gesture cue (bending her knees) and a verbal cue (the word "Whirl").

Amanda and Colbie demonstrate "whirl"

Colbie spins backwards at a remarkably high rate of speed, using gentle touches with Amanda's legs as a subtle guide as she travels. The impressiveness of this move is enhanced by Colbie's enjoyment and her happy play face as she zooms around.

How did Amanda teach this unusual behavior? (And, why does Colbie love it so very much?)

The answer lies in the use of positive reinforcement (+R) and shaping. The technical term for shaping, successive approximation, refers to teaching small increments of a behavior sequentially, with the end behavior attained only as the dog succeeds at each (successive) approximation. This and other indispensable dog training techniques are the topics of this chapter.

It's time to have some fun – let's train!

Selecting Reinforcers: If we are to concentrate on staying within the +R quadrant as much as possible, then the selection of pleasurable consequences as reinforcers is essential. Chapters 7 and 8 discussed the differences between pleasurable and aversive consequences and their inherent reinforcing properties (primary vs. conditioned stimuli). For reasons that we should now agree on, desirable consequences (positive reinforcers) are most effective for use in dog training.

Gimme those treats: The term primary reinforcer refers to the many things that a dog naturally enjoys and responds without a need for prior conditioning or exposure. For the vast majority of dogs, food treats are one of the most, if not *the* most potent primary reinforcer.

Years ago, I attended an obedience seminar given by a highly successful competitive trainer. He was discussing various types of food treats to use as +R for dogs. An attendee raised her hand

and asked him what to do with a dog who did not like treats. She stated that because her dog would not eat food treats, she could not use food as a reinforcer. The trainer paused for a few seconds, and responded: *"Well, telling me that your dog does not eat treats is strange. All dogs gotta eat. If they don't eat they die. You need to find something that your dog eats."*

Sarcasm aside, I agree with his response. If a trainer truly has that much trouble finding a type of food that has reinforcing properties for their dog, then their next trip should be to the veterinarian, not to the training center. Even if a dog *only* likes her dry food (or raw or dehydrated), then the trainer can use bits of her daily ration as training reinforcers.

Other primary reinforcers: In addition to food, other primary positive reinforcers for dogs include verbal praise, petting and opportunities to play a favorite game such as retrieving or tug. Verbal praise in the form of a single word or phrase can be further strengthened through association with a primary stimulus and used as a conditioned reinforcer (more about this later).

Ranking reinforcers: I live with Golden Retrievers, who consider pretty much anything that fits into their mouths (plus several things that do not) as potential food treats. But even among the chow hounds of the world, individual dogs often have very specific treat preferences. We can use these preferences to select not only the best treats to use with a given dog, but also to rank treats and other reinforcers according to their respective value to the dog. For example, my youngest Golden, Ally, loves the peanut butter flavor of a particular brand of soft-moist treats. Cooper on the other hand turns cartwheels over smelly bits of dried salmon. Similarly, the favorite play activity for both Alice and Cooper is retrieving – they will fetch their favorite toys all day long if I allow it. Interestingly, each dog's favorite retrieving toy is very "dog-specific". Alice loves her rubber ring toy, while

Coop is completely enamored with anything in the shape of a stick. We can put this information to good use when differentially reinforcing behaviors (discussed later in this chapter). The general rule of thumb is *"the most difficult or least desirable task (for the dog), is paired with the highest ranked reinforcer."*

Passive vs. active reinforcement: A primary reinforcer should also "match" the type of behavior that is being trained. At AutumnGold, we refer to these distinctions as "passive" vs. "active" reinforcement. Any new behavior that requires a measure of physical or emotional self-control on the part of the dog is reinforced with passive reinforcement. This includes a quiet, soft voice, crooning "good Ally, good stay", gentle and soft petting and handing a treat to the dog (not tossing it). Conversely, highly active exercises or those in which a dog is asked to work independently are ramped up and reinforced actively – loud and happy voice ("GOOD girl!!!"), a game of retrieve or tug, and perhaps a tossed treat.

Conditioned (Secondary) Reinforcers: Numerous research studies have shown that positive reinforcement must occur within one second or less of the behavior that it is intended to influence. If reinforcement follows the behavior by more than one second, the dog will be already offering another behavior, and it is this behavior that will be (mistakenly) reinforced. There are numerous situations in dog training in which it is difficult or impossible to provide a food treat or other primary reinforcer at the exact time that the dog is offering the targeted behavior. Examples include when the dog is not physically close or is offering a behavior that is incompatible with reaching for a treat.

Herein lies the beauty of using a word or a click (or both) as conditioned reinforcers. These tools improve our ability to precisely time our reinforcement because the word/click effectively *marks* the exact behavior that we intend to reinforce at the time the dog is offering it. (Note: The concepts and benefits of conditioned reinforcers were addressed in detail in Chapter 8). Although almost any type of stimulus can be used as a conditioned reinforcer, in dog training, the two most common are a selected word or a clicker:

- *Word:* Almost any word can be used as a conditioned reinforcer, provided the use of that word and the tone/manner in which it is uttered is reserved for use *only* when paired with the primary reinforcer. For this reason, many trainers use "YES!" or "Bingo!" rather than "Good", simply because we tend to use the word "good" frequently in everyday speech with our dogs. Of course, verbal praise alone also has primary reinforcing properties for dogs. However, pairing a specific word with a primary food reinforcer (word then treat) consistently results in that particular word becoming a conditioned reinforcer.

- *Click:* As a conditioned reinforcer, the clicker produces a sound that is unique and of short duration, properties that contribute to its effectiveness. Unlike a word, which can vary significantly in tone and pitch, the sound that the clicker makes does not vary and so sends a clear and consistent signal to the dog *"That's it! That behavior you are offering at this moment is what I am reinforcing. A treat will be arriving shortly!"*

Charging a conditioned reinforcer (word or click): The connection between the word/click and a treat is established by classically conditioning the sound of the word or the click with presentation of the primary stimulus, the food treat. As with all classically conditioned responses, the word or click must immediately precede the provision of the treat. *Always – word/click then treat. Never – treat then word/click.* Here are a few tips for "charging your word or clicker:"

182

- *Rapid-fire pairing:* Begin by offering your selected word or a click and immediately follow with a treat. For most dogs, several repetitions of click-treat (or "YES!"- treat) leads to a visible "startle response" to hearing the click/word. When the dog clearly begins to look for a treat upon hearing the word/click, the trainer has successfully introduced the conditioned reinforcer.

✓ *Mark a behavior:* The next step is to select a very simple behavior that your dog offers spontaneously. Examples are eye contact or simply looking up. The trainer waits for the dog to offer eye contact, and immediately marks the behavior with the word/click and a treat. After several repetitions, the dog should begin to increase the frequency of offering eye contact, presenting increased opportunities for marking and treating.

✓ *Vary the connection*: Once this connection is established, the temporal (time) relationship between the word/click and the treat can be varied. A reasonable span is between less than a second (immediately) to a few seconds. Never wait more than 5 or 6 few seconds, however. This training step teaches the dog to expect a treat within several seconds of the behavior being marked and is imperative for the use of the clicker in exercises in which the dog is physically separated from the trainer.

Which to use? Word or Click? The decision of what to use as a conditioned reinforcer is completely up to the trainer. For many years, when I was competing in obedience trials, I used the word "Yes!" more frequently than I used a clicker, simply because I could take my voice, but not a clicker into the ring with me. These days, in our classes at AutumnGold, some of our students choose to use a word rather than a clicker because they do not want to worry about one more thing to manipulate in addition to their dog, the lead, and treats. And of course, some dogs show their preferences. Although it is relatively uncommon, we do see dogs who are highly sensitive to the sound of a clicker, even the muted version, and so do best when trained with a word as their conditioned reinforcer.

Personally, I like to teach both to our dogs. While I am 100 percent a clicker trainer when working with my dogs at our training facility, I also do a lot of hiking with my dogs, and I rarely carry a clicker when I am hiking. In those circumstances, as well as in many spontaneous training situations around the house and yard, I use "Yes" rather than a clicker. Because dogs can and do respond well to both, it behooves the trainer to teach both and use them as dictated by circumstances.

Now that we have our reinforcers – both primary (food treats, petting, praise, play) and conditioned (word and/or click), let's move on to how and when to use reinforcement during training practice. The first application is a big word for a simple concept – differential reinforcement.

Differential Reinforcement: Differential reinforcement is a fancy term for simply reinforcing some responses that a dog offers and not others. This concept underlies all operantly-based dog training because when a trainer selects one particular behavior to target and reinforce, for example eye contact, she is *not* reinforcing other behaviors that the dog may offer *instead* of eye contact - looking away, yawning, pawing, sighing, or lying down. These alternate choices are simply ignored. Differential reinforcement is also used during shaping when a trainer begins to shift the criteria for reinforcement (see later in this chapter) and when we are solving behavior problems by reinforcing alternate and incompatible behaviors (see Chapter 14).

Reinforcement Schedules: These are sets of rules that the trainer may use when delivering differential reinforcement. Although these rules have been intensely studied and tested in experimental settings, they have varying degrees of practical use in dog training. The most important and the easiest to use is a continuous schedule.

- *Continuous schedule:* This is what it sounds like - reinforcing every correct response that the dog offers. A continuous reinforcement schedule should always be used when new behaviors are being introduced and continued until the dog is reliably offering the desired behavior in response to the selected cue. Consider that this reinforcement is vital information to your dog, reliable feedback, saying *"That is IT! That is what I would like you to do! Thank You!"*

- *Intermittent schedules:* Intermittent reinforcement schedule refer to offering reinforcement *occasionally* as the consequence to the desired behavior. An analogy that is often used is gambling behavior. A person who is addicted to the slot machines of Las Vegas is responding to an intermittent schedule of reinforcement. "Slot-machine playing" behavior is strongly maintained because it is occasionally and unpredictably reinforced by the arrival of money. Similarly, a dog who has been trained to come when called and gradually switched from continuous (+R for every correct response) to intermittent reinforcement (+R for some correct responses) will continue to offer "coming when called" behavior in anticipation of *possibly* receiving reinforcement. The theory is that using an intermittent reinforcement schedule turns Muffin into an unrepentant canine gambler and strengthens her come response.

Several types of intermittent reinforcement schedules have been devised. These include variable interval, fixed interval, variable ratio and fixed ratio. These are described in the table below:

TYPE	DEFINITION
Continuous	Reinforce every correct response (use when teaching new behaviors)
Variable Interval	Reinforce at *irregular time* intervals (For example; a food treat is given to a dog during a sit/stay at 30, 40, 90, 130, 145, 180 seconds)
Fixed Interval	Reinforce at *regular time* intervals (For example: a food treat is given to a dog during a sit/stay at 30, 60, 90, 120, 150, 180 seconds)
Variable Ratio	Reinforce after an *irregular number* of correct responses (For example: A food treat is given to a dog for coming when called after the first, second, fifth, and seventh correct response)
Fixed Ratio	Reinforcement is provided after a *regular number* of correct responses (For example: A food treat is given to a dog for coming when called after the first, fourth, seventh and tenth correct response)

Are They Practical? Intermittent schedules of reinforcement have been shown to have advantages in laboratory settings and under controlled conditions. For dog trainers who love to get down into the weeds of learning theory and who pay very close attention to their dog's response frequencies, using a particular type of ratio or interval schedule may be helpful. However, for the average dog owner and even for most trainers, the prescribed schedules are not practical and are often ignored. The good news is that these two simple and alternative rules of reinforcement work quite well:

1. ***Continuous for learning:*** Use a continuous reinforcement schedule when you are teaching a new behavior or when you are modifying a behavior by changing criteria for reinforcement. Go a bit longer than you feel is necessary as a safety margin, to ensure that your dog truly understands the behavior that is earning her the +R.

2. ***Differential for maintaining:*** Switch to differential reinforcement once the dog is reliably offering the new behavior on cue. Positively reinforce renditions that are exceptionally nice or steady. Offerings that are less than stellar either get nothing or are reinforced with a lower ranking reinforcer (kibble, not liver). Note: Switching to a variable interval schedule with stay exercises is easy to use and effective (see Chapter 13 for details).

Onward – time to talk about shaping.

Baby-Steps – The Power of Shaping: Because operant conditioning relies upon the consequences of behavior, the dog must first be able to offer at least a bit of a targeted behavior so that there is something to reinforce. However, many of the behaviors that we are interested in reinforcing in our dogs occur at low frequencies or are not being offered at all. An example is Amanda's whirl move. If Amanda had waited for Colbie to spontaneously offer *"spinning around her legs going backwards"*, she would clearly have had to wait a very long time indeed.

Okay, she would have to wait forever. It would not happen.

This is where shaping, the reinforcement of successive approximations of a desired behavior, comes in. Shaping entails starting with a small piece or an *approximation* of the desired behavior and reinforcing that little piece. The dog should offer this little bit at a high enough rate to allow the trainer to target it and dif-

187

ferentially reinforce it. As the dog becomes aware that it is this behavior that is "working" (earning her the +R), she begins to offer it more frequently. Once the dog is consistently offering the approximation, the trainer shifts the criteria and begins to reinforce the next level.

In the case of Colbie's whirl trick, Amanda began by marking and reinforcing when Colbie moved just a bit backwards (#1, below):

When Colbie was reliably offering one step back, Amanda shifted the criterion and now waited for Colbie to take a couple of more steps (# 2, above). This behavior was marked and reinforced until it was reliable….Amanda shifted the criteria again…..and so on. Once Colbie was spinning (backwards!) all the way around, Amanda began to reinforce the end result that we saw at the start of this chapter.

Monitoring progress: One of the most common mistakes that new trainers make with shaping is to expect too much too soon. Proceeding gradually ensures that the dog is successful (and understands) each little piece before asking for a more difficult response. Trainers must always be willing to drop back to an earlier stage if their dog experiences difficulties. When used correctly, successive approximation is a powerful tool because very complex behavior patterns can be achieved and many problem behaviors can be solved without the need to use negative reinforcement or punishment.

Luring vs. Free-Shaping: New behaviors that are targeted for shaping can either be lured or captured via free-shaping. Luring refers to showing the dog a food treat (the lure) to induce a bit of the targeted behavior, which is then reinforced with the lure. At AutumnGold, we refer to luring as *"jump-starting"* behaviors as this label conveys that the lure is helpful to get a behavior started but will not remain part of training for long. For example, a young dog may not be inclined to offer even the first part of lying down (moving front feet out in front of her) simply because she is an active youngster and is distracted. Her owner can lure the first portion of lying down by slowly moving a hand containing a food treat (the lure) from the dog's nose towards her front toes.

Free-shaping refers to waiting for the dog to offer a desired behavior (or, more practically, a little piece of the behavior), and then immediately reinforcing it. Trainers often refer to free-shaping as "capturing" behaviors because, when performed correctly, it involves targeting a dog's naturally occurring behaviors and gradually shaping them to approach the final desired behavior. A common example of free-shaping is teaching a dog to shake hands. Many dogs naturally use their paws to request attention or during play. The owner waits until the dog offers even a slight paw lift and immediately marks and reinforces that slight lift. Once her dog begins to increase the frequency of "lift paw," the trainer then shifts the criterion slightly and reinforces a higher lift - the paw touching a hand.

Although trainers often debate the pros and cons of luring vs. free-shaping, in actuality, *both* approaches are useful and have a place in practical dog training. At AutumnGold, we use lures for many basic behaviors when working with new dog owners – sit, down, come, stand. In all of these cases, we quickly remove the lure from the hand and turn the prompting hand into a cue (more about this in Chapter 13). We also teach many new behaviors, such as tricks, freestyle moves and platform exercises using free-shaping. This is most common in our advanced classes with dogs who have a strong grounding in reward-based training and will readily offer new behaviors for reinforcement. In my view, both are important tools in a trainer's tool box.

Here is a summary of the benefits and limitations of each and a few suggestions for where they may fit into a training program:

LURING
Benefits: Luring allows the dog to rapidly learn from positive consequences. This reduces the frustration that can occur with free-shaping and enhances the rate of learning.
Risks: If not used carefully, the lure can become associated with the behavior and becomes the cue for the dog to offer the behavior.
Precautions: The lure must be removed as early in the learning process as possible and replaced with a cue.
FREE-SHAPING
Benefits: Free-shaping increase a dog's willingness to offer new behaviors and allows shaping of new and unusual behaviors
Risks: Can be frustrating for the dog if unusual or complex behaviors are targeted because the dog will not experience many opportunities for +R.
Precautions: If the dog is not successful, the trainer must either lower the criteria for reinforcement or introduce a lure to "jump-start" learning.

Putting Behaviors "On Cue": Cues are the verbal cues or hand signals (gestures) that we use to ask for trained behaviors. Common verbal cues are "sit," "down," "come," and "get it." A few examples of gesture cues are a hand motion downward (for lie down) and an arm swing into the body (for come). While traditional dog training would introduce the cue at the same time that the behavior was introduced, it is actually more effective to add the cue (verbal, gesture or both) shortly *after* the dog has learned to offer at least part of the new behavior. This may appear backwards but it is actually more effective because it prevents incorrect responses and reduces confusion for the dog. Using the down example, once the dog is consistently lying down for a lure - food treat in hand – the owner can introduce the verbal cue "down", immediately prior to the hand prompt (movement of the hand downward) or the lure, if still present (food in the hand).

Verbal or gesture cue? Like many dog trainers, I use both verbal and gestural (hand) signals as cues with my dogs. With our students at AutumnGold, we introduce these at the same time, but generally emphasize verbal signals because this is what most pet owners prefer to use with their dogs.

If a trainer wishes to change the cue that is used to elicit a behavior, this can be accomplished with classical conditioning. The new cue is give immediately prior to the established cue, each time the behavior is requested. Over time, the new cue becomes classically conditioned to elicit the behavior without being paired with the established cue.

When emphasizing verbal (and fading a gesture), we "*lead with the verbal cue and follow with the gesture*", thus establishing a classical relationship (verbal signal predicts gesture signal). This connection allows the trainer to gradually fade the hand signal and eventually to rely primarily on the verbal cue:

191

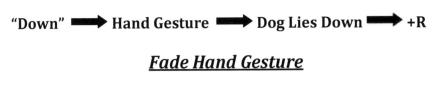

"Down" ➡ Hand Gesture ➡ Dog Lies Down ➡ +R

Fade Hand Gesture

"Down" ➡ Dog Lies Down ➡ +R

Conversely, if the trainer prefers to emphasize a hand signal rather than a verbal cue, the order is switched:

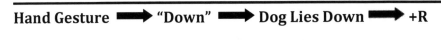

Hand Gesture ➡ "Down" ➡ Dog Lies Down ➡ +R

Fade Verbal Cue ("Down")

Hand Gesture ➡ Dog Lies Down ➡ +R

Stimulus (Cue) Control: Stimulus (cue) control refers to ensuring that the dog offers the behavior (lying down) only in response to the word or gesture, "down." A lack of cue control means that the dog tends to offer behaviors when they are not asked for or in response to a different cue. Anticipating a cue is a common example of a lack of cue control. For example, a dog who offers "shake" prior to the verbal cue is offering a correct behavior, but he is not offering it in response to the cue. Another example is the dog who happily rolls over in response to his owner's cue, "shake." Although the dog is offering a trained behavior, he is not offering the correct trick for the stimulus (cue) that the trainer has given.

Cue control is a part of the normal training process that must be consciously taught. If it is not, most dogs will simply choose be-

192

haviors that they most enjoy (or that are easiest for them to do or have the strongest reinforcement history), and offer them repeatedly in response to various cues. Others will continue to happily offer their favorite trick to anyone who even remotely appears to be getting ready to offer them a cue. While this is not a terrible problem to have in the grand scheme of dog ownership, trainers are most successful if they consciously teach stimulus control once they have a behavior on cue.

Using the "down" response as our example, the four rules of attaining stimulus control are:

> *ALWAYS reinforce* correct responses. Each time that you ask for "down" and Muffin responds correctly (lies down), you must +R. This is important when training for cue control because the pairing of the verbal cue ("down") with an opportunity to earn a treat must be consistent.
>
> *NEVER reinforce* spontaneous offerings. If Muffin lies down but you have not asked for it with a cue, simply ignore, reset or cue another behavior.
>
> *NEVER reinforce* the correct response (down) for an incorrect cue (sit). Although it is tempting to reinforce a new behavior when the dog offers it in response to a different cue; not reinforcing the incorrect response is a more effective approach to gaining stimulus control.
>
> *NEVER reinforce* an incorrect behavior (sit) for the correct cue (down). This is the opposite of the previous mistake. Release Muffin, ask again (back up and prompt if necessary) and +R when she responds correctly!

A Final Note: Training our dogs should be fun – both for our dogs and for us. It is important to not get so caught up in the science of training that we lose the enjoyment that we all experience when spending time with our dogs, teaching them new behaviors and strengthening the bonds that we have with them.

We turn more to the importance of these emotions in the next chapter. First though, let's have a little chat with Joe.

TALKING TO JOE

Talking to Joe: Neighbor Joe stopped by for a visit recently with his Aussie-mix, Lucy. Joe says that Lucy is a great dog – she is good with his kids, loves meeting other dogs, and enjoys going for walks in the neighborhood. However, Joe confides that he thinks that "Lucy is not the shiniest coin in the fountain" (his words). When asked why he believes this, Joe replies "*Well, I have been training her to sit and stay and she is failing miserably. I use food, like you showed me, and I have gradually increased how long I want her to stay, just like you explained. But, she is not getting it – in fact, she now jumps up to greet me every time I walk back to her. She is a great dog, but I don't think she is very smart.*"

Okay Joe, show me what you are doing to train Lucy to sit/stay:

🐾 Joe tells Lucy to sit and verbally reinforces her ("Good girl, Lucy"!). He waits 5 seconds and releases Lucy with her release word "okay." Lucy leaps up, and Joe praises her exuberantly and gives her a yummy food treat.

🐾 Joe repeats this sequence several times, varying the time between 5 and 30 seconds before releasing Lucy. Each time, af-

194

ter he releases Lucy with "okay" he praises her exuberantly and gives her a treat.

🐾 Indeed, after several repetitions, Lucy starts to wiggle and squirm during her stay, and then jumps up on Joe as soon as he moves back towards her.

Okay Joe – Got it.
First – Great that you are using yummy food treats and praise with Lucy! (And that you have dropped the dominance obsession). Yay Joe!

🐾 This is a simple timing problem, Joe. That is all. Instead of reinforcing the behavior that you want in Lucy - sitting calmly and staying in position – you are unintentionally but consistently reinforcing "*jump up exuberantly*!" by giving Lucy praise and treats *after* you release her from the stay rather than *during* the stay.

🐾 Remember, if positive reinforcement (petting, praise, food treats) is provided while Lucy is sitting quietly in position, *that* is the behavior that will be reinforced, Joe. Think of the "good girls", gentle petting and food treats as information to Lucy that what she is doing at the moment that she receives these nice things, is what you would like her to continue to do.

🐾 Give this a try, Joe: While Lucy is sitting, walk back frequently to praise her quietly, pet her gently and give her treats (passive reinforcement for control exercises). When you release Lucy, just calmly say "okay" - but *no treat* for the release.

🐾 Success! Lucy learns quickly that the behavior that is "working" now is sitting and staying, while jumping up afterwards earns no reward. (More about training duration and distance with stays in Chapter 13).

Evidence

D'Aniello B, Scandurra A, Alterisio A, Valsecchi P, Prato-Previde E. The importance of gestural communication: A study of human-dog communication using incongruent information. *Animal Cognition 2016; DOI:* 10.1007/s10071-016-1010-5.

Donaldson J. *Culture Clash: A Revolutionary New Way of Understanding the Relationship between Humans and Domestic Dogs.* James and Kenneth Publishers, Oakland, CA, 1996; 221 pp.

Fukuzawa M and Hayashi N: Comparison of 3 different reinforcements of learning in dogs (*Canis familiaris*). *Journal of Veterinary Behavior* 2013; 8:221-224.

Fukuzawa M, Mills DS, Cooper JJ. More than just a word: non-semantic cue variables affect obedience in the domestic dog (*Canis familiaris*). *Applied Animal Behavioural Science* 2005; 91:129–141.

Lindsay SR. *Handbook of Applied Dog Behavior and Training, Volume 1: Adaptation and Learning.* Iowa State University Press, Ames, IA 2000; 410 pp.

Mills DS. What's in a word? A review of the attributes of a cue affecting the performance of pet dogs. *Anthrozoos* 2004; 18:208–221.

Pryor K. *Don't Shoot the Dog.* Bantam Books, New York, NY 1984; 187 pp.

Pryor K. *Karen Pryor on Behavior.* Sunshine Books, North Bend, WA, 1995; 248 pp.

Reid P. *Excel-Erated Learning: Explaining How Dogs Learn and How Best to Teach Them.* James and Kenneth Publishing, Oakland, CA 1996; 172 pp.

Chapter 11
Emotional Outcomes

There is a well-known psychological phenomenon called the *Ben Franklin Effect*, named after the founding father himself. It has its origins in a story about Franklin's time in political office, when Franklin successfully turned a bitter political rival into an ally by doing something pretty simple – asking the man for a favor.

Being kind towards someone (or to your dog) makes *you* like *them* better: Typically, we think that we do nice things for the people we like and we do less nice things to the people that we dislike. We also believe that doing something nice for someone (i.e. loaning them a book), makes them like us better. But what the psychology behind the Ben Franklin Effect reveals is quite the opposite, a reverse-engineering of attitudes that takes place as we grow to like people for whom we do nice things and dislike those to whom we are unkind. This effect influences not only our attitudes towards other people, but towards our dogs, as well.

How the BF Effect works: Current self-perception theory tells us that our brains often behave like an outside observer, continually watching what we do and then contriving explanations for those actions, which subsequently influence our beliefs about ourselves.

Our observing brain doesn't like it when our actions don't match the views we have about ourselves, a situation commonly referred to as *cognitive dissonance*. So, whenever your behavior is in conflict with your beliefs (for example if you do a favor for someone you may not like very much or vice versa, when you do something bad to someone you are supposed to care about), this conflict immediately sets off alarm bells. Your brain has a clever response to this conflict - it goes about *changing* how you feel in order to reduce the conflict and turn off the alarms. So, if you believe that you don't like someone, but then you help them or do something nice for them, your brain simply changes how you think about that person. You start to think *"Gee, this guy is pretty cool; I actually do like him after all."* Similarly, if you have been snarky toward someone you care about, your brain convinces you that the person must have deserved the poor treatment and suddenly *you start to find fault with the person and like him less.*

Ben Franklin Effect and Dog Training: Many studies have demonstrated this effect, but one in particular relates directly to training dogs. Study volunteers acted as "trainers" and were asked to teach a group of human students a simple task. They worked with each student individually and were instructed to use one of two teaching methods, which were randomly assigned to each student:

- **Method 1 (+R):** Teacher offers encouragement and praise when the learner performs the task correctly.

- **Method 2 (-R):** Teacher criticizes and insults the learner when he/she makes a mistake.

After working with all of the students, the trainers completed a questionnaire that asked them to rate how likeable they found each student to be. A big difference was observed. Trainers rated students who they had praised and encouraged (i.e. used +R) as pleasant, likable, and friendly. Conversely, they rated students who they had criticized (-R) as unlikable and unattractive. The researchers concluded that the trainers' *treatment of each student formed their perception of that student.* They liked the students who they were required to be kind to and they disliked the students who they were required to punish.

Emotional Outcomes: The Ben Franklin Effect works in both directions - kind behaviors create positive perceptions while hurtful behaviors lead to unfavorable perceptions. Most dog trainers and researchers typically focus on the effects that positive and negative reinforcement have upon the *dogs*. As we saw in Chapter 8, there is evidence that dogs who are trained with reward-based methods tend to be less stressed and are more willing and motivated to learn.

However, we don't always consider the effects that these two approaches may have upon the dog's *owner*. The Ben Franklin Effect suggests that how we treat our dogs during training influences how we think about them as individuals - specifically, how much we like (or dislike) them. When we do nice things for our dogs in the form of treats, praise, petting, and play to reinforce desired behaviors, such treatment may result in our *liking them more*. And, if we use harsh words, collar jerks, or physical reprimands in an attempt to change our dog's behavior, then, well, if good ol' Ben is correct, *we will start to like our dog less*. If the Ben Franklin Effect is correct, we are heavily (and unconsciously) inclined to like the dogs who we treat well (use +R) and to dislike the dogs who we treat poorly (-R).

Think about it. When you see someone yelling at their dog or using harsh corrections.......does that person really appear to *like* their dog? Is cognitive dissonance (and the BF effect) leading them to conclude that their dog must be bad, poorly behaved, dumb, unlikable, unattractive, since he is deserving of such correction? Similarly, does the regular use of positive reinforcement, telling our dogs "*Yippee, you did it!! You are SO smart and so very good!*" subconsciously also encourage us to love them more?

The evidence tells us that it does.

Flipping Emotional Responses: In this chapter, we examine the emotional side of training practices – emotions of the dog *and* those of the owner. I will review tried and true behavior modification practices that trainers and behaviorists use to reduce problem behaviors and to modify dogs' emotional responses from fear or anxiety to calmness and pleasure. At AutumnGold, we refer to the emotional outcomes of these techniques as *"flipping a dog's emotional response."* Though we do not generally tell our students this, we also focus on flipping the owner's emotional responses to their dog's unwanted behaviors, an important part of strengthening bonds and promoting harmony between dogs and their people.

Let's begin with a powerful tool – Counter-conditioning.

Counter-Conditioning: Counter-conditioning is a specific type of classical conditioning in which we attempt to change a dog's emotional response to a stimulus that is causing the dog to be fearful, anxious or defensive. We also use counter-conditioning to tamp down a dog's emotional response – for example, teaching a dog to respond more calmly to situations that previously triggered high excitement or over-arousal. Unlike simple classical conditioning in which the dog has not yet developed a response to a particular stimulus, when we use counter-conditioning we are starting with a dog who has already developed an unpleasant or unwanted emotional response to something. We are attempting to "counter" the undesirable emotional response (fear, anxiety, or overstimulation) with more favorable responses, such as calmness, happiness and an absence of stress. (For a review of the principles of classical conditioning, see Chapter 6).

Counter-conditioning works like this. Eating yummy food treats is a pleasurable activity for most dogs and almost always evokes joyful emotions (remember, I live with Golden Retrievers –

mealtime is always a time for celebration). For this reason, high value food treats are the most valuable primary stimulus that we have for counter-conditioning. For dogs who do not respond strongly enough to food, high value toys can sometimes work, but are generally not as effective. The goal is to pair the appearance of something that previously evoked an unwanted emotional response with something that the dog finds to be highly desirable and pleasant.

Ready? Here are the rules for counter-conditioning:

1. ***Identify the triggers:*** Owners usually know what is causing their dog's fear or over-arousal. Common stress-inducing triggers include visiting unfamiliar places, meeting new people, loud noises, or seeing unfamiliar dogs. A few triggers that cause over-excitement in dogs may be riding in the car, hearing the doorbell ring or seeing a doggy friend. (Note: Details for solving several specific behavior problems are addressed in Chapter 14).

2. ***Classical pairing: Trigger, then treat:*** This is the same sequence that we use to classically condition dogs to enjoy handling using the "Touch then Treat" training method (discussed in Chapter 6). The difference is that instead of simply building a *new* association, we are now attempting to change (flip) the dog's emotional response to something that is causing the dog distress. Just as it was important for touch to always predict a treat, in this case, the trigger (introduced at the lowest level possible) should be a consistent predictor of a treat. The timing is always "*Trigger then Treat*" and never the opposite.

203

Trigger Appears ➡ Treat, Treat, Treat! ➡ Happy Dog!
  (CS¹)   *(US)*   *(UR)*

After Frequent Repetitions

Trigger Appears ➡   ➡ Happy Dog!
  (CS²)   *(CR)*

CS¹: **The trigger is classified as a conditioned stimulus because the dog already has a learned (negative) response to the trigger**
CS²: **After counter-conditioning, the trigger now should be associated with pleasant emotions.**

3. ***Trigger disappears – Treats stop:*** This part of counter-conditioning is often overlooked, but it is an important component of the sequence. While treats should "rain from the sky" each time that the trigger appears, those treats should stop raining down at the moment that the trigger is no longer present. This type of "on/off" conditioning strengthens the connection that the trainer is forming between the trigger and pleasure in the dog because treats are now precisely paired with a stimulus appearing and then leaving.

4. ***Train an alternate behavior, if desired:*** Although not always necessary, some trainers will add an alternate and incompatible behavior, once the dog has started to associate the trigger with food. This is called *operant counter-conditioning* (also called response substitution). For example, the owner may ask the dog to offer eye contact or to sit in response to the trigger, and that behavior is subsequently reinforced. In many situations, however, simply using "*trigger then treat*" provides the owner with the tools that are needed

to help their dog to flip his emotional reaction to an unpleasant stimulus.

5. **Ben Franklin Effect:** There is also an important Ben Franklin effect in play with counterconditioning. Dogs who are stressed, anxious or fearful often react to the "scary thing" by trying to escape, barking or whining, jumping on their owner, and sometimes, showing aggression. These behaviors almost inevitably cause the owner to feel stressed, embarrassed, or even angry. Using high value treats to redirect the dog and to change the *dog's* emotional response typically has a similar benefit for the owner, who begins to feel more relaxed and competent during training sessions. It is basically an emotional win-win for dog and owner alike.

Systematic Desensitization: Systematic desensitization is often paired with counter-conditioning and involves introducing the fear-inducing stimulus at a very low level of intensity and counter-conditioning at that level until the dog is calm and relaxed. The level of intensity is then increased slightly and the sequence is repeated again until the dog is desensitized (i.e. not reacting). This is repeated in step-wise increments until the dog is emotionally comfortable at the full intensity of whatever the scary or over-stimulating thing happens to be.

Is it practical? Systematic desensitization can work if the triggers are clearly identified and if they can be effectively controlled. This approach also relies upon having an owner who is dedicated to completing a prescribed (and sometimes tedious) training program. For example, a dog who is fearful of unfamiliar men can be systematically desensitized using an ordered introduction of men - gradually reducing distance and introducing different men (two variables). This takes persistence and patience and also requires that the trigger is limited to, in this case, unfamiliar men. (It also requires that the owner knows and can successfully enlist for help a range of men varying in age, appearance and even fashion preferences. A pretty big order, indeed).

In real life, things are often not this simple. Although systematic desensitization is a very popular textbook solution to behavior problems in dogs, the reality is that we often do not know all of the triggers for a dog (i.e. it is more complex than a simple "he does not like men with beards" scenario). Even if we do, triggers in the real world are often not under an owner's complete control. An added factor, and perhaps the most important, is owner compliance. While there are certainly owners who will carry out each step of a desensitization program (and who have enough friends to help them), there are also many owners who are simply not going to be willing or able to complete all of the steps of a detailed desensitization program with their dog.

Is there perhaps some middle ground here? I believe there is.

A realistic solution: As we have discussed, counter-conditioning is the best tool that we have for flipping a dog's (and the owner's) emotional response. Not only does it work well, but it also is simple for dog owners to learn and use. The benefits of including systematic desensitization is that it allows gradual introduction of the trigger, thus preventing exposure to intensities that could cause the dog to relapse. However, these programs are often associated with high attrition. There is a middle ground in which the owner can use counter-conditioning and can (usually) avoid exposing her dog to the unwanted trigger during training.

Two simple rules allow for this:

- ***Trigger-treat in all controlled and low intensity situations:*** The owner uses counter-conditioning in any and all situations that her dog notices the trigger (for example, an

206

unfamiliar man across the street), but does not react (i.e. the intensity is low enough that learning can occur). Owner treats until the trigger moves on. This is conducted in all situations that the owner either sets up and controls or does not set up but the trigger is not close enough to cause a reaction in the dog.

- *Back-out (escape) in any situation that the trigger cannot be controlled or is too intense:* This rule tells the owner to simply leave the area with her dog in any situation that the trigger is occurring at too high a level. Using the previous example – an unfamiliar man approaches rapidly. If the owner thinks her dog may react with stress, she simply turns, crosses the street, walks in another direction, or perhaps even picks up the dog. This prevents relapse scenarios in which the dog feels compelled to react. An added benefit of the back-out rule is that the dog quickly learns that the owner is a reliable source of help and security – she will not allow exposure to triggers that are in danger of causing a reaction and will quickly remove the dog from that situation.

Together these two rules provide an approach for owners who have the counter-condition part established and also want to ensure that their dog is not exposed to high intensity triggers during training. Because the back-out rule allows the owner to avoid unpleasant scenarios with her dog, it also reduces the owner's stress and anxiety during training. An emotional win-win once again for both the dog and the owner!

Extinction: The principle of extinction states that if no reinforcement is provided for an unwanted behavior, over time the dog will decrease and eventually stop offering that behavior. The unwanted behavior is said to be *extinguished*. Extinction can also be applied when attempting to change undesirable classically learned associations. This is accomplished by repeatedly presenting the conditioned stimulus by itself in the absence of the unconditioned stimulus, resulting in a gradual decline (or extinction) of the conditioned response. Two common examples that are used to illustrate each of these forms of extinction are:

- **Extinguishing an operantly learned behavior:** Using extinction to stop a dog from jumping up on people in greeting. Extinction in this case means removing *the person*. Because greeting the dog with petting, attention and affection is what positively reinforces and thus maintains jumping up, extinction involves telling the owner to ignore her dog by turning her back, backing away, or walking away from the dog whenever he attempts to greet by jumping up.

- **Extinguishing a classically learned association:** Dogs with separation stress begin to associate predictors of their owner leaving with impending isolation. For example, a dog may pace and become anxious whenever his owner picks up the car keys because picking up car keys has become a reliable predictor of isolation. Extinction of this association is accomplished by picking up the keys repeatedly without following the action with leaving.

Does extinction work? Extinction can only be successful if the operant behavior is never again reinforced and if pairing of the conditioned and unconditioned stimuli are permanently disassociated.

These are high (if not impossible) bars to clear, on both counts.

Extinction is also only useful as a training tool when the trainer has complete control over the reinforcers for the unwanted behavior. For example, if a dog is barking because he is chasing squirrels out of his yard, extinction is not an option since the reinforcer for this behavior is the squirrels running away, something that the owner cannot control. Similarly, some behaviors have self-reinforcing properties and will not respond to extinction. A dog who barks when excited will not generally stop if ignored because barking is an expression of excitement and is innately enjoyable and possibly stress-relieving for the dog.

Even if an owner *can* control all reinforcement and is able to consistently remove it, there is recent evidence that using extinction causes stress in dogs and can lead to new (and unwanted) displacement behaviors. For example, ignoring a dog who has been previously reinforced for jumping up to greet can cause the dog to initially increase his bid for attention (extinction burst) by jumping more emphatically on the owner or visitor. If the ignoring continues, the dog may become frantic, and begin to bark, nip or mouth in his requests for affection and interaction with an owner who is suddenly (and rudely) ignoring him. The emotional fall-out for the owner is not great either. It is not a happy owner who feels compelled to completely ignore her happy and loving dog when he rushes to greet her after coming home from a long day at work.

Bottom line - Although extinction continues to be recommended in popular training books, on the internet, and by neighbor Joe, in reality extinction is difficult to implement consistently and there is evidence that it causes unnecessary emotional stress to dogs. The good news is that its use is unnecessary because we have a more effective technique – operant classical conditioning (response substitution), discussed earlier in this chapter. Using the jumping up example, an alternate and incompatible behavior that can be differentially reinforced is "sit or stand for petting", completely eliminating the need to use extinction (details for this are provided in Chapter 14).

The Premack Principle (*"If you don't eat your meat, you can't have any pudding!"*): Even those who are not Pink Floyd fans understand this principle. *"You cannot have dessert until you first eat your vegetables"* means that you can only have the thing that you *really* want if you first complete a task that you are far less motivated to do. Parents everywhere use this technique. By rewarding vegetable-eating with dessert, mothers attempt to make Johnny's vegetable-eating behavior more likely to happen (or so the theory goes). Behaviorists refer to this as using a high probability behavior to reinforce a lower probability behavior – aka *The Premack Principle.*

Dessert reinforces eating vegetables; going swimming reinforces getting the yard mowed; drinking a glass of wine reinforces finishing the vacuuming. You get the picture.

The Premack Principle is not only popular with parents; a lot of dog trainers also seem to like it. Often referred to as "life rewards," this principle is in play when trainers use the opportunity to greet a friendly person (something the dog *really* wants to do) as a positive reinforcer for approaching slowly or sitting prior to greeting (the dog is not so keen on doing this). Another popular example in the literature (but I have yet to see it work well in real life) is attempting to teach a dog that walking on a loose lead will be (eventually) rewarded by an opportunity to sniff a bush at the end of the block. In these two examples, sitting first and loose-lead walking are the vegetables. Greeting and getting to sniff are the dessert. Sounds great, right?

Sure. Except that it generally does not work very well with dogs. (Nor with kids, I would argue). Just as with extinction, attempting to reward something that the dog finds difficult or does not want to do with something that he wants to do very much, can cause unwanted emotional fall-out. Here's why:

Problems with Premack: The problem is that Premack ignores the emotional components of the behavior it is meant to influence. Let's return to little Johnny and his vegetables for a moment. Imagine Johnny, finishing the green beans as instructed, only so that he can get his pudding. Do we expect this approach to increase Johnny's enjoyment of vegetable eating? Probably not because vegetable eating is turned into a means to an end when Premack is in play. There are three possible outcomes when Johnny (and dogs) are told *"Do something that you rather dislike in order to get a reward that you really like:"*

1. **Rushing through:** Johnny rapidly shoves the remaining green beans into his mouth, choking them down as quickly as possible in order to get to his dessert.

2. **Stonewalling:** Johnny folds his arms and refuses to eat the dreaded green beans. He reasons (correctly) that at some point his mom will capitulate and allow him at least to leave the table (which he would like) if not actually receive dessert.

3. **Scamming the system:** Johnny hides the vegetables under his plate or, if he is lucky, slips them to his vegetable-loving dog who is waiting under the table.

Of course a fourth possibility is that the promise of future dessert causes Johnny to suddenly take a new look at those green beans and decide that he really *does* love vegetables! Perhaps, but highly unlikely because the Premack Principle does absolutely nothing to increase the value of the behavior that is of interest – in this case eating and enjoying one's vegetables.

And so it goes also with dogs.

In many of the situations in which a low probability behavior (sitting to greet, loose-lead walking) is presumably being rein-

211

forced by a high probability behavior (greeting or sniffing), the dog does exactly what Johnny did. She will attempt to rush through – walking rapidly and frenetically (perhaps even throwing in a vertical leap and frustrated whines) while still (trying to) maintain a loose lead. She may stonewall by avoiding the target behavior altogether (lying down), or she may try to scam the system by offering another (equally unwanted) behavior (barking in excitement). Regardless of the dog's response, the emotional outcome is *not* going to be a dog who enjoys sitting to greet or walking on a loose lead precisely because Premack turns these behaviors into a *means to an end* and does absolutely nothing to make the behavior itself enjoyable (reinforcing) for the dog.

Beef up the behavior you want: An alternative approach is to increase the value of the behavior you wish to affect. In Johnny's case, perhaps his mom could prepare green beans in a way that is more palatable for little kids, or make a game out of eating each bean, or have Dad sit at the table with Johnny and make a show of how much he loves to eat vegetables. For dogs, it is even simpler. At AutumnGold we call this "*beefing up the behavior you want.*" Positively reinforce desired behaviors as they are occurring and use differential reinforcement as the dog becomes proficient. Loose-lead walking, sitting for greeting and almost all other "low probability" behaviors can be turned into high probability behaviors by reinforcing these behaviors directly. By not turning these into means to ends, we can increase a dog's enjoyment of the targeted behaviors and reduce the frustration that is associated with making dogs "*eat their vegetables in order to get their dessert.*"

Talking to Joe: Joe and his new dog Ranger are out walking in the neighborhood and stop to chat. Ranger, a two-year-old Spaniel mix, is a sweetheart – he wiggles up to greet with a happy face and relaxed body posture. Joe says that he and his wife adore their new dog and that Ranger is "perfect in every way" except for one concerning issue. It seems that whenever Ranger sees an unfamiliar dog approaching, he becomes fearful and anxious. He moves behind Joe's legs, barking and eventually lunging as the other dog comes closer. Joe says that this has become such a problem that he is nervous and tense during his daily walks with Ranger.

Joe goes on to say that he heard a celebrity dog trainer say on TV that owners must never "reward fear" in their dogs because it will make them continue to be fearful. The celebrity trainer advised owners to yell "NO!!" whenever their dog barked or lunged at an approaching dog and to give the dog several hard leash yanks as a reprimand. Joe says he has tried this, but Ranger continues to be anxious with approaching dogs when they are out walking.

Here are some tips for helping Joe to "flip" Ranger's emotional response to other dogs from fear to calmness:

🐾 First, Joe, you should never worry about "rewarding" fear in Ranger by comforting him or providing him with security.

213

The belief that fear can be reinforced in dogs is incorrect. Think about it like this. I know you have a very strong and understandable fear of clowns, Joe. If I were to comfort you when a clown was nearby, would that reward your fear and make you *more* fearful of clowns? Of course it would not. We cannot reward fear in dogs because, just like you with your clown fear, Ranger has no control over being afraid of unfamiliar dogs. What we can do to help Ranger is to teach him that unfamiliar dogs are not threatening to him and that you, as his owner, will always have his back and keep him from harm.

🐾 *Start with counter-conditioning*: Joe, take a bunch of yummy treats with you on your walks. When Ranger sees another dog at a distance immediately begin giving Ranger lots of yummy treats, and if possible, stay at a distance that Ranger can tolerate. Continue to give treats until the dog has moved away, then stop giving treats.

🐾 *Use a back-out when needed*: When you see a dog who is approaching too quickly or too closely and you know that Ranger may react, "back out" of that situation. Turn 180 degrees and walk away in the opposite direction, cross the street, or duck into a side yard. This prevents Ranger from reacting fearfully in circumstances that you cannot manage.

🐾 *Management:* I know it is not always possible, Joe, but try to walk with Ranger only in areas where other owners keep their dogs on lead and do not allow their dogs to come running up. It is a good idea to stay away from dog parks with Ranger, as he could become more nervous or defensively aggressive when multiple unfamiliar dogs approach him.

🐾 *Benefits for Joe:* An added benefit to this approach is that you should find that you become more relaxed and less tense when you see other dogs during your outings with Ranger. Because you can control most of the interactions, can help Ranger, and will probably seem some rapid improvements, I predict that you and Ranger both will start to enjoy your walks in the neighborhood a lot more, Joe!

Evidence

Bentosela M, et al. Effects of reinforcement, reinforce omission and extinction on a communicative response in domestic dogs (*Canis familiaris*). *Behavioral Processes* 2008; 78:464-469.

Jakovcevic A, et al. Frustration behaviors in domestic dogs. *Journal of Applied Animal Welfare Science* 2013; 16:19-34.

Jecker J and Landy D. Liking a person as a function of doing him a favour. *Human Relations* 1969; 22:371-378.

Ley J, et al. Assessing fear of novel and startling stimuli in domestic dogs. *Applied Animal Behaviour Science* 2007: 104:71–84.

Miltenberger R. *Behavior Modification: Principles and Practices.* Brooks/Cole Publishing, Pacific Grove, CA, 1997; 392 pp.

Shopler J and Compere J. Effects of being kind or harsh to another on liking. *Journal of Personality and Social Psychology* 1971; 20:155-159.

Yin S. Classical conditioning: Learning by association. *Compendium of Continuing Veterinary Science, Small Animal Practitioner,* 2006; June: 472–476.

Chapter 12
Puppy Smart

I love having a new puppy in the house. I love a pup's enthusiasm, silliness, curiosity, and insatiable need to investigate all that is new. The world is indeed a puppy's oyster, and as their humans, we get to share in their enthusiasm and joy as they discover all of the fun that life has to offer. In our home, Alice, now two-years-old, has been our most recent puppy.

Like all puppies, she was cute. Really cute.

Alice, 8-weeks-old

Cute is a universal puppy attribute. This is a good thing because puppies are a *lot* of work and they can try our patience, deplete our energy, and test our love, often all within a single afternoon. When Alice first came home I was starting the research for this book. I typically set up a structured writing schedule for large projects and had planned on completing research within two months.

Best laid plans, and all.....

By the second week, the schedule had been abandoned and I was spending a large part of my free time playing with Alice, training Alice, keeping Alice safe, and accomplishing very little else.

In my view, that time was neither wasted nor begrudged. Alice and I had tons of fun together, we accomplished her house training (mostly), established harmony among all of our animals (including Pete the Cat, who has become one of Ally's besties), started Ally's basic handling, grooming and obedience exercises, and taught her to swim and retrieve. At the time, one of AutumnGold's instructors also had a new puppy, allowing Alice and Dembe' to enjoy regular puppy play sessions together. Though little else was completed during those weeks, I knew that puppies grow up fast and that this was the time to enjoy those days, do the work, and fall in love with our newest family member.

And fall in love, we did.

Alice, 2-years-old

Puppyhood challenges: Of course, not all new puppy owners are able (or willing) to spend the large amounts of time and energy that puppies often demand and can struggle mightily during those early puppy weeks. The folks who make up our student base at AutumnGold often have busy lives and are trying to juggle career demands, kids, household responsibilities, and a new puppy. They may also have unrealistic expectations of puppy behavior and the time that is involved, based on sentimental memories of a childhood pet or a beloved elderly dog. Naturally, many new owners receive plenty of advice from others, including neighbor Joe, who has raised a *lot* puppies (and who happens to know a lot about dogs). Therefore, it should not be surprising that puppy owners are often confused and frustrated, while still falling head-over-heals in love with their new family member, just as I did with Alice.

For this chapter and those remaining, I provide details about AutumnGold's specific approach to puppy training, adult dog training (Chapter 13), and solving commonly reported behavior problems (Chapter 14). My school's methods are evidence-based and are consistent with our current understanding of canine behavior and learning theory. For puppies, our goal is to help owners to raise a well-adjusted, well-behaved and happy dog without feeling that they must quit their day job in order to do so. For this reason, as I discussed in Chapters 10 and 11, AutumnGold uses training methods that are easy to learn and are practical for the average dog owner. These methods all also consistently adhere to our two Golden Rules:

1. Stick with the science (just the facts, Ma'am).

2. Emphasize reward-based training.

As I discussed in the book's introduction, you are welcome to use and reproduce the AutumnGold Guidelines that I provide in these remaining three chapters. If you instruct classes, work with private clients and their dogs, educate potential adopters through a rescue group or shelter, train your own dogs, or find yourself trying to help *your* neighbor Joe with his dog, I hope that you will find the methods that are used and the guidelines in these chapters helpful to you.

Let's begin with three frequently reported puppy issues that owners report that they are concerned with: House training, nipping/mouthing, and chewing inappropriate items.

Housetraining: Housetraining problems continue to be one of the most common complaints of new puppy parents. There appear to be several reasons for this, with a lack of sufficient supervision and having unrealistic expectations for pups at the top of the list. In response to this, our message is a simple one: *Supervise, supervise, supervise* (and then supervise some more). Below are the housetraining guidelines that we provide to our students:

AutumnGold Guidelines
Successfully House Training Your New Puppy

Housetraining involves teaching your dog to reliably eliminate outdoors and to not eliminate indoors. Because young puppies naturally avoid using the areas that they sleep, eat and play as "potty areas", we capitalize on this tendency when we teach them to eliminate in outdoor areas only. Here are a few simple rules for success:

- *Supervision, supervision, supervision*: Puppies are curious and love to explore. However, unsupervised exploring leads to chewing on forbidden items and eliminating in different rooms of the house. The best way to avoid accidents is to keep your puppy in the same room with you. A crate or small puppy-proofed area can be used to safely confine your pup when you cannot closely supervise him. As your puppy matures and becomes more reliable in his elimination (and chewing!) habits, you can gradually increase his freedom in your home.

- **Establish a regular feeding and exercise schedule:** Feed your puppy two or three times a day, on a regular schedule. Dogs who are fed this way are regular in their elimination habits, which helps with housetraining. Similarly, puppies thrive on a daily and regular exercise routine. Set aside time each day for walks, play, and training. This will not only help with housetraining, but is important for creating good house manners.

- **Frequent trips:** One of the most common mistakes that new owners make with young dogs is to wait too long between trips outdoors. Puppy bladders are small and young dogs have a limited ability to control their elimination habits. Do not wait for your puppy to indicate his needs to you – when in doubt, take him out!

- **Positive results:** Accompany your puppy outside so that you can be sure that he eliminates. As he begins to sniff and circle or starts to urinate, introduce a cue such as "go potty" or "hurry up". Eventually this cue can be used to encourage him to eliminate when you are traveling or in a rush. Stay with your puppy and praise quietly as he eliminates. (Note of caution: Keep your praise moderate – too much enthusiasm may interrupt him)!

- **Avoid unrealistic expectations:** Puppies less than 12 to 14 weeks of age have limited control over elimination and *must* be taken outside frequently. It is a myth that puppies younger than this age can be completely housetrained. More realistically, most begin to be reliable when they are about 5 to 6 months of age (or older, in some cases). Once housetraining is complete, young dogs and adults should still be provided with multiple opportunities per day to go outside for elimination.

- **When "accidents" happen**: If your puppy is well supervised and taken outside frequently, house accidents should be rare. However, if you do find an accident in your home, _never_ punish your pup. Punishment only serves to create fear and puppies do not associate the presence of their waste with the act of eliminating. If you witness your puppy eliminating in the house, quietly interrupt and carry him outside to finish. Clean the spot thoroughly with a biological cleaner designed for pet waste and intensify your supervision and housetraining techniques.

One more thing: We occasionally field questions from new owners regarding when they can expect their dog to "ask" to go out. The perception seems to be that the dog not only must learn *where* to go, but also that he must also reliably *request* elimination breaks, either by alerting the owner, standing by the door, barking, or (ugh) ringing a bell. My opinion about this spurious requirement (and therefore the position of my training school) is that once a dog is dependably eliminating outdoors and is not eliminating indoors, he is house trained. Period.

As the human side of this relationship, we are in complete control of almost all aspects of our dogs' lives. We decide when, what and how much our dogs eat; when and for how long (and if) they go for walks; where they are allowed to rest and sleep; the amount and type of health care that they receive; *and* where and when they are allowed to relieve themselves. Cannot we give

222

them just this one little thing then - regular opportunities during the day to go outside to eliminate without putting additional training conditions upon it? Sure, if a dog naturally learns to ask, that is fine. But I see no reason at all to make "asking" a requirement of successful house training. It is not difficult - just take the dog out regularly to eliminate – in the morning when she arises, after eating, after playing, every couple of hours, and before bedtime at night. Do our dogs this courtesy and do not require that they have to *ask* for something so basic and necessary as elimination.

Nipping and Mouthing: Although individual puppies vary in intensity and frequency, almost all mouth and nip when playing with people and with other puppies. Owners must teach their puppy to inhibit the intensity of nipping during play and to stop nipping and mouthing when asked to do so. Contrary to popular belief, puppies will not learn this on their own, nor will they outgrow this behavior. A puppy who is not taught to stop play biting while young may develop into an adult dog who uses his mouth too roughly while he is playing.

At AutumnGold, we use redirection (play with a toy, not my hands) and play interruptions to teach puppies to play gently without biting. All play sessions with puppies include a preselected chew toy or interactive toy that is durable and safe. The toy is brought out only for play sessions and all nipping and mouthing is redirected to the toy and away from hands or clothing. Gentle tug-of-war games can be introduced and used as an opportunity to teach the puppy "give" and "get it" cues (see Chapter 14 for details). After several play sessions, the puppy begins to associate the special toy with play and focuses his nipping and tugging on the toy, not on hands or clothing.

Play interruption is a form of response substitution. We teach puppies to come when called away from play (for a very high

223

value treat) and to respond to a "sit" or "down" cue as a method to tamp down over-arousal and to reinforce calm behaviors. These exercises are included with all play sessions, as they provide a positive way to moderate the puppy's energy and arousal levels, and provide an opportunity to positively reinforce relaxed behavior. Here are the guidelines that we provide to puppy parents in our classes:

AutumnGold Guidelines
Good Puppy Manners: Teaching Your Puppy to Play Gently

Contrary to popular belief, most puppies do not outgrow nipping. Teaching your puppy to not use his mouth during play will lead to an adult dog who plays gently and safely. Here are a few guidelines for helping your puppy to learn proper play behaviors with you:

- **Redirection:** During play sessions, redirect your puppy's nipping behaviors to a favorite toy. Store a special toy in a secure place and present it to your puppy at the start of every play session. Your puppy will begin to associate the toy with play and focus his nipping and tugging to the toy, not on your hands or clothing!

- **Interrupt play:** Once the come and sit/down exercises have been introduced to your puppy (as taught in class), begin to use these cues to periodically interrupt his play. Use these regularly, *not* just in response to nipping. When your puppy becomes too excited and tries to use his mouth, cue him to sit or lie down. Praise quietly (passive praise) and give him high value treats to reinforce him for coming or responding correctly.

- **Time-outs:** A short time-out can be used when your puppy becomes overly excited during play or persists with nipping

224

despite the previous techniques. Stop the play session and carry your puppy in an area that is "puppy-safe", such as his crate or a small, secure area. When he is calm, return and release him and begin interacting again, starting with cueing him to come or sit/down and reinforcing him with yummy treats. (Caution: Take care not to overuse this technique because of the risk of your puppy forming a negative association with confinement).

One more thing: Negative punishment is often recommended for stopping nipping and rough play with puppies. Some trainers advise stopping the play by walking away, while others get a bit more theatrical and encourage owners to "yelp loudly" or exclaim "OUCH!" I am generally not a fan of these approaches. While, in theory, negative punishment (removing something the puppy wants to stop a behavior) is effective, in practice it does not work well. Yelping loudly, saying "ouch" and attempting to walk away paradoxically further incite puppies to chase and play roughly, either out of frustration or simply because they perceive the yelping as escalated play. Teaching a puppy to put his mouth only on toys (never on people) and to respond positively to "come" and "sit" during play works well without the need for additional (though admittedly entertaining) theatrics.

Exploratory Chewing: Because puppies learn about their environment by smelling and chewing on novel items, chewing behavior is not considered to be a problem behavior, but rather a normal behavior that must be directed to appropriate items. (There are a variety of reasons that *problem* chewing behaviors can develop in adolescent and adult dogs. These are discussed in Chapter 14). Management of a puppy's home environment is the most effective approach for preventing undesirable chewing and for teaching puppies which items are their own and which are not. Here are the guidelines that we give to our students (following page):

AutumnGold Guidelines
What to Chew? Teaching your Puppy Good Chewing Habits

Puppies are curious creatures – they learn about their environment by smelling, touching, and sometimes chewing on novel items. Therefore, chewing behavior in puppies is not considered to be a behavior problem, but rather is a normal behavior that puppies must be trained to direct to appropriate items. Here are guidelines for teaching good chewing habits to your puppy:

- **Prevent mistakes**: Manage your puppy's home environment to prevent undesirable chewing and to keep your puppy safe from consuming dangerous objects. Keep all forbidden items away from your puppy and supervise him when he is loose in the house.

- **Select appropriate toys:** Provide a variety of interesting chew toys for your puppy and offer these to him frequently. If your pup picks up something that is not his, simply remove it from his mouth by making a trade with a yummy treat and redirect him to one of his own toys. Make it a habit to praise your pup quietly when he is chewing on appropriate items.

- **Rotate toys:** Puppies and adult dogs enjoy novelty in their toys. Therefore, select a variety of types of chew toys for your puppy and rotate them frequently. If your puppy has not seen a particular toy for a few weeks, he will be more excited to play with it when it is reintroduced!

One more thing: In addition to managing the puppy's environment and providing plenty of varied and interesting chew toys, we recommend teaching "leave it" (*"Don't grab that and come to me for something of higher value"*) and "give" (*"Give that to me in exchange for something of higher value"*) to all puppies. These exercises are actually fun games to teach and we introduce them in all of our puppy and adult classes (see Chapter 14 for details).

Doggy Dens or Puppy Prisons? In today's dog training landscape, many dog advice websites, blogs, and booklets include instructions for teaching a young puppy to accept being confined to a crate. The underlying assumption is that all dogs benefit from being crate-trained and that using a crate is an essential component of successful puppy raising. Conversely, there are other dog training sources that extoll the potential harms of crating dogs and advise (often adamantly) *against* their use.

Unfortunately, there is no evidence that demonstrates either benefits or risks of crating dogs. Many dogs (my own included) enjoy sleeping and traveling in their crates and have no issues whatsoever with being crated for short periods of time. However, we also encounter a reasonable number of clients at AutumnGold who prefer not to use a crate with their puppy because they see it as too restrictive, believe crates to be unnecessary, or simply do not have space for a crate in their home or car.

So, what are the generally reported benefits and risks of crate-training puppies, how is crate-training accomplished, and what are some alternatives?

What is crate-training? Crate-training is an approach to safely confining puppies or newly adopted adult dogs when they cannot be adequately supervised. Dog crates also provide a method for safe car travel. A variety of crate types are available for dogs and are typically constructed from either metal, plastic or fabric. When sizing, a crate should be large enough to allow the dog to stand up, lie down comfortably, and turn around. (For puppies, a large crate can be reduced to an appropriate size by blocking off part of the space). The ultimate goal with crate-training is to have a dog who is comfortable being confined to a crate for short

227

periods of time and who can be left in a crate when isolated without experiencing stress or anxiety.

Risks - Crate overuse: While crating is an effective way to keep a young dog safe when alone and to prevent house soiling and chewing damage, crates can be easily overused or abused. Isolation is stressful for puppies, and this stress can be worsened by confinement in a crate for excessive periods of time. Although a crate environment can be enriched by including food delivery toys, it is *still* an impoverished environment, lacking in stimulation and restricting the dog's natural movement. Because an owner *can* crate their dog for long periods of time (the dog really has no choice in this matter), crates can be easily overused. If a crate is serving as a "dog storage device" in which the dog is spending a large part of her day, rather than as a (preferably temporary) training aid, it is being abused.

Are there alternatives? Of course there are. Successful house training and safety training relies partially upon having an area that a young dog can be safely confined when unsupervised. This space can be a crate, but may also be an exercise pen, a small room or an area that is partitioned off with baby gates. Unlike a crate, baby gates offer the flexibility of being able to change or increase the area of confinement as the puppy matures and becomes more reliable. Crates are convenient and a helpful tool for house training and keeping puppies safe, but they are not essential.

AutumnGold's approach: We generally recommend crate training at AutumnGold but also provide alternatives for owners who prefer to not use a crate. We view crates as a means to an end – not as an end in itself. Once a dog is reliably housetrained and can be trusted not to damage household items when alone, a crate should no longer be needed in the home. Overall, the ultimate goal is a dog who can be safely left alone, loose in the home

228

or a designated room, for several hours a day. Crates are a tool, nothing more, to help attain that goal. Here are the guidelines for successful crate training that we provide to our students:

AutumnGold Guidelines
Teaching Your Puppy to be Comfortable in His Crate

Whenever possible, your puppy's crate should be located near you when you are at home. This will encourage your pup to enter the crate when he is tired and needs to rest. Here are the steps for teaching your puppy to accept his crate as a comfortable place to relax:

- *Toss treats:* Introduce the crate to the puppy by periodically tossing treats into the open door during the day. Allow your pup to enter the crate to find these treats, and to come out as he desires. (Do not push or force your pup into the crate).

- *Meal time:* Puppies can learn to associate their crate with meal time by feeding them in the crate while leaving the door open. When your pup seems comfortable in the crate, the door can be closed and reopened *before* he finishes eating.

- *Short naps:* Crate your puppy for short periods of time while you are home with him and he is tired and ready for a nap. This helps to prevent an association between the crate and isolation and teaches him that his crate is a pleasant place to get away and rest.

- *Limit time:* The time that your puppy is confined to his crate can be gradually increased and should always be paired with a high-value food delivery toy or chew toy that your pup enjoys. Do not overuse the crate. A general rule of thumb is that a dog should never spend more than 3 to 4 hours of uninterrupted time in a crate during the day.

One more thing: I need to address a bit of advice that continues to be promoted, far and wide (aka on the internet). I am referring to recommendations that the owner should never let their puppy out of the crate if he is crying or whining and to always wait until the puppy stops to open the crate door. The rationale behind this erroneous advice is that by responding to a crying puppy, the owner will reinforce the puppy's crying (i.e. his distress). Ugh. Do we really need to continue to address this? Just as we cannot reinforce *fear* in dogs, we also *cannot* reinforce distress or anxiety. A young puppy who is not accustomed to isolation and simply wishes to be with his family is not using crying to get what he wants. He is crying because he is isolated and upset. Rather than wait so long that a puppy becomes distressed in his crate (a sign of overuse), owners should release the puppy *before* he becomes upset. Certainly, the occasional little whine or short cry can be ignored, provided the pup does not become increasingly distressed and settles in. However, truly upset and distressed puppies should be released from the crate, and the owner should do a reset – reduce the amount of time the pup is in her crate and continue to build positive associations with the crate using stuffed toys (aka a "safety cue" – see following).

Home Alone Training: Isolation can be stressful for dogs, especially if time alone is not introduced gradually and with the proper use of classical conditioning. Once a puppy has arrived in her new home, she must gradually learn to be comfortable with periods of isolation. There are two essential components to successful home alone training: meeting the puppy's needs and gradually introducing alone time using a safety cue:

First, meet all of the puppy's needs: It must be emphasized that puppies cannot be expected to quietly accept alone time if they are not receiving regular and daily periods of attention, exercise, socialization, and play. Puppies are most active immediately after rising in the morning, after they have had a meal and following a nap. Play and walk sessions should be scheduled to coincide as much as is possible with these periods. Play can include short training sessions, walks in a safe area (i.e. avoid places where many dogs visit until the puppy is fully vaccinated), games such as fetch, tug and find it, and visits with friends and if possible, other puppies. Once the puppy has become acclimated to his schedule and the owner is aware of the times that the pup is generally sleepy during the day, short periods of isolation in a crate or small, confined area, paired with a safety cue, can be introduced.

Introduce a "safety cue:" Home-alone training is first practiced when the owner is at home, and the puppy is crated or confined in another room. Alone-time is always paired with a specially selected toy or chew bone - the "safety cue." This is provided immediately before the period of isolation and at no other time. We use durable rubber Kong™ toys with our dogs that can be stuffed with small biscuits, soft treats or canned food (then frozen). Pet supply stores carry a variety of treat delivery and stuffable toys that are designed for this use. The most important criteria is that the safety cue must be something that takes a fair bit of time for the puppy to consume, as opposed to something that is rapidly eaten or played with and cast aside.

As always with classical conditioning, the sequence of events is important. The owner approaches the crate (or resting area) with the puppy, gives the pup the safety cue in the crate and leaves the area. In this sequence, the desired outcome is that after several repetitions, short periods of alone time become associated with an opportunity to enjoy the special safety cue toy. If a highly desirable toy is provided and the puppy has received adequate attention and exercise, most puppies immediately become engaged with the toy. The owner returns within 5 to 10 minutes, removes the safety cue, and releases the puppy from her crate or confinement area. The alone time training is complete for that session.

The amount of time that the puppy is left alone is varied and slowly increased, always pairing the crate or other area of confinement with presentation of the safety cue and pairing the termination of alone time with removal of the special toy. While the puppy can and should have access to other toys, the safety cue toy must be provided *only* in association with periods of isolation. This serves to maintain the toy's high value and as a signal for quiet, alone time. This training is an effective approach to reducing or completely preventing isolated-related stress at an early age and teaching puppies that alone time can be pleasant rather than distressful.

Puppy Socialization Classes – Are They Helpful? I addressed developmental periods and the types of helpful (and not so helpful) socialization for puppies in Chapter 3. In addition to socialization experiences that owners can directly provide, a properly conducted puppy class can offer additional benefits to pups and owners alike. At AutumnGold, we offer a 5-week puppy class entitled "Puppy Pre-school and Social Club." This class includes instruction for housetraining, prevention of chewing and nipping, teaching proper play manners, handling (touch-then-treat) exercises, and an introduction to manners training and basic obedience exercises.

An additional benefit is that socialization classes provide puppies the opportunity to play with other pups of about the same age, something that is often not available to them. We structure these play periods rather strictly at AutumnGold and never allow the chaos of all puppies running loose, playing *en masse*. In my opinion, that type of puppy play leads to bullying behavior by some pups and fear and avoidance in others. Rather we assign puppy play pairs each week in which pups are matched with each other according to age, personality and play styles. Owners are taught to closely monitor introductions and play and also repeatedly practice "calling out of play" and calming exercises with their puppies. These play sessions also give us the chance to teach owners how to recognize normal and relaxed play signals and to avoid stress or over-arousal in their puppies.

Finally, an added but often overlooked benefit of puppy classes is the social support that they offer to owners who often have the same worries and concerns about their puppies. Not only do owners have the chance to get to know each other and share puppy-raising stories, but their dogs often become friends and offer new opportunities for puppy play sessions and dog walking outings together.

Puppy training = dog training: A final benefit to a puppy class is that it can introduce new owners to the concept that their puppy can learn to enjoy learning at a very young age. While many owners are concerned about the puppy behaviors that we have addressed in this chapter, puppy class also can introduce training methods for teaching basic manners, loose lead walking, coming when called, tricks and much, much more. In the following chapter, I present the approach that we use at AutumnGold to teach basic manners to dogs, including several "life skills" that we include in our shorter series of classes and as private in-home lessons. All of these behaviors can be introduced to young puppies as well. Before we tackle that topic though, let's chat with neighbor Joe about puppies.

TALKING TO JOE

Unfortunately, neighbor Joe believes a number of things about raising puppies that are antithetical to humane training and to our understanding of puppy development and behavior. Here are a few suggestions for helping Joe to move into the 21st century regarding his puppy training views:

- Joe, I know that your parents and their parents before them used a rolled-up newspaper as a housetraining tool, but those days are long gone Joe (and good riddance, I say). Punishing a puppy for having an accident in the house does not work and can make your puppy afraid of *you*. Put away the paper, Joe and instead use supervision, plenty of trips outside for elimination, and restrict your pup to small areas in the house until she is reliably housetrained.

- I hear that your new pup is stealing socks and underwear Joe. This is normal puppy exploratory behavior. However, while you might think that your pup will grow out of this behavior as he matures, that is often not the case. Try picking up more diligently or partition your pup in an area of the house where he cannot get into mischief.

- Hey Joe, I heard that you just got a new puppy for your three kids, who are all under 10 years of age. Yes, I agree that kids

234

love dogs, Joe, but puppies have some special needs and small children are not generally capable of doing all of the puppy training without a lot of supervision. While I am sure your kids love the new puppy (and vice versa), you should drop the expectation that your children can be completely responsible for her care and training. Bring your kids with you to our puppy class, Joe and we can teach them how to be respectful and gentle with the puppy. They can even teach her a few fun tricks. At home though, make sure that the adults in the house are supervising interactions and oversee most of the new pup's care and training.

🐾 Of course you can start to train your puppy at this age, Joe! The idea that a recently adopted puppy is "too young" for training isn't true. Puppies are already learning rapidly by the time that they arrive in their new home. It's entirely up to you to make sure your pup learns what you would like him to learn. You just need to tailor the lessons to a pup's shorter attention span and physical limitations. Give me a call and we can have one of our instructors come over to give you and your kids some private lessons, Joe!

Chapter 13
Manners for the Civilized Dog

A popular class at AutumnGold is our basic manners class, also called beginning obedience. Eligible dogs are those who are 5 months or older at the start of class. A typical class includes a mix of dogs coming from our puppy class and adolescent dogs who have had no prior training. Manners training is also the primary reason that clients request private in-home lessons, which are offered by several of our instructors.

As I discussed in Chapter 5, AutumnGold uses a detailed behavior profile form for dogs' entry into our group classes. Dogs with problem aggression or severe fear responses are not accepted into group class, but rather are provided with in-home private lessons. What we do accept and see in our beginning classes are plenty of dogs who are excitable, highly-aroused, and lacking in basic manners. Our goal in this class is to provide owners with all of the tools that they need to shape their dogs into well-mannered family companions, who are a pleasure to be with at home and when out in public.

AutumnGold's Approach: In this chapter, as in the previous, I describe the training methods that we use at AutumnGold. Our approach focuses on reward-based methods that are supported by the science that is presented in earlier chapters. That said, I am mindful of the fact that the majority of our clients, like many pet owners, are not interested in either the science or the evidence underlying dog training. Rather, they are most concerned with teaching their dog to behave and with solving bothersome behavior problems. For this reason, we distill the science in a way that remains accurate while providing a set of rules and training guidelines that are easy to learn and remember. In this chapter you will see less training jargon and more handy mnemonics for when you are working with the other end of the lead – students, friends, family members, and of course, neighbor Joe, (who already knows a lot about dogs).

The Basics: In our manners class, the primary exercises that we teach include: (1) Sit/Stay and Down/Stay; (2) Walk on a loose lead; (3) Come when called; (4) Accept and enjoy grooming and handling (touch-then-treat), (5) Greet new people and other dogs politely; and (6) Respond to "Leave it" and "Give" (covered in Chapter 14). We also include information regarding dogs' needs for daily exercise, attention, affection, and mental stimulation and we encourage owners to find several mutually enjoyable activities to share with their dogs. On the first night of class with dogs, we start off by introducing a simple behavior that both dogs and owners enjoy and learn quickly - default eye contact.

Default Eye Contact: This behavior is easy to teach and is almost instantly rewarding to both the owner and the dog. At AutumnGold we refer to this as a "default" behavior simply because we train it with an extremely strong reinforcement history and because we often ask for it prior to introducing a new behavior. It is a great exercise for practicing timing and to prevent dogs from focusing on the food in the owner's hand or treat pouch. Our memory aid for this exercise is: *"It's the behavior, not the hand."* Here are the guidelines that we provide to students for teaching default eye contact:

AutumnGold Guidelines
Default Eye Contact
It's the Behavior, NOT the Hand

We occasionally use lures (food in your hand) to jump-start new behaviors. Examples include using a food lure to initiate eye contact and luring your dog to lie down using the "nose-to-toes" method. While helpful, lures must be removed from the exercise as soon as possible. The goal is to teach your dog that the presence of a lure is not necessary and that "*It's the behavior, not the hand*" that earns him the good stuff. You can teach your dog this rule while training default eye contact:

1. ***Wait for the look:*** Begin with your dog sitting at your side or toe-to-toe with you. Wait until he spontaneously looks up into your eyes. If he is distracted, you can cue him with his name or lure the behavior with a treat in your hand, moving the hand up towards your face. Reinforce your dog immediately (Good! Treat!) for any glance into your eyes.

2. ***Add your cue:*** Continue to reinforce all glances into your eyes. When your dog is offering the behavior spontaneously, add your cue word ("watch", "look") and reinforce.

3. ***Change position:*** If you started this training with your dog at your side, move so that you are now toe-to-toe (with your dog looking directly up into your face). If you started toe-to-toe, switch to by your side.

4. ***Add duration:*** Wait two to three seconds before reinforcing eye contact. If your dog looks away, simply re-cue. Ask for extended periods (up to 5 seconds) of uninterrupted eye contact before reinforcing.

5. ***It's the behavior, not the hand:*** This part of the exercise is to teach your dog to ignore treats in your hands. Place several pieces of food in each hand. Place your hands by your sides, in your dog's line of sight. Cue your dog for eye contact and wait. If your dog stares at your hand, continue to wait. At some point, (possibly after becoming a bit frustrated), your dog will glance up into your eyes. Immediately reinforce from one of your hands. Return your hands to your sides and repeat, alternating the reinforcing hand. After several repetitions, your dog will be on to this game – *"Oh! It is "watch" that earns me the praise and treat, NOT staring at the hand! Yay!"*

6. ***Up the ante:*** Once your dog understands that the food treat will come from your hand in response to him looking into your eyes (and not at your hands), change the position of your hands. Hold them out at your side (see photo below), over your head, or resting on your knees. Only reinforce your dog (Good! Treat!) for maintaining eye contact, and never for staring at your hands. Up the ante even further by placing your treat-holding hands on your dog's back or face, and reinforcing her for default eye contact!

Alice offers default eye contact

Teaching Sit and Down: At every Beginner Class orientation, I ask our new students if they have taught their dog to sit on cue. Invariably, almost everyone holds up a hand. Sit seems to be a universal exercise that people teach to a new dog. This works out quite well for us because it allows me to introduce the use of positive reinforcement (+R) with a simple exercise that most of the dogs are already reliably offering. We send students home from orientation with instructions for the timing of +R for sit, and how to introduce lie down from a sit, using a lure.

Introducing sit:: For pet dog owners, the sit and the down lend themselves well to lure training because the movement of the hand holding the food lure can be faded to a prompt and then to a hand-signal when the dog becomes proficient. To teach sit, the owner stands directly next to or in front of the dog. A food treat is held in the left hand and the hand is placed directly in front of the dog's nose (allowing the dog to smell the treat). The owner slowly moves her hand up and forward slightly (in a diagonal direction). This movement of the lure encourages the dog to lean forward and to look up, shifting weight forward and off of the hind legs. Because this posture naturally makes sitting the most comfortable option, most dogs will sit. The treat is provided immediately as the dog sits (for a refresher on the importance of timing with operant conditioning, see Chapter 7). As the dog eats the treat, the owner continues to praise quietly using passive praise - "*Good sit...that's a beautiful sit.*" After several repetitions, as the dog begins to offer sit in response to the hand movement, the owner adds in the verbal cue "sit" in a pleasant voice, timed immediately as the dog begins to offer a sit.

Introducing down ("nose-to-toes"): In our manners classes, we first teach dogs to lie down from a sit position. We eventually train this behavior from a stand position and when moving, but these exercises are introduced only when the dog reliably responds to a verbal cue to lie down from a sitting position. Train-

240

ing begins with the dog sitting at the owner's side. The owner holds several small food treats in one hand and may be either standing or kneeling next to the dog. The treat-holding hand is placed in front of the dog's nose, allowing the dog to sniff at the treats in the hand (the lure). The hand is then moved slowly downward, from the dog's nose to a point on the floor just slightly in front of the dog's front toes. The verbal cue "down" can be introduced with the motion of the hand. If the dog readily follows the food and lies down, the owner immediately opens the hand and reinforces with a treat and with calm verbal praise (*"good girl, that's a good down"*) and gentle petting.

Because the down position is similar to a submissive body posture and perhaps because some dogs feel more vulnerable lying down, some resist moving into a down position, especially in a group class. If this occurs, the owner can use successive approximation (shaping), first reinforcing a foot coming forward or head lowered toward the ground. Holding several food treats in the hand at once allows rapid and continuous shaping as the owner gradually shifts the criteria for reinforcement in the direction of a complete down position.

Cooper learning down with "nose to toes" method

Removing the lure: For both the sit and the down, the lure should be removed from the gesturing hand once the dog is offering the behavior. The primary reinforcer (food treat) is now delivered immediately as the dog sits or lies down from the opposite hand and is no longer presented as a lure. If the owner wishes to train their dog to respond primarily to a verbal cue, the gesture cue (hand movement) is gradually faded and the voice cue alone is emphasized (see Chapter 10 for details about removing lures and fading cues).

Teaching Stay: A reliable "stay in position" has many practical uses. In the home, a dog who remains quietly in a down stay next to the dinner table reaps the benefits of being with her family during dinnertime without begging or being disruptive. A stay cue can also be used when teaching a dog to "go to her spot" when visitors arrive, or to remain in position for brushing and petting. In all of its uses, stay is an exercise that allows owners to repeatedly reinforce calm and relaxed behaviors in their dog.

When training a dog to stay in position, three criteria are shaped. We call these the *Three D's*. These are (1) *Duration* - the length of time that the dog stays in position; (2) *Distance* – the physical space that separates the dog from the owner; and (3) *Distractions* – environmental events and interruptions that dogs must learn to ignore. These three criteria are isolated and trained separately. At AutumnGold, we train duration first, introduce distance once the dog reliably stays for ~ one minute, and begin to introduce distractions as the final stage of training.

Letting the dog choose: While some dogs are more comfortable in a sit position, others prefer a down. These preferences may be related to an individual dog's physical structure, temperament or training history. We encourage owners to start teaching the stay exercise with their dog's preferred position. This helps to achieve early success and reduces errors (dog changing position). If the dog has no clear preference, the owner can teach stays in both positions simultaneously.

The first D – Duration: Training duration is accomplished by positively reinforcing very short periods of time during which the dog maintains the targeted position (sit or down) with the owner standing very close. The owner reinforces continuously with treats, quiet praise, and gentle petting. The time that the dog remains in the sit/down position (and is consistently reinforced) is increased gradually on a varying time schedule (a variable interval schedule – see Chapter 10 for details). Duration is only increased as the dog shows proficiency during shorter periods (measured in seconds for most dogs). Movements out of position are ignored and the dog is simply re-cued to sit or lie down. The owner must stay close to the dog for duration training and most dogs benefit by keeping a lead attached to their collar or harness. With many owners, the staying close part is the biggest challenge. Many seem to want to "test" their dog prematurely by walking away or even leaving the room. We encourage owners to remain close and increase duration until their dog is "rock solid" steady with his or her stay response. (Warning: With the neighbor Joes of the world, you may feel like you are talking to a wall on this one).

No treat for the release: Following a successful sit/down response and/or stay, the dog is released with a pre-selected word. The verbal cue "okay" is commonly used, while some trainers prefer "free". When the release word is given, all treats, petting, and praise stop. Deemphasizing the release draws the necessary distinction between "stay" (the targeted behavior) and movement. As explained in Chapter 10, although it is common for dog owners to believe that they are "*rewarding a job well done*" when they praise their dogs at the end of the stay, this in actuality reinforces the release (jumping up), *not* staying in position. If this mistake is made repeatedly, from the dog's point of view the stay becomes simply something to get through in order to earn a reward for the release. Concentrating on providing the good stuff (treats, praise, and petting) *during* the stay and stopping the good stuff upon the release correctly targets the desired behavior and prevents the owner from unintentionally rewarding the release. This is especially important because being released from a stay is highly self-reinforcing for most dogs - moving around freely is innately more enjoyable than sitting or lying in one place. At AutumnGold, the mnemonic that we use to remind our students to reinforce the behavior that they want (sit/stay or down/stay) as opposed to reinforcing too late is: *"No Treat for the Release!"*

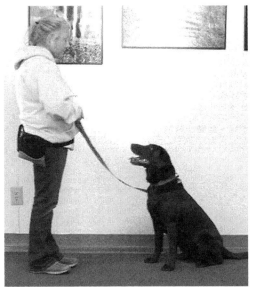

Sharon and Barrel training sit/stay duration

The second D – Distance (yo-yo training): The second criteria, increasing distance, is introduced when the dog is consistently staying in position for up to one minute with the owner standing close. The owner begins by simply taking one step away from the dog and immediately returning to reinforce the stay. The owner then takes a step away again, in another direction, and again immediately returns to reinforce. We call this *"Yo-Yo Training"* as distance is introduced in the absence of duration – the owner is a yo-yo moving away and back repeatedly to the dog, without asking the dog to stay for a long period of time before the owner returns to reinforce the stay. As the dog becomes reliable with increasing distances, the owner begins to walk away in different directions, circles the dog, and eventually, moves to spots outside of the dog's line of vision. Similar to training duration, any movement out of position is ignored and the dog is helped and repositioned. Repeated errors are interpreted as information and signify a need to drop down to a previous criterion and to retrain at that level.

Combining duration and distance: Duration and distance are trained together when the dog reliably stays in position for a predetermined duration of time (with the owner close) and for a predetermined distance (with the trainer leaving and immediately returning). As with all training, combined criteria are shaped slowly, starting with incremental increases of both time and distance. When the dog is reliable for time and distance together, training then focuses on generalizing the stay in other settings and in the presence of distractions - the third D.

The third D (Beefing up the stay): Dogs vary tremendously in the types of things that they find to be distracting. For some, an approaching person is enough to turn them into a whirling dervish of excitement, while others react dramatically to a squirrel across the street or another dog. At AutumnGold, we ask owners to identify the types of distractions that affect their dogs and to rank these in order from easiest to most difficult for their dog to handle. They can then introduce these gradually, beginning with the distraction that is easiest for the dog to manage. We introduce this in class using an exercise that we call *"Beefing Up the Stay."* Because many dogs are challenged when greeting a friendly stranger, an instructor approaches the dog, who is maintaining a sit or down stay at the owner's side. The instructor stops several feet away (low intensity distraction) as the owner simultaneously "beefs up" the stay by reinforcing continuously with high value treats and calming praise. When the approaching instructor turns away, treats and praise stop. We emphasize the importance of always pairing difficult exercises (distractions) with extremely yummy (high value) treats. Although many dogs will still become excited about greeting strangers and other distractions, "beefing up" the stay can help dogs to improve self-control and learn to gradually handle difficult distractions.

Walking on a Loose Lead: In my view, one of the best benefits of living with dogs are the walks. All of my dogs love to hike and run and we spend time together almost every morning at our local forest preserve. The dogs enjoy the exercise and have opportunities to explore, sniff and play, while Mike and I exercise, enjoy the outdoors and spend quality time with our family. Seriously, what's not to like?

Dog walks can also be social events. A friend and I meet regularly at different parks to go hiking with our dogs. We enjoy exploring new trails and rotate favorite parks so that the dogs get to experience and enjoy a variety of outdoor areas. Group walks are also a regular part of AutumnGold's open floor training nights and are great fun for the dogs and for us.

AutumnGold Group Dog Walk

For most dog owners, it comes as no surprise that walking with our dogs is good for us. There is evidence that as a group, dog owners are more physically active than are non-owners and that acquiring a dog often leads to an increase in activity level. Other studies have found that dog owners report physical and psycho-social benefits of walking with their dogs. They get to know other dog walkers in their area, have increased opportunities to meet new people, and develop a sense of community in their neighborhoods.

However, walking with a dog who is pulling incessantly and has no leash manners is not enjoyable for anyone. Teaching loose-lead walking is an important goal for most dog owners and is central to our training philosophy at AutumnGold. The primary objective of teaching loose-lead walking is to teach a dog to walk at the owner's side without pulling and to sit politely when the owner stops.

Training Challenges: Paradoxically, while loose-lead walking is something that most owners engage in daily, it can be one of the most challenging behaviors to train. A primary reason for this is that pulling on-lead often has a strong reinforcement history, even in young dogs. Dogs pull because they enjoy going for walks and have learned that pulling forward is rapidly reinforced by "getting to go," which leads to the many rewards of walks – new smells, sights, and opportunities for interactions with other people and in some cases, other dogs. Many dogs have experienced a long and highly satisfying reinforcement history for pulling by the time that their owners decide that they no longer enjoy walking with a dog who almost dislocates their shoulder.

A second reason that loose-lead walking is difficult to teach is related to the type of behavior that it is. Walking on a loose lead is a *place* rather than a distinct behavior. Even worse, that place is a moving target. Teaching a dog to walk at the owner's side within a "no-pull" zone requires that the dog learns to maintain a position that keeps the lead loose relative to wherever the owner is located – and the owner is usually moving. This requires that the dog not only learns to maintain his position in a rather arbitrary spot (from his point of view) but that that spot is in constant motion. To illustrate the difficulty of this, owners can be asked to attempt "heeling" next to another person who is constantly changing direction – trying this brings new awareness of the difficulty of this task for our dogs!

Training Collars and Harnesses: Our ultimate goal at Autumn-Gold is to have all dogs walking on-lead while wearing a flat buckle collar or walking harness. However, many of the dogs who we see have been pulling into their collar for an extended period of time and can benefit from either a head-collar or a harness that is designed to reduce pulling. The types of equipment that we recommend are provided in these guidelines:

AutumnGold Guidelines
Suggested Training Equipment for Loose Lead Walking

It is a training goal to teach your dog to walk on lead at your side without pulling, wearing only a buckle collar or harness. However, many dogs require some type of training collar or harness to assist with teaching them to walk on a loose lead. Here are several recommendations:

- *Flat collar or walking harness*: Many young dogs or small dogs can be trained exclusively using a flat buckle collar or a walking harness. However, very exuberant youngsters and large, strong dogs may need training equipment that provides a little more control.

- *Head halter collar:* Head halter collars restrict head movement and exert pressure around the dog's muzzle when the dog pulls forward. Head halters are recommended for boisterous dogs and for large dogs who have learned to pull into their collar. At AutumnGold, we use the Gentle Leader™, but there are several types of head collars to select from.

- *No-pull harnesses:* No-pull harnesses reduce a dog's tendency to pull by applying pressure around or across the dog's chest. At AutumnGold, we use and recommend Freedom™ harnesses, but there are a wide variety of these available on the market. Select a harness type that works well with your dog's body conformation and temperament. No-pull harnesses do not work with all dogs, but can be very effective with dogs who do not need or will not tolerate a head halter.

Reinforcing the "Sweet Spot": The first criterion for loose lead walking is training the dog to maintain a loose lead while the owner is standing still. This is an easy exercise to learn and it lends itself well to pet dog training because the owner can practice this several times per day in the comfort of their home. At AutumnGold, we call this *"Reinforcing the Sweet Spot."*

To begin, the owner puts the lead on the dog. This action has often become a conditioned stimulus that predicts walks and so evokes great excitement (including pulling forward) in dogs. The owner's treat pouch contains plenty of high value, yummy treats. The owner plants her feet, and waits. Any movement that the dog makes toward the owner's left hip (the sweet spot) that allows the leash to be slack is immediately reinforced (Good! Treat!!). The goal is for the dog to develop a strong reinforcement history of staying close to his owner's hip while maintaining no tension on the lead. Remaining stationary while introducing "maintain a loose lead" minimizes all of the distractions and reinforcers that have served to strengthen pulling on lead in the past. This approach also allows the owner to achieve a very a high rate of reinforcement (lots of treats and praise) and enables the dog to be rapidly successful.

The sweet spot dance: Once the dog is noticing that it is the left hip (or right hip, or both) that he needs to stay near to get all of the good stuff, the owner can begin to take a single step in various directions, reinforcing "loose lead" when the dog moves alongside to keep the leash slack. Because there are few distractions, most dogs quickly learn this and enjoy the game of keeping the lead loose to earn treats. Pulling behavior is simply ignored and if needed the owner can do a bit of luring to initiate the dog moving into the desired position. Multiple small treats should be provided and every attempt that the dog makes to stay close to the left hip is reinforced.

Add movement: Once stationary loose lead has been introduced, the owner can begin to reinforce loose lead walking. A verbal cue such as "Let's go" or "Heel" is used. The owner provides the verbal cue in a pleasant voice and steps forward. Initially, each step that the dog takes while keeping the lead loose is reinforced. At this stage, we instruct our students that they should be literally "raining treats" to ensure that their dog maintains a loose lead and stays in that all-important sweet spot. After several repetitions of reinforcing each step, we switch to *"Three-step heeling"* in which the owner reinforcers every 3 to 5 steps.

Whenever the dog moves out of that spot and causes the lead to become tight, the owner stops moving forward and waits. If necessary, the owner can lure the dog back into position to avoid the dog becoming frustrated. Stopping removes all opportunity for the dog to be reinforced by continuing to walk. When the dog looks back or moves back toward the sweet spot, the owner immediately reinforces the behavior and begins to walk again – reinforcing at a very high rate to prevent the dog from lunging forward again. An important caution - Because stopping when the dog pulls is a form of is negative punishment (remember, I am not a fan), stopping as a method for teaching loose-lead walking can be extremely frustrating for dogs and so should be used prudently. The most important component of this training must always be to positively reinforce a loose lead as the dog remains in the sweet spot near the owner's hip.

Be a dog time: As an alternative to negative punishment (stopping), we encourage our students to give their dogs frequent opportunities to "be dogs" during walks. Short stretches of loose lead walking should be combined with frequent opportunities to stop for a sniff (or three), explore a bit, greet a friend, and simply enjoy the outdoors. We suggest that owners view loose lead walking as an important *part* of their walks with their dog, but never as the *entire* walk. A release word that means "you are free to snort around, greet someone, or play" is used ("okay" works fine for most dogs). The dog is then allowed some unstructured time either on-lead near the owner or off lead depending on the circumstances and the dog's level of training. When the owner is ready to move on, loose lead walking resumes. By including plenty of "be a dog" time in a walk, both owners and dogs can fully enjoy their outings together.

Teaching Come When Called: Having a dog who comes when called and reliably stays close during walks allows off-lead exercise and a more stimulating and enjoyable life for the dog. However, similar to walking on a loose lead, not coming when called or even worse, running away, have often had a strong reinforcement history when we first see dogs. This can occur because the owner has simply never trained his dog to come when called, or more insidiously, because the dog has learned (quite well) that being called is a reliable predictor for the end of fun.

It is an unfortunate habit that owners can all fall into – only calling the dog to them when they are preparing to leave home (and the dog will be confined), when the dog is out playing and the owner will be ending his fun, when the dog is doing something undesirable such as digging or chasing, or when the owner is getting ready to do something unpleasant such as cutting nails or administering a medication. These associations can accumulate into a classically conditioned response in which the dog learns – *"When mom calls me, fun stuff will stop or unpleasant stuff will ensue."* Multiple events of this type result in a dog who has no love for the words "Rover, Come!"

Please stop using that word: At AutumnGold, the first step that we use to weaken prior negative associations with the word "come" is to ask owners to do us a favor. We ask them to *stop using that word* with their dog, except in several specific circumstances. Those circumstances are when the dog is highly motivated to come to them and is already on her way. An example is when the dog has been home alone and the owner arrives at the door. As the dog rushes to greet and say hello, the owner throws in the dog's name, followed by *that* word *"Muffin, Come!!"* Muffin arrives (she was already happily on her way), and the owner provides tons of positive reinforcement – petting, praise and yummy treats. This works similarly when owners are preparing to feed their dog a meal. The dog may be just a few steps away, but we ask them to throw in *that word* as their dog is happily approaching them for dinner. You get the picture. Calling the dog *only* when she is already happily and voluntarily on her way helps owners to break any unpleasant (classically learned) associations that their dog may have with the word "come" and to begin to build a very positive (classical) relationship – the word "come" now reliably predicts good things happening! (For details regarding the classically learned association between cue words and reinforcers, see Chapter 6).

After two weeks of this rule, we begin to actively train come when called. The behavior of coming when called is composed of two elements: (1) Turn to your name, and (2) Return to your owner close enough to be touched.

Turn to your name: Although this is a step that is often overlooked, teaching a dog to turn to his or her name is an important first step when teaching come when called. This is especially important in homes in which the dog's name has been overused or worse, has been used as an aversive cue - yelling the dog's name in a harsh tone to interrupt an unwanted behavior or as a form of punishment. The goal of teaching "turn to your name" is a dog who turns and gives the owner her attention and anticipates another cue will follow.

The owner selects a quiet area in the home. Standing close to the dog, the owner quietly speaks the dog's name. If the dog turns her head to look, the owner immediately reinforces with a praise and a high-value treat (Good! Treat!) This sequence is repeated 10 to 20 times, with the owner standing close to the dog and maintaining a high rate of reinforcement. Once the behavior of "turn to your name" is reliable, the owner begins to move around – stepping behind or to the side of the dog, repeating the training sequence.

Come when called: Teaching "come" begins once "turn to your name" is reliable. When teaching a dog to come when called, it is important that the owner continues to call the dog in circumstances in which the dog is still highly motivated to respond. The same examples discussed previously can be used, with the difference that the owner now provides the cue *"Muffin, Come!"* before the dog is on her way. In this minor timing shift, the dog (who has been well primed to respond under these circumstances) will readily turn to her name and come running for a happy reunion, food treats and affection. Upon arrival, the owner now briefly touches the dog's collar (or harness) immediately before giving the treat. Other scenarios include having one family member hold the dog while another calls the dog from different room, playing "hide and seek" in the yard or house, and using a long-line or flexible lead to practice come when called during "be a dog" periods on walks.

The dog must also be prevented from *not* responding (or, worse, running away) when she is called. To prevent this, the dog should either have an attached long line or retractable lead in all situations in which she is free and has the option to choose not to respond. In accidental situations in which this happens, we ask owners to not use *that word* and walk out to meet the dog instead. Once a dog is highly reliable with confined space training and when trained on a drag line or flexi-lease, we introduce steps to teaching off-lead come when called. At AutumnGold, because we view off-lead coming when called as a critically important behavior, we dedicated an entire LifeSkills class, "Rollicking Recalls" to teach this (see below).

LifeSkills Training Classes: In addition to our puppy and manners classes at AutumnGold, we also offer tricks, K-9 Nosework, canine freestyle and informal agility classes as advanced classes. In recent years, we have added a series of short courses, called "LifeSkills Classes." These sessions focus on one or two specific life skills that our students have identified as important for their dogs. For example, last year we offered "Rollicking Recalls" for off-lead coming when called, "Mind Your Manners" for teaching dogs calm greeting behaviors in the home and in public, "Keep Calm and Master the Mat" for training dogs to relax on a bed or mat, "Show Me a Sign" for teaching hand signals, and "Give and Take" for preventing and solving food and toy possessiveness. Each year we identify new LifeSkills courses based upon the needs and interests of our clientele. This keeps the courses fresh and interesting for all of our instructors and provides something new for our returning students and their dogs.

TALKING TO JOE

Talking to Joe: Neighbor Joe has a lot of beliefs about how to best train his dog. Here are a few tips for encouraging the Joes in your life to embrace dog training methods that are based upon sound science and are pleasant to use and are enjoyable for dogs:

255

🐾 Hey Joe, I heard you tell neighbor Rose that she should avoid looking in the eyes of her Shih Tzu, Taffy because it will cause Taffy to think that her status is being threatened and she may react by attacking. I know you think that dogs perceive eye contact as a threat, Joe, and there is some truth to that if the gaze is unfriendly or a hard stare. However, just like people, dogs respond positively to friendly eye contact and can even be trained to offer it on cue. Here, give it a try with your dog, Captain. I bet you both will enjoy "default eye contact." It has an added benefit of giving you a tool to keep Captain's attention when he is distracted.

🐾 I see that Captain loves to greet your friends as they come into your gate, Joe. He is an exuberant boy and when he leaps up he can be a bit intimidating, eh? You know, you can teach Captain to sit and stay at your side using lots of those yummy treats that Captain loves. Practice this by the gate, when no one is visiting and then start to "beef up" Captain's sit/stay when a family member comes home or when someone approaches the gate but does not enter. You can use this exercise to help Captain to gain some self-control over his exuberant personality when you have visitors.

🐾 What's that, Joe? You do not want to use food treats to teach Captain to lie down because you think it will teach him to only listen when you have food in your hand? Here's the thing, Joe. Whenever we use a lure to jump-start a behavior, such as teaching down with food in your hand, it is important to remove that lure early in the training. Once Captain has started to respond, remove the food from your gesturing hand, and always reinforce him from the opposite hand once he has lied down.

🐾 I know that you saw a celebrity trainer on TV say that dogs who pull on their leads are demonstrating dominant behavior towards their owners. This is simply not true, Joe. The explanation is actually more simple. Captain pulls into his lead when you are out walking because he is eager to be out. In addition, all of the great smells, sights and opportunities for meeting people and other dogs during walks in the past have rewarded his pulling forward. We can start to change this behavior by having you reward Captain for staying by your side with a loose lead. Begin this training in the house with Captain, while you are not moving and gradually introduce movement, giving Captain lots of good stuff for maintaining a loose lead. Intersperse Captain's walks with opportunities to sniff, investigate things, and "be a dog" so that you both can continue to enjoy your outings together.

🐾 I know that all of these training rules can be confusing and difficult to remember, Joe. Here are a few memory aids to help you to keep them straight:

🐾 *"It's the behavior, not the hand"* – Take care to make sure that Captain offers the behavior that you ask for without following a lure in your hand (or staring at your hand or at your treat pouch).

🐾 *"Nose-to-Toes"* – You can use a lure in your hand, moved slowly from Captains nose and down to just in front of his toes to jump-start his response to "down."

🐾 *"No treat for the release"* – A reminder to reinforce the behavior that you want at the time it is occurring. Give Captain the good stuff while he is staying or walking at your side, not when the behavior has ended, when he jumps up or is released to go play.

🐾 *"Yo-yo training"* – When training Captain to reliably stay in place, you can increase the distance that you walk away from him gradually by going back and forth repeatedly (like a yo-yo) from varying distances and directions.

- 🐾 _"Beefing up the stay*"_ – Whenever you are introducing something new that challenges Captain's staying in place (*or walking by your side), remember to "beef up his response" by providing lots of high value treats and praise.
- 🐾 _"Reinforce the sweet spot"_ – Remember that staying by your side and keeping the leash loose is highly challenging for Captain, Joe. You can help him to maintain this "spot" by your side by making sure that you provide lots of yummy treats when he is close to your hip and walking or standing with a loose lead.
- 🐾 _"Stop using that word"_ – Captain has a great "come when called" response, Joe. Take care to maintain his belief that coming when called always predicts good things happening (treats, love from you) and never predicts bad stuff. So, avoid "using that word – come" when you are frustrated with Captain, when you know he will not come, or if you are going to reprimand him. In circumstances in which Captain may not come – train those situations using a long-line or retractable leash with him. You will see positive results – I promise! Good Dog, Captain!
- 🐾 _Touch then Treat:_ You can teach Captain to enjoy being handled and brushed using this simple exercise, Joe. Have a bunch of yummy treats close by and sit on the floor with Captain. Touch his collar – give a treat. Touch a paw – give a treat. Touch an ear – give a treat. Work up to areas of Captain's body that he may be a bit sensitive about – always following a light touch or bit of handling with a yummy treat. After a few sessions of this, Captain will be "leaning in" to handling rather than avoiding it. A fun game for you (and your kids) to play with Captain!

Chapter 14
No More Misbehavin'

The prescreening behaviour profile that we use at AutumnGold asks students to identify the behavior problems that they are experiencing with their dog. We provide the following list:*

Housetraining	Excessive chewing	Barking when alone
Running away	Not coming when called	Pulling on the leash
Fear of other dogs	Nipping during play	Stealing forbidden items
Fear of strangers	Destructive when alone	Jumping to greet
Rough play	Lack of car manners	Barking for attention
Chasing cats	Rushing out of doors	Fear in new places
Chasing wildlife	Barking for attention	Possessive with toys
Digging in yard	Fear of a family member	Guards food bowl
Barking in yard	Raiding the garbage	Hyperactivity
Counter surfing	Anxious when alone*	Aggression/biting*

Of this list, the most common problems that owners select are pulling on the leash, not coming when called, hyperactivity, and jumping up to greet. A substantial number of owners are also concerned about chewing, destructive behaviors, and dogs who steal forbidden items.

---

* Dogs with problem aggression, separation anxiety, and extreme fear reactions are screened from group class and provided with private, in-home sessions. These topics are outside of the scope of this book.

The majority of these problem behaviors are normal dog behaviors that are expressed in circumstances that are not appropriate or in situations that distress the owner. For example, stealing food and counter-surfing begins as normal exploratory behavior in dogs and then persists because the consequences are very pleasurable (*"I found cake! I love cake!"*). Similarly, jumping up to greet is the sign of a happy and friendly dog who has not been trained to greet politely and without physical contact. Chewing, barking, digging? Normal, but certainly not compatible with a pleasant and harmonious household.

Fulfilling a Dog's Needs: Problem behaviors that owners consider to be unruly or disruptive often reflect the exuberance of a young dog who has not been trained and who may lack regular and adequate opportunities for attention, exercise, and mental stimulation. Discussions regarding how to fully meet their dog's physical and emotional needs are a central component of our training philosophy at AutumnGold and a primary theme of this chapter.

Meeting a young dog's needs can be challenging for a variety of reasons. Some of our students possess rose-tinted memories of a former beloved dog and conveniently forget those early months when that dog was a puppy or exuberant adolescent. Some owners simply lack understanding of a dog's complete needs and mistake over-activity and a lack of manners for deliberate disobedience (neighbor Joe is guilty of this one). Unfortunately, in this day and age, a considerable number of people lack sufficient time or resources for a dog and have failed to account for the changes in their lifestyle and routines that a dog naturally requires. And last, sadly, some owners are just not strongly committed to dog ownership and are unwilling to put in the time and work to train and exercise a dog.

The paradox is that spending time interacting with and training a dog not only helps to prevent unruly and disruptive behaviors, but strengthens the love that we have for our dogs and subsequently our commitment to them. A dog friend and I refer to this level of commitment as the "throw yourself in front of a bus" stage because once we have this degree of love and commitment to our dogs, we truly do feel that we would lie down our lives to keep them from harm.

But as an instructor, I realize that not everyone attains the "in front of the bus" level of commitment. As trainers, we need to meet our students where they are, teaching rather than preaching. In this chapter I examine a set of the most common behavior problems that we see in dogs at AutumnGold and provide the approaches that we use to help owners to prevent and solve these problems. Our ultimate goal is to keep the dog in the home and to encourage an enduring bond of commitment and love (and in some cases, getting to that "bus" stage).

First and foremost is the importance of providing for all of a dog's needs; physical, emotional, and social. Here are the guidelines that we provide to our students to help them to achieve this:

AutumnGold Guidelines
Meeting Your Dog's Daily Needs

We know that you are dedicated to providing for your new dog's physical and emotional needs and incorporating her care into your daily routines. Here are a few tips for achieving this in ways that you and your dog will find enjoyable:

Together Time: There are a host of fun and exciting activities to share with your dog – pick a few that appeal to you both!

- **Walks:** Walking is one of the most enjoyable activities that we share with our dogs. Take at least one extended outing per day to keep your dog physically fit and to give her opportunities to explore. Visiting different parks and public areas and taking different routes will keep the walks interesting for both of you.
- **Call a friend:** If your dog has one or two dog friends, set up play and walk dates with their owners to meet and explore together or allow the dogs some supervised play time.
- **Games:** Retrieving, chase games, tugging, playing hide-and-seek, and scent games are fun for you and for your dog. Select a few play activities that your dog enjoys and incorporate these into your daily routines.
- **Time to train:** Include manners training exercises in your daily walks and play time. This will keep training interesting and fun and will help your dog to generalize her responses to new settings.
- **Dog sports:** There a variety of organized sports and activities that you can enjoy with your dog. These include flyball, agility, canine freestyle, Rally obedience, tricks, Frisbee (disc dog), tracking, herding, and carting. Enroll in a local class to discover if one of these sports is for you and your dog.

Home Alone Time: In today's busy world, most dogs spend at least a few hours of each day alone. Here are a few tips for helping your dog to relax and be comfortable during these periods:

- **Food puzzles:** A variety of food puzzle toys are available. If your dog enjoys playing with these toys, find a type that is safe for him and that he enjoys but does not become frustrated with. Use these occasionally as one option for keeping your dog engaged during times when you are not available.
- **Chew toys:** Most dogs need regular opportunities to chew. Select chew toys and bones that your dog enjoys, that are

safe if consumed and that do not break off in chunks or damage your dog's teeth. To increase a chew's value, pair one or two special chew toys with alone time and use them only in those circumstances.

- *Limit alone time:* Dogs thrive when they are with their family and receive regular attention, exercise and love. As a rule of thumb, limit your dog's alone time to 4 to 5 consecutive hours each day, especially if your dog is young and active. Dog sitters, dog walkers, and well-supervised doggy day care services can all help you to provide for your dog's needs if you must be away for long periods of the day.

Jumping Up to Greet: Jumping up to greet is almost universally identified on our behavior forms as a behavior that owners wish to change in their dogs. Although this behavior is unwanted and may cause unintentional injury, jumping up is usually an expression of friendliness in an untrained and exuberant dog. In addition to greeting, some dogs jump up to solicit attention. In these cases, jumping up may be accompanied by non-aggressive mouthing and barking.

Once established, jumping up to greet can be difficult to stop because the owner has been inconsistent (*"You can jump on me when we are playing but not when I am dressed for work"; "You can jump on me but not on visitors"*), and has repeatedly reinforced jumping up with petting and attention. Because jumping up is inherently reinforcing to dogs, every episode in which this behavior occurs provides positive consequences and strengthens the behavior. The good news is that these self-reinforcing properties can be used to teach dogs that interaction and petting during greeting are still available as a consequence of an alternate behavior: sitting for greeting. At AutumnGold, we practice this exercise multiple times with each owner-dog pair at the start of each class.

Meet and Greets at AutumnGold

Here are the guidelines that we use for training dogs to greet politely:

AutumnGold Guidelines
Teaching "Meet and Greet" Manners to Your Dog

It is impossible for a dog to be sitting and jumping up at the same time. Teaching a "sit for greeting" lends itself nicely as an alternate behavior to prevent your dog from jumping up. Here are the steps for this training:

1. ***Train a solid sit/stay:*** Teach your dog to maintain a sit/stay by your side, on a loose lead, in the absence of distractions. Train in a variety of settings, including those in which your dog is likely to greet people (such as the doorways in your

home), but without visitors present. Increase duration until your dog will reliably sit by your side for up to 30 seconds.

2. ***High value treats – from you:*** Once your dog understands sit/stay at your side, you can begin to introduce greeters. If possible, begin with a family member or friend who your dog sees often. Using high value treats, hold several in your hand, and reinforce sit/stay (treat, treat, treat!) *before* the greeter approaches. Continue to "beef up" sit/stay as the greeter walks towards you (starting *before* your dog becomes excited). You are a treat machine – *lots and lots* of treats for staying. Allow the greeter to approach, say hello and then walk away. As the greeter walks away, treats stop. Repeat with a variety of greeters in different settings.

3. ***High value treats – from greeter:*** Begin this step only when your dog has developed self-control with *you* providing him with praise and treats. Give a handful of treats to the greeter. Continue to "beef up" your dog's sit/stay as the greeter approaches. In addition, the greeter now cues "sit" as he approaches and reinforces your dog (in addition to you) as he maintains sit-to-greet. Keep greetings short in duration so that your dog can be successful and does not become overly excited.

4. ***Practice, practice, practice:*** Remember, having a dog who is excited and jumps up to greet simply means that you have a very friendly dog – not the end of the world, really, is it? Practice sit for greeting as often as possible so that you can build up a strong reinforcement history for this behavior. Introduce a variety of greeters in many different situations as your dog becomes more reliable.

Inappropriate Chewing: Regular chewing is a normal way in which dogs explore and learn about their environment. Although puppies tend to chew most vigorously and frequently, most dogs enjoy chewing throughout their lives and should be provided with a variety of appealing chew toys. Young dogs come into homes without an understanding of which items are acceptable chew toys. As they explore their new home, dogs will be especially attracted to items that can be shredded (pillows, children's stuffed toys, clothing) and objects that can be gnawed (furniture, shoes). Training includes management to prevent access to forbidden items, positively reinforcing the use of appropriate toys, and when mistakes are made, redirection.

Happily for dog owners today, an understanding of the types of materials that are attractive to dogs and recognition of the dog's natural need to chew has led to the development of a wide variety of suitable and safe chew toys. These include hard natural bones, synthetic bones, chew devices constructed of hard nylon, plastic, or rubber, and a variety of interactive food delivery toys. Owners can select different types of chew toys to determine their dog's chewing preferences. The table below provides examples of several types of suitable chew toys:

TOY TYPE	DESCRIPTION
Interactive Toys	These are toys that owners and dogs play with together and include retrieving toys and balls, tug toys, and scent toys for nose work games. To maintain high value to the dog, interactive toys should be brought out only for play time and then put away again.
Food Delivery & Puzzle Toys	These include toys that can be stuffed for use as a "safety cue" for home alone training and toys that must be manipulated in some way to deliver bits of food. While all of these can provide entertainment and stimulation, caution is advised. Just as a crate can be overused for confinement, food delivery toys can be overused and should never replace regular opportunities for interactions with people and exercise.

TOY TYPE	DESCRIPTION
Chew Bones and Toys	Hard bones for dogs are constructed with a variety of materials and provide opportunities for extended chewing and gnawing. The type that is selected should match the dog's interest and chewing intensity. In general, a safe and appropriate chew bone is one that takes a dog several weeks to destroy or consume, does not damage teeth or gums, and which cannot be broken into large or sharp chunks.

Proactive training: In addition to providing a variety of attractive chew toys and bones (and encouraging their use), owners must also *proactively* prevent their dog's undesirable chewing through household management:

- *Pick up!* Objects that are potential chew targets must be secured out of sight and out of reach. Pay special attention to kitchen trash, counter tops, laundry and kid's toys.

- *Supervise!* Young dogs must be supervised whenever they are loose in the home. If your dog picks up something that is not his, simply remove it (or ask him to "give" – see below) and redirect to one of his own toys. Always praise quietly (passive praise) when your dog is chewing on his own chew toys (don't forget this part!).

- *Avoid reprimands:* Similar to house training, the use of verbal (or worse, physical) reprimands when your dog steals or chews on a prohibited item rapidly teaches him to avoid you and to chew out of your sight. These behaviors do not mean that your dog *"knows he is wrong."* Rather, avoidance indicates that he has learned through experience to stop chewing in your presence in order to avoid punishment. In severe cases, this can lead to fear or even an aggressive response.

Teaching "Leave it" and "Give": Finally, in addition to managing a dog's environment and providing varied and interesting chew toys, dogs can be trained to respond to cues for "Leave it" (*"Don't touch it if you are thinking about it"*) and "Give" (*"Hand it over if you already nabbed it).*" We provide instructions for these two behaviors in our basic training classes:

AutumnGold Guidelines
Teaching "Leave It" and "Give" to Your Dog

All young dogs naturally investigate and chew on novel items. Teaching your dog to "leave it" and "give" provides an extra tool to use when your dog is learning about which items are his toys and which are not. Here are the steps:

Teaching "Leave It: "Leave it" is used when your dog is attempting to pick up or steal an object or food that you do not want him to have. This command should only be used *before* your dog has possession of the item. (If he already has it, use "give" – see following).

- *Select a low value object:* Select an item that your dog is mildly (but not intensely) interested in. Attach a lead to his collar and place him in a sit/stay ~ 2 feet away from the object. Stand at his side, slightly behind him.
- *Lure - Turn to me:* Hold a high value treat in your hand; allow your dog to sniff it. Cue "Leave it" in a pleasant voice and lure your dog away from the object and toward you (i.e. jump-start the behavior). Reinforce turning toward you immediately. Repeat. Continue teaching "leave it" from the sit position until your dog readily offers turn toward you. Remove the lure when he has offered several turns and reinforce from the opposite hand.
- *Prevent mistakes:* If your dog attempts to reach for the forbidden object, say nothing. Stop him with the lead and redi-

268

rect him toward you. Use the lead only to prevent him from reaching the object, not as a correction.

- **Standing/walking:** When your dog is responding consistently from a sit position, place him in a stand position and repeat. Begin walking him towards the object, cueing him to leave it. Reinforce each time with praise and a high value treat.
- **Increase object value:** When your dog is responding consistently from a stand and while walking, progress to different objects (increasing value) and in varying settings. If your dog is a sock-stealer, train with socks. If he has a passion for your kid's stuffed toys – train with those. Garbage raider? Ditto. You get the picture.
- **Caution:** Regardless of how well trained your dog is, all dogs will occasionally grab items that are not safe. It is our responsibility as conscientious owners to keep our dogs out of harm's way by ensuring that dangerous objects are out of reach and by carefully supervising our dogs during walks.

Teaching "Give": "Give" is used to take possession of any object that your dog has in his mouth. This training teaches your dog to release the object into your hand. This means that he will open his mouth and move away from the object, *not* that you will pull it from his mouth.

- **Toys and fetch:** Fetch games are a great time to teach dogs to "give". If your dog occasionally (or not so occasionally) decides to play "catch me if you can" during a game of fetch, attach a long line to his collar during this training. When he returns to you with the toy, tell him to sit before you attempt to retrieve the toy from him.
- **Make a trade:** Praise your dog for sitting, and reach to take the toy. Hold your hand directly under his jaw. Do not attempt to pull the toy out of his mouth. Hold your hand still, and show him a food treat with the other hand (lure). When

269

he has focused on the food treat, tell him "give" in a pleasant voice. When he opens his mouth for the treat, take the toy, and reinforce him with the food treat.

- **Manners, please:** Do not allow your dog to jump for the toy or to try to take the toy back after eating his treat. If necessary, ask him to sit again and reinforce the sit, before resuming your game.

- **Remove the lure:** After several successful repetitions using the lure, switch to reinforcement - do not show him the treat prior to asking him to "give." Provide your dog with a treat (and praise) as soon as he gives you the toy.

- **Practice with a variety of items:** Continue to use a food treat to positively reinforce "give" when your dog reliably releases toys. Add other objects, playing the "make-a-trade" game each time, reinforcing your dog for releasing items into your hand with a food treat and praise.

Objectionable Barking: As we learned earlier (Chapter 4), barking is a normal form of vocal communication in dogs and is used in a wide variety of contexts. Dogs bark to alert their owners to visitors, during greeting, when they are excited, and when they are anxious and stressed. Many owners also encourage their dog to bark and train a "speak" command. So, like most behaviors, barking *itself* is not a problem. It only becomes so when it occurs in situations that an owner finds objectionable. For example, barking to ask to go outside or to warn of intruders are typically encouraged and appreciated. Alternatively, the dog who barks "too much" when a visitor appears or when he would like to come in from outside is considered to be ill-behaved.

Hmm.....

The similarities between these two scenarios of "desirable" and "undesirable" barking illustrate a common paradox in our relationships with dogs. Desired contexts (*"It is acceptable to me that*

270

you bark at the door when someone arrives") and undesired contexts (*"It is not acceptable to me when you bark at the window when someone walks by"*) can be almost identical from the dog's point of view. In many of these cases, it is unreasonable to expect a dog to understand the distinction between them. Therefore, when diagnosing and treating problem barking in dogs, we must identify not only the triggers for barking (visitors, isolation, boredom), but also the owner's (often unrealistic) expectations.

Repetitive Barking (aka "nuisance barking): Repetitive barking in dogs is unfortunately often labeled as "nuisance" barking. This mislabeling reflects the effects of excessive barking upon the dog's owners and in some cases, their neighbors, rather than focusing upon the underlying cause. Because really, if we asked these dogs to tell us why they are barking, I am pretty certain that they would NOT say: "*Oh, because I want to be a nuisance.*" Rather, a list of the underlying causes of excessive barking in dogs, in no particular order, are:

- I am bored because I spend too much time alone.
- I am stressed because I am uncomfortable being alone.
- I feel territorial around my home's doors, windows, or yard.
- I am responding to noises in my neighborhood such as other dogs barking, vehicles approaching or people walking by.
- I am responding to the sight of people or other animals outside or near my home.

Once the underlying cause of undesirable barking has been identified, changing this behavior involves managing the context, removing triggers and counter-conditioning an alternate response (if needed). Repetitive barking is most commonly observed in dogs who spend long periods of time alone, are isolated in yards or kennels, or who are experiencing separation stress. Dogs who spend many hours in a yard are under-stimulated and experience isolation in the same way as a dog who is left alone indoors for long periods. Management and treatment include:

- **Reduce isolation:** Decrease the time that the dog spends isolated in the yard or in a kennel or alone in the home.
- **Response substitution:** Train an alternative behavior, such as coming away from the barrier (fence, property edge) or if in the home, resting on a bed or mat (see target training guidelines later in this chapter).
- **Manage triggers:** Prevent the dog's ability to see/hear the triggering stimuli (privacy screens, bring the dog indoors).
- **Provide for needs:** Increase the dog's daily exercise, mental and emotional stimulation so that the dog spends less time isolated and more time with people (if necessary hire a dog walker or use a reputable doggy day care).

Attention-Seeking Behaviors: Stealing forbidden items, playing "catch me if you can", barking, chewing, excessive play solicitation and mouthing can all be forms of problematic attention-seeking behavior in dogs. Following the basic rules of operant conditioning, dogs who steal, chew or bark for attention have learned that these behaviors "work" for them because the end result is desired interaction with the owner. Attention-seeking chewing can be distinguished from exploratory or boredom-related chewing in that it is always conducted in the owner's presence. The dog may even approach the owner while holding the forbidden object, play bow, and then dance teasingly away. There may also be a history of the owner chasing the dog when he has taken a forbidden item. Similarly, dogs who bark for attention direct this behavior at their owners, typically in situations when the owner is distracted or engaging in an activity that does not involve the dog.

Those pesky needs again: Attention-seeking behaviors are both normal and desirable in dogs. My dogs frequently seek me out for affection and games and walks. I do not consider the fact that my dogs request petting and affection and play to be a problem behavior. These behaviors may only become problematic when they are excessive and interfere with the dog and owners' daily lives together. The first step when addressing potential attention-seeking problems is to ensure that the dog is receiving sufficient daily attention and exercise and love. If walks, opportunities for play, and mental stimulation are not currently part of the dog's daily routine, these must be established. A dog who is receiving regular exercise and who has learned to expect regular interactions with his owner is less likely to develop problem attention-seeking behaviors. For many dogs, increasing exercise and introducing some form of mental stimulation such as manners training, teaching retrieving or find-it games, or walking in a new area several times a week, reduces or eliminates problem attention-seeking.

However, when pawing, barking, play solicitation, and other problem behaviors persist and have clearly been reinforced with attention, we use two approaches to treatment – preemptive redirection and response substitution (for example, target training to a mat).

Preemptive redirection: Dogs who chew, steal, or bark for attention usually have very specific circumstances that trigger these behaviors. For example, a young dog may show attention-seeking behaviors every evening when her family sits down to dinner or later at night when her owner is watching television. It is helpful to ask owners to pay attention to these patterns and to identify the times of day and circumstances in which their dog shows the unwanted behavior. They should specifically note the triggering events that precede the unwanted behavior.

Preemptive redirection involves providing the dog with an interactive toy *before* the problem attention-seeking occurs. For the meal-time attention seeker, a bone is stuffed with cheese or soft treats before the meal begins and is given to the dog to chew. The dog can be attached to a lead and is trained to maintain a down-stay on a mat or bed as she chews on her special bone. For dogs who steal items when the owner is watching television or reading, the owner can hide several food-delivery toys around the living room just before sitting down (i.e. *before* the problem behavior is triggered). These toys provide an appropriate chew toy to the dog and effectively prevent attention-seeking chewing when they are provided before the problem behavior is triggered. Alternative solutions are for the owner to play a "touch-then-treat" training game or have a grooming session with their dog as they sit down to watch TV.

For dogs who get the evening "zoomies", we suggest adding in a short walk to their routine and take the dog out for this outing several minutes *before* the evening acrobatics begin. Preemptive redirection works to both prevent the onset of attention-seeking behaviors and also allows the triggers that had previously signaled "opportunity to steal/chew and get the zoomies" to become associated instead as predictors for opportunities to chew on a favorite bone, search for a toy or enjoy an evening walk.

It's all in the timing: Preemptive redirection differs significantly from waiting until the dog offers the problem behavior and then replacing the toy with an appropriate toy or offering a chew on a mat, a solution that is commonly recommended. Waiting for the behavior to occur before redirecting the dog is not generally effective because this approach does not prevent the problem behavior and if used repeatedly can actually serve to unintentionally reinforce the unwanted behavior.

Finally, basic manners training is very important for dogs with any type of problem attention-seeking behavior. A reliable "come when called" is needed so that a dog who steals items can be

274

cued to bring them back. Similarly, as discussed with problem chewing, teaching the cues "leave it" and "give" are indispensable tools for gaining control with a dog who chews or steals prohibited items.

Mat training: Teaching dogs to "relax on your bed or mat" is a helpful behavior to train as an alternate behavior for several types of problem behaviors, including attention-seeking. For this training, the dog is taught to move to a bed or mat, lie down and relax. Dogs should be trained to "go to your mat", in the absence of any triggering stimuli (see target training below). The owner gradually shapes the behavior until the dog can be commanded to "go to your mat" from different parts of the room or house. As with all operant responses, a very high value food reinforcer is selected and is reserved for this training. Remote training aids such as a Pet Tutor™ or Manners Minder™ can also be used to deliver treats periodically as the dog maintains his stay on the mat. Here are the guidelines for introducing target and mat training that we use at AutumnGold:

AutumnGold Guidelines
Tips for Target Training with Your Dog

Target training can be used for teaching your dog manners, preventing and solving certain problem behaviors, and for teaching fun tricks! You can train your dog to touch a specific target with her feet and/or with her nose.

Teaching Nose Touch: Most dogs intuitively examine a novel object with their nose, so "nose touch" is an easy behavior to jump-start. Here are the steps:

- *Touch hand or stick:* You can use either a touch stick or the flat of your hand (palm facing your dog) for this training. Present your palm or the end tip of the stick to your dog, directly in front of her nose. As soon as she sniffs the target, reinforce (Good! Treat!). Repeat several times, always immediately following a sniff or touch with reinforcement.

- *Add a cue:* When your dog has "touched" several times, add in your verbal cue ("Touch!") and continue to reinforce.
- *Move the target:* Move the touch stick or your hand into different positions, such as above and below your dog's head, to the side, or several feet in front of your dog. As she begins to understand and moves reliably towards the target to touch (and get a treat), you have your touch behavior!
- *Cue control:* Take the time to achieve cue control with this behavior – it is really worth the extra training! Your dog should touch the stick only when cued and not in response to the presentation of the touch stick or your hand. This will allow you to use your "touch" cue for many different behaviors and tricks.
- *Nose touch tricks:* Nose touch can be used as a lure to guide your dog to different locations and to teach a variety of body positions. Examples include "put your head down", "turn on the lights" and tricks such as spin in place, shake your head yes/no, and crawl.

Teaching Paw Touch: The paw touch can be more challenging to teach because not all dogs are naturally aware of how they use their feet. Dogs who use their feet to hold and manipulate toys or who paw when they want attention are usually more "foot aware" and more likely to quickly learn "hit it." Give this a try – your dog may love it!

- *Select a target:* A small carpet square or computer mouse pad work well as paw touch pads. Place the target on the floor near your dog's front feet and reinforce any interaction of your dog's feet with the target (Good! Treat!).
- *Add a cue:* Begin to move the target to different spots and reinforce her whenever she touches it with her feed. Add in

your cue word (Hit it!") and provide several yummy treats while she remains on the target for several seconds.

- **Go to your bed:** The "hit it" targeting behavior works great for teaching your dog to go to her bed or a mat. Simply place the target on the bed and begin with your dog standing immediately next to the bed/target. Gradually move your dog away from the target, shaping her to "go to your bed" from different areas.
- **Relax:** If you would like to add a "relax on your bed" behavior to your dog's repertoire, begin to reinforce a down/stay and calm behavior while your dog rests on her targeted bed or mat. Begin this training when your dog is tired and there are no distractions. Add in a stuffed toy for her to enjoy while relaxing and gradually increase the amount of time that you ask her to stay on her mat.

TALKING TO JOE

Talking to Joe: Neighbor Joe stops by for a visit with his 9-month-old dog, Tyler. Joe tells you that Tyler was a perfect puppy – he came when he was called, was easy to house train, played nicely with his kids and did well in his puppy classes. However, once Tyler reached about 8 months of age, Joe said that he started to show several behaviors that Joe does not particularly like. Tyler has been stealing bits of laundry, chewing up Joe's shoes, and has been barking incessantly when left outside in the yard. Rather than give Joe detailed instructions for each of the problems on his list, instead you offer Joe a few general rules to fol-

277

low when thinking about some of the unwanted behaviors that Tyler offers and that Joe would like to change:

☙ *Give Tyler what he needs:* You know Joe, dogs thrive on a regular routine of exercise, attention, training and being with their family. Since Tyler is older now, he can go for longer walks with you in the morning and will probably also enjoy playing fetch your kids and other games such as "hide and seek" and "find your toys" in the house. Enlist your kids to help you to give Tyler his daily walks and training. Even something as simple as brushing Tyler while they are watching TV at night is positive time with him. While I know you think he loves the yard, Joe, you should avoid leaving Tyler out in the yard for more than a few minutes. Contrary to what some folks believe, dogs are *not* happy when isolated in yards and can begin to bark from boredom or frustration if left alone for too long. If Tyler gets plenty of time with you, he is less likely to steal things for attention or get into mischief when you are not home with him.

☙ *Be proactive rather than reactive:* Most dogs who get the zoomies, bark for attention, or steal laundry and then play "catch me if you can" develop a daily pattern of these behaviors. For example, Joe, you mentioned that Tyler always gets the zoomies right after you eat dinner. Since you know this is a pattern, perhaps take him out for a short evening walk immediate after dinner (before the onset of the zoomies), or play a game of "find your toy", or give him a stuffed toy to chew on as you do the dishes. Being proactive simply means doing something before Tyler begins the behaviors that you dislike. This is a win-win, Joe, as it prevents Tyler from doing the unwanted behavior and teaches him that interacting with you in the ways that you would like him to is much more enjoyable!

🐾 *Use preemptive redirection:* Timing is everything, Joe. It sounds like Tyler has developed a real love for dirty socks. Your daughter told me that he will follow her into the laundry room when she is sorting clothes, poised to grab a sock (or two) and run! Your daughter can be preemptive in this situation by storing a few of Tyler's favorite toys in the laundry room and giving one to him each time that he follows her into the room (and before he lunges for a sock). It will also help to manage the situation a bit by putting all socks up and away from his reach, as well. Pretty soon, Tyler will be thinking more about his favorite toys (that suddenly seem to live in the laundry room) rather than stealing socks.

🐾 *Target train:* Your younger daughter told me that she loves playing games with Tyler and teaching him new tricks. So, Joe, here is a hand-out for teaching dogs to touch targets with their nose and their paws. Your daughter can teach Tyler several tricks with "nose touch" and also can train him to go to his bed and relax, a great behavior to have when you need Tyler to settle in and chew on a yummy bone. Your daughter will have fun and you will get some new (and desired) behaviors trained with Tyler as well. Have fun with your boy, Joe. He is a great dog!

CONCLUSION
Smart Dogs & Dog Smart Owners

We live in exciting times for the dog world. The changes that have occurred during the last 50 years have guided us to training methods that are not only humane and reward-based, but that also encompass current scientific evidence regarding how dogs learn, respond emotionally to training, and demonstrate their very unique ability to communicate with and understand their human partners. All that we have learned, and continue to learn, informs us not only about how to train, but also how to live with, love and respect the dogs with whom we share our lives.

Personally, looking back, it has been an amazing journey. All of the dogs who I have lived with have brought boundless love, joy, laughter, fun, and understanding to my life. I miss those who are no longer with us, celebrate my current family of dogs, and am deeply, deeply grateful for being able to share their lives with them. I am also grateful to the many scientists, trainers, behaviorists, and researchers who so generously have shared and continue to share their discoveries and their knowledge with others. As we continue to learn about the complexities of the dog's mind and behavior, I am certain that we will also continue to modify training approaches and to shift our perceptions and understanding of our dogs.

Being *"Dog Smart"* can turn a crazy puppy, rambunctious adolescent or fearful new rescue dog into a well-behaved, happy and responsive dog, supporting harmonious homes for owners and their dogs. Training dogs well involves love and caretaking and compassion – it also includes science. Continue to pay attention to the evidence – it will inform and guide us as we continue to learn about how to best train and live with our beloved dogs. Happy training!

Books, Blogs & Cool Websites

Books

Alexander MC. *Click for Joy*. Sunshine Books, Inc., Waltham, MA, 208 pp., 2003.

Aloff, B. *Canine Body Language: A Photographic Guide.* Dogwise, Wenatchee, WA, 372 pp., 2005.

Burch MR, Bailey JS. *How Dogs Learn*. Howell Book House, New York, NY, 188 pp., 1999.

Case L. *Beware the Straw Man: The Science Dog Explores Dog Training Fact & Fiction.* AutumnGold Publishing, Mahomet, IL, 189 pp, 2015.

Coppinger R, Coppinger L. *Dogs: A Startling New Understanding of Canine Origin, Behavior and Evolution.* Scribner Publishing, New York, NY, 352 pp., 2001.

Csanyi V. *If Dogs Could Talk: Exploring the Canine Mind.* North Point Press, New York, NY, 334 pp, 2005.

Donaldson J. *Culture Clash: A Revolutionary New Way of understanding the Relationship between Humans and Domestic Dogs.* James and Kenneth Publishers, Oakland, California, 221 pp, 1996.

Hare B. *The Genius of Dogs: How Dogs Are Smarter Than You Think.* Penguin Random House, 384 pp, 2013.

Horowitz, A. *Domestic Dog Cognition and Behavior: The Scientific Study of Canis familiaris.* Springer, 274 pp, 2014.

Horowitz, A. *Inside of a Dog: What Dogs See, Smell, and Know*. Simon and Schuster, 368 pp, 2012.

Kaminski K and Marshall-Pescini S. *The Social Dog*. Academic Press, 418 pp, 2014.

Lindsay S. *Handbook of Applied Dog Behavior and Training (Volumes 1 – 3)*. Iowa State University Press, 2002.

McConnell PB. *For the Love of a Dog: Understanding Emotion in You and Your Best Friend*. Ballantine Books, 332 pp., 2006.

McConnell PB. *The Other End of the Leash*. Ballantine Books, 272 pp., 2003.

Miklosi A. *Dog: Behavior, Evolution and Cognition*. Oxford University Press, Oxford UK, Second edition, 274 pp, 2014.

Overall K. *Clinical Behavioral Medicine for Small Animals*. Mosby, St. Louis, MO, 544 pp, 1997.

Pryor K. *Karen Pryor on Behavior*. Sunshine Books, North Bend, WA, xxx pp., 1995.

Pryor K. *Don't Shoot the Dog*, Bantam Books, New York, New York, 187 pp, 1984.

Serpell J (editor). *The Domestic Dog: Its Evolution, Behaviour, and Interactions with People*. Cambridge University Press, Cambridge, UK, 268 pp., Second edition, 2017.

Tucker N. *The Good Enough Dog: Living with and loving the imperfect dog*. CreateSpace Press, Montreal, Canada, in press, 2018.

Blogs

Animal Emotions (Mark Bekoff)
https://www.psychologytoday.com/blog/animal-emotions

Canine Corner (Stanley Coren)
https://www.psychologytoday.com/blog/canine-corner

Companion Animal Psychology (Zazie Todd)
https://www.companionanimalpsychology.com/

Do You Believe in Dogs (Julie Hecht and Mia Cobb)
http://doyoubelieveindog.blogspot.com/

Dog Spies (Julie Hecht)
https://blogs.scientificamerican.com/dog-spies/

EileenandDogs (Eileen Anderson)
https://eileenanddogs.com/

The Other End of the Leash (Patricia McConnell)
http://www.patriciamcconnell.com/theotherendoftheleash/

The Science Dog (Linda Case)
https://thesciencedog.wordpress.com/

Dog Cognition Research

Arizona Canine Cognition Center
https://dogs.arizona.edu/

Canis Sapiens Lab
http://www.comportamentoanimale.it/en/

Dognition
https://www.dognition.com/who-we-are

Family Dog Project
https://familydogproject.elte.hu/

Horowitz Dog Cognition Lab
https://dogcognition.weebly.com/

University of Portsmouth Dog Cognition Centre
http://www.port.ac.uk/department-of-
psychology/facilities/dog-cognition-centre/

Yale University Canine Cognition Center
https://doglab.yale.edu/

Organizations

Academy for Dog Trainers
https://academyfordogtrainers.com/

Association of Pet Dog Trainers (APDT)
http://www.apdt.com

International Association of Animal Behavior Consultants
http://www.iaabc.org

Karen Pryor Academy
https://www.karenpryoracademy.com/

Pet Professional Guild
https://www.petprofessionalguild.com/

Think Dog!
https://www.thinkdog.org/

Index

About the Author

Linda Case is a dog trainer, canine nutritionist and science writer. She earned her B.S. in Animal Science at Cornell University and her M.S. in Canine/Feline Nutrition at the University of Illinois. Following graduate school, Linda was a lecturer in canine and feline science in the Animal Sciences Department at the University of Illinois for 15 years and then taught companion animal behavior and training at the College of Veterinary Medicine.

Linda owns AutumnGold Consulting and Dog Training Center in Mahomet, IL (www.autumngoldconsulting.com), a company that provides scientific writing and training programs. Linda is the author of numerous publications and seven other books, including most recently, *Beware the Straw Man: The Science Dog Explores Dog Training Fact & Fiction* (AutumnGold, 2015) and *Dog Food Logic: Making Smart Decisions for your Dog in an Age of Too Many Choices* (Dogwise, 2014). She also authors the popular blog "The Science Dog" (http://thesciencedog.wordpress.com).

Linda and her husband Mike currently share their lives with two dogs; Cooper and Alice, and Pete the cat. In addition to dog training, Linda enjoys running, hiking, swimming, and gardening—activities that she happily shares with her dogs.

Contact information:
Linda P. Case, MS
Owner, AutumnGold Consulting and Dog Training Center
www.autumngoldconsulting.com
http://thesciencedog.wordpress.com

15367853R00157

Printed in Great Britain
by Amazon